VOLUME TWO

THE BEST

WRITING

—ON—

WRITING

EDITED BY JACK HEFFRON

STORY PRESS

CINCINNATI, OHIO

Other fine Story Press Books are available from your local bookstore or direct from the publisher.

99   98   97   96   95   5   4   3   2   1

Library of Congress Cataloging-in-Publication Data

ISBN 1-884910-25-4

The Library of Congress has cataloged volume one of this title as follows:

The best writing on writing / edited by Jack Heffron.
     p.   cm.
 Includes index.
 1. Authorship. I. Heffron, Jack.
PN151.B58   1994
808'.02—dc20   94-13864
                                                      CIP

Designed by Clare Finney

The permissions on the next two pages constitute an extension of this copyright page.

The Best Writing on Writing, Volume Two is printed on recycled paper.

PERMISSIONS

CONTENTS

Introduction viii

MARGARET ATWOOD
   The Page 1
   from GOOD BONES AND SIMPLE MURDERS

T. ALAN BROUGHTON
   Some Notes on the Art of Lying 3
   from NEW ENGLAND REVIEW

ROGER ROSENBLATT
   Nine Antirules of Journalism 15
   from MICHIGAN QUARTERLY REVIEW

KATHLEEN NORRIS
   Degenerates 36
   from PLOUGHSHARES

MICHAEL NORMAN
   A Book in Search of a Buzz: The Marketing of a First Novel 42
   from THE NEW YORK TIMES BOOK REVIEW

CALVIN TRILLIN
   Paper Trials 71
   from THE NEW YORKER

WILLIAM H. GASS
   Anywhere But Kansas 74
   from THE IOWA REVIEW

WILLIAM GOLDMAN
   Butch Cassidy and the Nazi Dentist 82
   from WILLIAM GOLDMAN: FIVE SCREENPLAYS

STEPHEN SPENDER
My Life Is Mine; It Is Not David Leavitt's 96
from THE NEW YORK TIMES BOOK REVIEW

LEE UPTON
The Closest Work 106
from FIELD

ANNETTE GRANT
One Song, Start to Finish: A Music Lesson 113
from THE NEW YORK TIMES MAGAZINE

NANCY WILLARD
What We Write About When We Write About Love 120
from THE WRITER

JUSTIN KAPLAN
A Culture of Biography 131
from THE YALE REVIEW

LYN LIFSHIN
The Writing of "Mint Leaves at Yaddo" 144
from WRITER'S DIGEST

DAVID CARKEET
Dear Reviewer. . . 155
from SAN FRANCISCO REVIEW OF BOOKS

CHARLES BAXTER
Dysfunctional Narratives or "Mistakes Were Made" 158
from PLOUGHSHARES

DAN GREENBURG
Writers Have Had It Up to Here:
The Latest on the Authors' Strike 175
from THE NEW YORK TIMES BOOK REVIEW

DOROTHY ALLISON
Believing in Literature 178
from SKIN: TALKING ABOUT SEX, CLASS AND LITERATURE

JOYCE CAROL OATES
"JCO" and I 194
from ANTAEUS

THOMAS E. KENNEDY
Realism & Other Illusions 196
from AWP CHRONICLE

RICHARD LEDERER
Conan the Grammarian 208
from ADVENTURES OF A VERBIVORE

LINDA SIMON
Foreign States of Mind 224
from AGNI

MAXINE KUMIN
Menial Labor and the Muse 238
from WOMEN, ANIMALS, AND VEGETABLES

About the Authors 242

About the Editor 244

Index 245

INTRODUCTION

It's no easy task for writers to explain what they do. It's even tougher to put those explanations on paper. They may be able to discuss with confidence a story's genesis or analyze the strategies used in structuring a poem, but the creative process is, finally, enigmatic—as much a matter of instinct and imagination as conscious design.

In this second volume of *The Best Writing on Writing*, twenty-three writers undertake the task of explaining—or exploring—the mysteries of their craft. And they succeed in insightful, surprising, even moving ways. Some present methods for creating songs, stories, novels, screenplays, poems, essays and articles. Others offer insights into stirring the imagination. Still others examine key writing issues, put forth theories about the creative process, analyze the world of publishing, or discuss the writing life. A few poke fun, such as David Carkeet, who gives a chiding, tongue-in-cheek workshop for book reviewers in "Dear Reviewer. . ." Others simply have fun, such as Dan Greenburg, in his playful fantasy of a writers' strike in "Writers Have Had It Up to Here: The Latest on the Authors' Strike."

My goal in this collection, and in the series itself, is to gather in one place the best work published in a particular year on a variety of writing topics. To that end, I've cast a wide net. Many of these pieces you may not have seen or heard about when they were originally published. Other pieces—Michael Norman's "A Book in Search of a Buzz: The Marketing of a New Novel," for example—created quite a buzz themselves when they first appeared. *The Best Writing on Writing, Volume Two* seeks to present a rich brew of powerful voices, as diverse as they are compelling. It is a celebration of memorable writing that I hope you will find illuminating as well as useful to your own work.

I have not attempted to put forth a unifying theme or to champion a critical or aesthetic agenda. You'll notice, instead, that the contributors don't always agree. In "A Culture of Biography,'' Justin Kaplan presents a different perspective on writing biographies from that offered by Linda Simon in "Foreign States of Mind." William Gass, in "Anywhere But Kansas," challenges writers to be more innovative, to explore new forms, to, as he puts it, "shake up the system by breaking its rules, ridiculing its lingo, and disdaining whatever is in intellectual fashion." On the other hand, in her "What We Write About When We Write About Love," Nancy Willard suggests a much gentler approach. She tells us: "Death is so ordinary. Write about love."

Certain themes do emerge. One that resonates through a number of pieces is that artistic inspiration requires writers to perform a balancing act. Writers must investigate their material, must push it into fresh, new areas, and must develop the discipline and grit to explore the potential of an idea. At the same time, they must wait patiently, allowing inspiration to arrive as if unbidden. In "Degenerates," Kathleen Norris explores this paradoxical stance by comparing it to the lives of Trappist monks:

> "Listen" is the first word of St. Benedict's *Rule* for monasteries, and listening for the eruptions of grace into one's life—often from unlikely sources—is a "quality of attention" that both monastic living and the practice of writing tends to cultivate.

Maxine Kumin, in "Menial Labor and the Muse," echoes this idea as she explains how doing tough, physical chores on her farm and sitting daily at her writing desk must be tempered with silence and isolation:

> My writing time needs to surround itself with empty stretches, or at least unpeopled ones, for the writing takes place in an area of suspension as in a hanging nest that is almost entirely encapsulated. I think of the oriole's graceful construction.

In "Paper Trials," Calvin Trillin humorously outlines the dangers of grasping too eagerly for inspiration and perfection, sure ways to block creativity. He recalls a time when he tried to make a small sign to put in his car:

I took on the task of composing a sign to inform potential pillagers that it contained nothing of value. Hours later, my wife happened to ask me to do some little chore around the house and I heard myself saying, "I can't right now. I'm on the fourth draft of this sign."

You will surely find other themes as you make your way through this collection. But the one I hope shines brightest is a respect, even a certain awe, for the process of writing and for the creative people with the courage and the tenacity, the patience and the just plain willfulness to do it. The contributors here would agree, I think, that writing is both a craft to be learned and a mystery to be savored. Each beginning is an adventure, with all the attendant hopes and fears. In "The Page," Margaret Atwood sums up these feelings:

The page waits, pretending to be blank. Is that its appeal, its blankness? What else is this smooth and white, this terrifyingly innocent?

—Jack Heffron

MARGARET ATWOOD

THE PAGE

GOOD BONES AND SIMPLE MURDERS

1. The page waits, pretending to be blank. Is that its appeal, its blankness? What else is this smooth and white, this terrifyingly innocent? A snowfall, a glacier? It's a desert, totally arid, without life. But people venture into such places. Why? To see how much they can endure, how much dry light?

2. I've said the page is white, and it is: white as wedding dresses, rare whales, seagulls, angels, ice and death. Some say that like sunlight it contains all colours; others, that it's white because it's hot, it will burn out your optic nerves; that those who stare at the page too long go blind.

3. The page itself has no dimensions and no directions. There's no up or down except what you yourself mark, there's no thickness and weight but those you put there, north and south do not exist unless you're certain of them. The page is without vistas and without sounds, without centres or edges. Because of this you can become lost in it forever. Have you never seen the look of gratitude, the look of joy, on the faces of those who have managed to return from the page? Despite their faintness, their loss of blood, they fall on their knees, they push their hands into the earth, they clasp the bodies of those they love, or, in a pinch, any bodies they can get, with an urgency unknown to those who have never experienced the full horror of a journey into the page.

4. If you decide to enter the page, take a knife and some matches, and something that will float. Take something you can hold onto, and a prism to split the light and a talisman that works, which should be hung on a chain around your neck: that's for getting back. It doesn't matter what kind of shoes, but your hands should be bare. You should never go into the page with gloves on. Such decisions, needless to say, should not be made lightly.

There are those, of course, who enter the page without deciding, without meaning to. Some of these have charmed lives and no difficulty, but most never make it out at all. For them the page appears as a well, a lovely pool in which they catch sight of a face, their own but better. These unfortunates do not jump: rather they fall, and the page closes over their heads without a sound, without a seam, and is immediately as whole and empty, as glassy, as enticing as before.

5. The question about the page is: what is beneath it? It seems to have only two dimensions, you can pick it up and turn it over and the back is the same as the front. Nothing, you say, disappointed.

But you were looking in the wrong place, you were looking *on the back* instead of *beneath*. *Beneath the page* is another story. Beneath the page is a story. Beneath the page is everything that has ever happened, most of which you would rather not hear about.

The page is not a pool but a skin, a skin is there to hold in and it can feel you touching it. Did you really think it would just lie there and do nothing?

Touch the page at your peril: it is you who are blank and innocent, not the page. Nevertheless you want to know, nothing will stop you. You touch the page, it's as if you've drawn a knife across it, the page has been hurt now, a sinuous wound opens, a thin incision. Darkness wells through.

T. ALAN BROUGHTON

SOME NOTES ON
THE ART OF LYING

NEW ENGLAND REVIEW

We all know that art is not truth. Art is a lie that makes us realize truth,
at least the truth that is given us to understand. The artist must know
the manner whereby to convince others of the truthfulness of his lies.

—Pablo Picasso

I learned the virtues of lying at an early age.

I am on the school bus. I want my companions to listen to
my story of what happened at home last night. We all love to
tattle on our familes—grievances about strict mothers, arguments we have overheard through half-closed doors, the evil
schemes of siblings we have thwarted. But the telling does us
no good if the audience does not listen carefully and react with
the anger or laughter or sympathy that we want. Last night my
sister and I have, as usual, quarreled over who will be able to
keep the radio in the bedroom after homework is done. My
friends have heard this story before, and not just from me. I
finish my homework first. I put in my claim for the radio. She
is three years older and has more to do than I. "Not fair," she
howls when the radio is awarded to me.

So ends the historical narrative. She stays up later, so she gets
it back anyway. My friends sense this because it is what they
expect from their own lives. Only Rumpelstiltskin is so enraged
that he stamps his foot through the floor. I see their attention
wavering. Ben is putting in for his share of the trip to school.
"Hey, you know what my Dad said last night?" he says. But I'm

not to be silenced yet. "Listen," I say. "You won't believe it. She was so mad, you know what she did?" Now, as E.M. Forster would say, we not only have a story, we have a plot. They are listening again. "She took the radio out of her bedroom and brought it into the hallway and threw it at me. She missed. It smashed. Mom was so angry she smacked her right across the mouth."

Do they believe me? They don't care, they love it, and I hardly even feel like I'm lying. Even if she didn't, she wanted to. I could see that in her tight lips, hear it in the slammed door after I began playing the radio loudly in my room. In my story I am enabling her to do what she wanted to do—maybe even what I wanted her to do, given the imagined consequences. She would, at last, have been totally in the wrong. Of course, in my expanded version she's not exactly my sister anymore, but I and my friends' emotions are engaged in a drama true to the experience of our inner lives. And they are listening.

When friends of Gertrude Stein objected that she did not look like his portrait of her, Picasso is purported to have said, "She will." Everyone admits now that she does.

I have stolen some loose change from one of my mother's bureau drawers. I convince myself that if money is left there so negligently, she dosen't really want it. Besides, it is enough to pay for the Saturday afternoon matinee at the movies. I am not allowed to go to the movies alone.

"Where were you all afternoon?" my mother asks at dinner. I know she has been listening to the opera, and my father was at his office in the library where he always is except when eating or sleeping. My sister has filled the dinner conversation with descriptions of her latest water ballet rehearsal. I am ready for that question. I describe how I have been sledding on various hills around the campus. Was Charlie with me? No. I haven't had time to set up an alibi with him. I was alone. I see doubt, suspicion growing. I cull details from other times I have had some fine runs down the steepest hill behind the dorms. I tell how I swerved to miss the oak, tilted, veered across the stream that was, luckily, frozen over, coming to rest near the small dam—and there, just to distract them with wonder, I tell how

I saw a muskrat looking out through a hole in the bank. Yes, yes. I'm sure it was, I say to my sister's incredulity.

"If you're going to tell a big lie, don't tell any little ones," Swift is purported to have said about his fictional technique in *Gulliver's Travels.* All the details of my sledding afternoon are plausible. The stream is frozen, the hill is steep, my father has previously pointed out a muskrat to me near that pool. Composite details gleaned from other trips, other winters. All credible. The illusion of truth is all they really need, and years later, as a parent, I suspect they are unconsciously complicitous, glad to believe. Who wants to accuse his child of petty theft and buying forbidden pleasures?

And where have I actually been? In the great House of Illusion, watching the pictures flick by—Errol Flynn with a sword leaping over the taffrail, swinging from ropes, the deck ablaze— and after dinner I go to my room and become that man on the deck of my bed. So many levels of illusion for all of us in only one afternoon and evening.

But beware. A week later my mother has been walking in a new-fallen snow. She comes home to say she has seen no sight of the muskrat in that pool. What muskrat? I ask her. The one you saw when you were sledding last Saturday. Sledding? For a moment I draw a blank. The story has faded. All those details I found, the experience I described so vividly to them because it was as real as it might have been, is of no use to me afterwards, and is erased. Oh, yeah. Sledding, I say, remembering only the movie, hoping she won't recall any more of the details I have forgotten.

When I write a novel I live in a parallel world as real to me as my waking life in which I teach, cook, buy the groceries, take my son and his friend to school. When the book is finished, I am a little weary of those people I have come to know better and better but never well enough, yet I am also sad to have to part from them. A few years later, talking to someone who has read the book, I cannot remember their names. My friend asks me about a scene, mentions a few details. He knows those characters now much better than I do. They served their purpose for me, and I have expediently dismissed them. I have no room for them in my life because I am already working on a new lie and trying to make it seem as true as possible.

"In twenty-five words or less," the voice announces on the weekly broadcast of Superman, "tell us why you like Good and Plenty candy."

I don't like Good and Plenty. I do covet an Erector set, the kind with a small motor that can be attached to various constructions. The winner will receive one. For three days I sit and imagine and struggle with word counts. The gist of the story is that I have been on a camping trip with friends in the woods. I become separated from the group. Lost. Overnight in the woods alone. But I have my box of Good and Plenty. Two days later when they find me, I'm still OK. Water in the nearby stream, candy in my pocket have saved me. I send in my entry and forget about it.

Two months later my cousin calls to ask me, was I listening to Superman that afternoon? No. "You won," she says. "You won." It's a national contest. They have read my entry over the radio. My uncle relates it to my parents. I wait uneasily. They laugh. They think it is very imaginative. Clever of me. Quite a yarn. What's wrong with them, I wonder. Nobody has said the word "lie." I am awarded the Erector set. I also receive a year's supply of Good and Plenty. Superman's revenge.

Ambition has been rewarded. I began by wanting an Erector set. I lied and got it. What else can stories get you? When I was younger I believed being a writer might bring fame, or at least fortune. When publication brought neither of those, I hoped it might provide a decent living for me and my family. Despite what I think of as a modestly successful career (four novels, four books of poetry, a collection of short stories, hundreds of poems and stories in various journals, a number of grants and awards) I would not be able to support my needs without teaching. But I have had the good fortune of loving that second vocation, so I have felt little disappointment since my earlier hopes were dashed. Perhaps being a poet has preserved my sanity in all this. In this society, to be a poet is to be involved in a business that runs constantly in the red.

But luckily if you do it often enough, you come to like the

making of stories and poems so much that the making itself is what they get you. I do have faith that at least my imagination can leap tall buildings at a single bound.

My father is a Classicist, an historian. Anyone who knows him is in awe of his memory. He can recall names, dates, places, lines from poems he learned when he was in school (at the time of this writing he is 93)—and facts not just from his life and the lives of those close to him but from all the vast amount of history he has studied. I have been and am in awe of it. But it was, in my teenage and early adult years, a cause of contention. Not that I ever argued with him about those facts, or even one from my own past. But his capacity made him hard to argue with.

I do not have that memory. I am awash in emotions, vaguely situated in my own history, able to keep an eye on the clock sufficiently to catch planes and make it to appointments on time, but incapable of distinguishing one year from the other in the mat of my memory. I am not a scholar. Names of stories and novels and poems are gone soon after I read them. The books I love are part of me, but I would not dare to discuss them without having read them within the past few days. I walked away from the Ph.D. program at the University of Washington with a sense of relief duplicated only by leaving a bad marriage or two.

For years I compared my memory to my father's and felt insufficient. Then I began to remember times when that memory was a curse for him. Conversational anecdotes, stories, movies, anything that touched on history but fudged on its facts made him squirm. Literally. I remember sitting next to him often in movies that had historical references. "No," he would be saying in a whisper to himself in one scene after another, his legs shuffling uneasily, one hand quietly but impatiently patting his thigh. "No, no." Afterward he would tell us that Caesar could not have appeared in that scene. He was not alive in that year. My father had not been affected by the plight of the characters in the story—those little lies had destroyed his ability to enter into the illusion. Time and again the truth I experienced in the story, the one made by lies that convinced me of the justness of the character's feelings, were only an agony of misrepresentation to him.

Then, in my middle age, I realized my father could never have written novels or poems or stories. It is not that I lack a memory. I have come to believe that I possess all I have lived through, imagined or experienced, but that it is not to be recalled except indirectly in dreams and fictions; the details are held in store available for the transformations needed to make the illusion effective. It is impossible to make a world if all you remember remains located in and bound to the world of its origin. I can only tell the kinds of lies that might make truth if I can lie to myself and not know it. I was a good liar because I could believe my lies. My father finds truth in a faithfulness to the exact nature of the event, and from the storehouse of history finds and extracts truths no less exquisite than any I could make. I find my truths in the lies my imagination gives me—those real toads in imaginary gardens.

But of course he and I are of a passing generation. Historians and the writers of nonfiction have appropriated the methods of novelists and poets, believing that all aspects of knowing are the subjective imaginings and raving of deluded points of view. My adolescence today would have had to find its arguments in other matters.

When I wrote a novel using my first trip to Rome, Italy, as a fifteen-year-old, I invented a mother and son and sent them there in the same year I had gone (1950-51). I used the place carefully, consulting maps to locate scenes, giving streets their proper names, making certain events I mentioned from history were possible. By this time I had developed a respect for those "small lies" Swift mentions. I had a student who had imagined a fine strategem for a story—a man, who is desperately shy, wants to meet women, have a lover, but cannot come out of his reticence. However, he is an excellent cook. He finds he can meet other people if inviting them to dinner where he feels supremely confident. On the night of the story, he invites a woman he is particularly obsessed with. They will begin with a pasta dish. The ingredients are lovingly described by the writer.

But the writer is not a cook. He has the man cook the spaghetti well before the guests arrive. Suddenly we no longer believe in the protagonist's ability to cook. The story is wobbling, falling apart because the little lies have not been carefully maintained. Worse than our doubting the protagonist, we begin to doubt the author. If he does not even know how to cook a good pot of spaghetti, what can he know about human nature?

So I was punctilious about the facts in my novel, and I even let events occur in a small school like the one for English-speaking children I had gone to. Then, to give me the self-confidence to begin, I used the first names of some people I knew there. I called the protagonist's young, Yugoslavian friend Mladen, his first name in reality, but changed the last, which sent me rooting around since I didn't know Yugoslavian surnames. Anyway, I told myself I could change the names when I finished writing the book, and I was careful to invent new surnames for them.

Of course as the book took over my life, as the characters became more real than my friends and family, I forgot they had any reference to an "outside" world and came to know them intimately by the names I had given them. I could not change them any more than I could change the names of my own children. The necessities of plot, action, characterization—the fabric of the book—took over, and they no longer seemed based on anything I had experienced. I was discovering their lives in the many versions I wrote. The book was published. I went on to the next.

The first rumblings of trouble came through a friend of mine at the university where we work. She had been to a class reunion. Someone she had known vaguely when she had been at college came up to her and said, "Don't you work at the University of Vermont?" Yes, she did. Did she know that bastard Broughton who had written that novel *Winter Journey*? Yes again, but he wasn't all that bad, really—or was she a previous wife? Good God, no. Who'd want to marry a lying s.o.b. like that? She spluttered and fumed on about the novel she had just read that was about the small school in Rome she had attended. In it she had found a number of her teachers and friends, only tenuously disguised by changing their surnames—but they had been defamed, libeled, distorted beyond belief. Why, one of them, a superb teacher, had even been presented as a homosexual. The author ought to be sued.

My friend, who like myself is both writer and teacher of literature, did her best to defend the noble art of fiction. Surely the difference between Art and Reality was clear, no? But like all of us in that argument, she was in a defensive position. Friends, family, all of those close to us who see fragments of themselves in what we write feel like those aborigines who will not have their pictures taken because the image on the paper has become a permanent trap for their souls. Their essence has been locked into the photograph and evil magic can be done to it there. She and I laughed about it, but secretly I was glad she, not I, had been there to take the heat.

Then, a year later, I am wakened at midnight by a call. A voice says, "Hello, this is Mladen." I am not fully awake. There is only one Mladen, and he is a character in a book of mine. The boy I knew in Rome has faded completely before the imagined one who became, and will continue to be, more real than any I have known. He tells me a story while I listen from my limbo, perched on the side of the bed. He has been to a bookstore in New York, browsing. He sees a book with the cover of Bernini's Triton fountain and wonders if it could be about Rome, that place he has continued to love since he was there in the fifties. On the back is a picture of a man who looks remarkably like someone he knew, although he has sprouted a mustache. Yes, that's the name. He remembers those nights when we lied, saying we were going to a movie, or perhaps a specific party, and all we did was wander the city freely, taunting the whores, watching people at fountains, eating from street stands. He opens the book. He finds himself in it. A boy named Mladen.

When I hear his voice I begin to believe in him, and I am moved in ways I cannot understand. Is it simply a validation that the illusions we inhabit so much as writers do have their connections to realities? Or is it that the book has been the means to discover a truth the book affirmed but which seemed only to be spoken to myself—how much I cared for that boy, how much we helped each other through that year? A message in a bottle. We spent twenty minutes talking. He was very tolerant about my use of him, eloquent about what it is like to find yourself encapsulated in someone's imagined world. He gave me an address, a number. We hung up.

We have never seen each other or spoken since, although I made a brief attempt a year later to contact him. The letter was returned. I called. No one with that name at that number. I am writing a sequel to that book and I have put him in it. He is an adult there, a terrorist working with the Red Brigades. I have sometimes wondered why I was not more aggressive about finding him after that call. My excuse is that I rarely go to New York City, but I also wonder guiltily whether I wanted to preserve my imagined Mladen. Is it another example of how the artist in me can sometimes sacrifice the living on the altar of a relentless need to make? I accepted that when I was younger. I abhor it now.

If there is a center to this labyrinth, I have not yet arrived.

Recently I completed a story concerning an event in my childhood so painful for me that I had hardly even faced it in memory, much less tried to transform it into fiction. When I was going to a small, private grade school, I had a homosexual relationship with a teacher there. He was young, energetic, popular with the kids and other teachers, and married to the school secretary. He would drive me home in the school van, leave the other students at their homes, then park with me in some field or on a back road. There was no violence—I was all too willing to be taken this close into the life of someone I worshipped, although the physical act of masturbating him in the front seat of a car seemed much less essential than the intimacy of his conversation, the special tone he reserved for me. But abuse is not just violence. He used my ignorance, my need for adult affection, my simple good will, if you wish, that was based on considerable innocence. Then, when he thought it getting dangerous, he shoved me away.

In my syllabus in the introductory course in writing fiction and poetry I warn my students, "When your work is being

SOME NOTES ON THE ART OF LYING 11

discussed you should understand that you do not have to defend your writing or yourself before the class; ideally you should present your work, listen to all the responses, and consider at leisure which remarks are useful and which are not. An important part of this process is learning how to be objective about your own work." It's a passage I lifted from the syllabus of a good friend who is a wiser teacher than I am. But it's a standard I think I've learned to live by in my own relationship to editors. Especially if the advice is offered on the phone ("Don't you think Hilda in that scene is really a twerp?") I have learned to count to ten, then say in an even-toned voice, "OK. Let me think that over."

The story, like all pieces that deal with the most intractable aspects of our lives, ones that we've hardly even faced anywhere but in our deepest dreams, took a few years to settle down—from novella to short story by jettisoning a number of scenes, even characters that had enabled me to evade the center of the story. Again, by the time it was ready to send out, the protagonist (although speaking through "I") was no longer myself, the events altered, some invented. But the essence was there.

The truths of the story had a strangely releasing effect on me. I still live in the penumbra of that—a form of acceptance that seems almost impersonal, as if I was given through writing it not so much a personal release, a private therapy, as some wider sense of what it is to be a member of the species, a descriptive knowledge of what that can be. It's not my story, it's Hank's, and by seeing the story through his life I enter the shared experience of the community.

David Milofsky at *Colorado Review* accepted the story. He called me about it, wanted a few changes, above all wanted to tell me how much it moved him. I listened to his astute, detailed suggestions, found myself even more confused than some of my sophomores must be—"Wait a minute, that's the way it happened," or, "Hey, that's my life you're talking about, go easy." Then he said, of the young man in the story who seduces the protagonist and drops him when his own needs are played out, "That bastard, that bastard." He meant it, an almost inarticulate rage at the abusive nature of what had happened. I found myself grateful that David was on the other side of the country and could not see me. He had said what I had never allowed myself to say. He had commented on an event in my life that I had never told to *anyone* but had made into a story, and I was weeping.

I am fifty-seven. I have been writing seriously for forty years. Tell me now, I said to myself as I lay in bed that night waiting for the next dreams I would forget, what is art, what is reality?

And here is one of my latest dreams. I sit down at my word processor and boot up. I am in WordStar. I open the file of a new novel I am working on. This is not quite my usual computer, though, because even as I am seeing the words, I am actually experiencing the presence of the characters in my room. They surround me, if that is the right way to describe how I am there at the keyboard but they are unaware of me. They are going about whatever it is that I am having them do. I am revising— but that very fluid stage of revision before the nitpicking, when they are still capable of initiating whole new scenes, showing me sides of their personalities I did not know were there.

Slowly I become aware of the fact that these are not just the characters in my novel. A friend or two has come into the room. Members of my family. They are mingling with my characters. Then, to my horror and yet as if it is simply part of my usual endeavor, I am revising them too. My son no longer needs his retainer. My daughter is deleted for a moment and then recreated verbally in another corner of the room, this time dressed elegantly in an evening dress. One of my former wives has tamed parakeets to perch on her breasts, and when she whistles five blackbirds flutter from her hair. My mother watches an arm vanish and my father stands beside her on one leg, erasures as painless as if I have only deleted a phrase. They look at the blank spaces to see if I will type them in again. I am dispassionate in all this, determined only to make the scene work.

Lately my seven-year-old has been having nightmares about his favorite stuffed bear, Bubba. The worst one is when Bubba is maliciously split into kindling and burned in the stove. We comfort him, especially at night before he goes to sleep when he is afraid he will have the dream again. We can find no reasons for these forms of self-torture. I am sure a child psychologist would merely mutter "developmental stage." Perhaps a new bank of chips has become accessible in the skull's computer.

The latest one is gentler and intrigues me. He and I call it The Two Bubbas Dream. "Sometimes," he says, "I dream I come across two Bubbas and I have to choose the right one." It is a vision of doubles. One is an imposter, perhaps wicked. The other is the good, reliable, loving Bubba. But my son says proudly, "Usually I can tell the false Bubba. I look at their eyes. The false one has bright blue eyes. Bubba's are gray." He is triumphant.

I can't help wondering if I am watching my son begin his voyage into his own world of illusions, of the search for truths among various fictions. Bubba is his primary fiction that he carries about the house in his waking hours. He brings him into the illusory world of dreams. Now, in this fiction within a fiction, he must find the "true," the "real" Bubba. Every morning I sit down to lie and then look for some truth in all the lies I tell. There are lies in my lies, and those are the ones I must weed out. All I ask is that the truth I find in the world of lies be convincing.

ROGER ROSENBLATT

NINE ANTIRULES OF JOURNALISM

MICHIGAN QUARTERLY REVIEW

I dedicate half of this talk (I've never dedicated half of a talk before, or a whole talk if it comes to that) to Avery Hopwood who, among other things, became rich at writing plays, which seems to me noteworthy. They say about playwriting that you can't make a living at it, but you *can* make a killing.

I would like to dedicate the other half to Larry Goldstein, editor of the *Michigan Quarterly Review*, because of the anxiety I have caused him, and continue to cause him. He requested, quite reasonably, that I give him the printed copy of this talk. I informed him, quite unreasonably, that I don't write out my talks, but that if someone would care to record and transcribe it, that would be fine with me. Goldstein shuddered, and is shuddering still.

The reason I don't like to write out talks is that I don't like to read things aloud in public, and I kind of like the fear of not knowing exactly what I'll say. I kind of like to look at the fear in *your* eyes, too. I don't even like the title of this talk, but being magnanimous, I conceded to Goldstein a title: "Nine Antirules of Journalism." Then I realized that I had to come up with nine.

I am leery of titles from my experience of working at *Time* magazine. My colleagues and I used to collect the titles of books that we most favored. These are titles of real books that came in over the years. We had a special shelf on which we would keep them. Office favorites included *God and Vitamins, Socialism for the Dead*, an animal book called *Do Reindeer Experience Religious Ecstasy?* This was one of a whole series of animal books, which we discovered sell very well. Alan Coren, the former editor of *Punch*, was always trying to write a best seller. One day he asked his agent, "Well, what kind of books sell? I mean, on what subjects should I write books?" And his agent told him, Nazis, cats, or golf. So Coren wrote a book called *Golfing for Cats*, with a swastika on the cover. My own favorite title on our shelf was a book called *1637, a Year of No Significance.* And the absolute favorite of the boys in the office, a computer book called *Using Your Wang for Business.*

When I saw the distinguished roster of Hopwood lecturers before me, I realized that I also had no *authority* to give this talk. This was not news to me. I have no authority, generally. Every time I try to establish authority, I always bring humiliation upon myself.

When at *Time* I worked for a wonderful editor, Ray Cave—very dour man, had a beard, looked like Rockwell Kent's illustration of Captain Ahab. My family and I were living in Vermont when Cave called me, and I very much wanted to work at *Time*. But I didn't want to look over-eager. I didn't want to look like a hick. So I drove down to New York and had a conversation with Cave, in which everything sounded fine. The hours were fine. The salary was fine—in those days any salary would have been fine. Fifty dollars okay? Fine, fine. But I wanted to show Cave that I had some gumption. So I said, "Well" . . . my voice cracking because I was about to tell a lie. I said, "Well, I'm used to four weeks vacation." Now this was both true and not true. At the *Washington Post* where I had worked before, I got three weeks vacation, but at a university where I had worked before that, I got three *months* vacation. So I figured the whole thing averaged out. "Well," I said, "I'm used to four weeks vacation."

I looked at Cave. Cave looked at me. I could tell he could tell he wasn't dealing with any corn-fed. I could tell he could sense my authority.

"All right, Roger," he said after a pause. "We ordinarily start with five weeks, but in your case we'll make an exception."

I only had one experience in my life in which I managed to

turn a humiliation into triumph. I've never told this story before. And the only reason I am recounting it at this university is that the incident involved a member of the English literature faculty here.

Richard Tillinghast and I were good friends at Harvard when we were in graduate school, and it so happened that we had our oral exam for our Ph.D. on the very same hour of the very same day. In graduate school I was quite undistinguished, quite unmemorable, but Richard was a star. Everybody knew Richard. That morning of our orals Richard and I decided to walk over to Warren House, where the English department was located, together. When we got to Warren House three professors greeted us, two congratulating me for being such a supportive friend as to walk Richard to his orals. One of the professors congratulating me happened to be on my board.

The orals began, Richard's taking place in the next room. I could clearly hear Richard's orals through the wall, as two of my examiners immediately went to sleep. I noticed that because the third examiner didn't show up. Meanwhile, through the wall I continued to hear raucous laughter, explosions of celebration. "That's great, Richard! Who would have thought of *that* before, Richard! Oh, the hell with this, Richard, let's go out and have a drink!" . . . while the tedium of my exam went on, and the seasons passed.

I interrupt this anecdote to bring you to another moment which I will then relate to the anecdote itself. Earlier in the year I was teaching a survey course in English literature. I like memorizing poetry, and I memorized Wordsworth's "Lines Composed a Few Miles Above Tintern Abbey," for two reasons. To show off was the first reason; and the second that it was easier to teach if I could just recite the poem freely and then talk about the lines. The students couldn't have cared less whether I had memorized the poem or not. Nonetheless, it rested in my mind throughout the term as I studied for my orals.

Back at the orals, where the professors are drowsily starting to awaken, the third examiner, an assistant professor, has finally remembered that this exam was to take place, and he bursts in the room wearing tennis togs, just off the court. He didn't want to appear foolish in front of his colleagues (he certainly didn't care how he looked before me), but he wanted to look like he was with it, you know, to rush into this exciting event with a question at the ready. "Where are we?" he asked the two others who of course, could not answer that question.

One of them said, "Wordsworth."

"Wordsworth! Ah, Wordsworth!" said the assistant professor, as if he had just come from Wordsworth's cottage and a chat with Dorothy. "Wordsworth, Wordsworth, Wordsworth," he said. "Mr. Rosenthal . . ." he began. (Who were the other two to correct him? I didn't have the energy.) "Could you, Mr. Rosenthal, tell us how the poem, 'Lines Composed a Few Miles Above Tintern Abbey' begins?" Before that son-of-a-bitch settled his fat ass in that chair, I gave him the whole poem right between the eyes.

In his characteristically gracious introduction of me, Nick Delbanco referred to my most recent humiliation: my publisher suggesting that they publish a collection of my work. I know that this may sound lofty; really it means that you're all washed up and that they just want to get the detritus out of the way and print the eight copies they send to reviewers, and then pension you off to some asylum. The humiliation consists of reading all the stuff that you've written, and realizing how little you are not suicidally ashamed of.

But I did discover something in the course of this investigation which became the seed of what I will try to make sense of today. I discovered that the one characteristic that defined this odd body of my work was mystery—not just the love of, or appreciation of, mystery, but a professional desire to dwell in mystery. I saw that it had done me good. That is, when I least understood a subject, when I was most overwhelmed with some experience, I was, strangely, most self-assured as a writer, most accurate as an observer.

It is in the interest of that idea of mystery that I concoct these nine antirules of journalism. These may be of use to those of you who would be journalists, but they really are intended to apply more generally to us as readers, writers, citizens, dealers in the experience of words. So I hope you won't mind if I present these antirules as if I were talking to young people about to enter that trade, because by this method I can most clearly state what I mean.

Let me start off simply by stating what these antirules are—you'll see why they are weird—and then I will try to explain them as I go along. 1) Be out of things, (2) Be slow, (3) Write dead stories, (4) Go to hell, (5) Distrust rational thought, (6) Be beside the point, (7) Avoid the company of people, (8) Betray your sources, and (9) the most important antirule, Do not understand it.

Be out of things. Oscar Levant said to Joan Crawford in *Humoresque*, "Don't blame me, lady, I didn't make the world; I barely live on it." That's the ticket. To be out of things you must create an atmosphere in which you deliberately generalize your knowledge and your experience. You must cultivate, believe it or not, the old general education. And this cultivation involves several decisions.

First, it involves the deliberate avoidance of the narrow focus, usually the assigned focus. If I could show all that journalism can and cannot do by using one movie, it would be *Citizen Kane*, which is largely about journalism. *Citizen Kane* is a wonderful example of how *not* to go about discovering a story.

You remember how *Citizen Kane* begins: there is the newsreel about all the high points of Charles Foster Kane's life spilling loudly on the screen, and then the newsreel winds down to that kind of awkward halt. The room is dark. The editor, unseen (always the best condition for an editor), says in effect to the reporters in the room, "Um, how do we go about this? I understand his last word was 'Rosebud.' Let's find out what Rosebud is. If we find out what Rosebud means, we will discover Charles Foster Kane." And so he sends a reporter on the quest to discover Rosebud, and that is the entire plotline of the movie. The reporter, of course, does not discover Rosebud. *We* discover Rosebud only at the end when the sled is in the furnace, and we are to conclude from this disclosure that an entire life might be defined by a single moment—when Kane as a little boy used this instrument of the sled to resist the force that was going to take him from his bucolic bliss to the world which he then began to command and mess up simultaneously. As if any life could be defined by so small a discovery. The reporter does, in fact, get to the life of Charles Foster Kane by talking to all the people who *cannot* identify Rosebud.

But it's an accident, and only a partial truth he discovers anyway. And even at the end of the movie we are not sure who Kane was, which is exactly what we were supposed to learn. Any quest that looks for the narrow answer is usually the wrong quest. Any quest that looks in the direction in which you were initially pointed is usually the wrong quest in the wrong direction. If you want to find Rosebud, look almost everywhere but at that sled and find almost everything *but* that sled.

Being out of things involves anti-specialization, and, unfortunately, we live in a world of specialization. In the most recent issue of the *Michigan Quarterly Review* someone writes, "The ego-self is being replaced by the eco-self." I wish it were true, but I do not believe it for a moment. We live in a time when specialties are becoming both stupid and dangerous. There are specialty markets, target audiences, specialty magazines like *Wood, Teeth, Aleut Life,* and so forth. But we are also living in a specialized country in which we divide ourselves among races, among regions, between sexes, and on and on. We live increasingly in a segmented world that defines itself by remorseless violence, as in the tribalism in Bosnia, or in New York, or in the Sudan, from which I have recently returned, and where I saw the work of specialists firsthand. Specialists in the north, specialists in a peculiar sect of Islamic fundamentalism specializing in "ethnic cleansing"—a high point of specialization. With sufficient specialization, eventually there will be nobody left but us, whoever the "us" is; through such specialization we live in and we will be living in a country that is the antithesis of the one that we anticipated and deserve.

Being out of things also involves avoiding the news. If anyone were interested in going into journalism I would tell him or her, "Do not read the news." I realize that is something of an encumbrance when it comes to conversations with one's employers, but there are ways that you can pick up the news secondhand.

Instead, read history, read poetry, read fiction, if you really want to understand something, if you want to get to the heart of something. We watched John McEnroe trying to make a comeback. And he would get so far and he would fall back; and he'd get a little further, and he would fall back. And you'd wonder what was happening here. People said, "Well, he's older than he was, his serve isn't as strong as it was." All the rational explanations for people who follow the news.

If you ask me, if you want to know why John McEnroe couldn't make a comeback, read Bernard Malamud's novel *The Natural.* The reason that McEnroe couldn't make a comeback is that he was a natural; he didn't believe in discipline. He couldn't work at tennis because he was so naturally good at tennis. And when all of those inborn reflexes failed him—as if he were shocked at the mismotion of his own arm, at the slowness of his own leg—then we understood John McEnroe.

The opposite of a McEnroe went to this University—the pitcher Jim Abbott, who worked and worked and worked at his craft. Abbott pitched with his left hand because he was born without a right hand. And here at Michigan he worked at and acquired the pitches that made him a star in the majors.

The nice and interesting thing about Abbott is that for all that sunny, farm-boy ordinariness about him, there is no doubt that he is eccentric too. What sort of boy at the age of five or six would look down and see emptiness at the end of his right wrist and say, "You know what I'm going to do? I'm going to be a pitcher." Naturally, he was also a quarterback. Do you want to understand what makes a pitcher? Don't worry about the physics of a curve. And surely don't read the sports pages. Read a poem by Robert Francis called "The Pitcher." It's a poem about deception. It's a poem about fooling people, which is what a pitcher does.

Do you want to understand George Bush—I don't know why you would—but if you want to understand George Bush read Ford Madox Ford's *The Good Soldier.* Bush was a man with no center. You could tell he had no center by his use of language. Referring to Vaclav Havel, then the president of

Czechoslovakia, George Bush praised Havel for having been in jail "and living and dying, whatever, for freedom."

"I think it no exaggeration," said Bush about his own election in 1988, "to say that the undecideds could go one way or the other."

I miss Bush. I hope that Larry Goldstein will forgive me for these digressions. I miss Reagan, too, for the same kind of stuff. Reagan once returned from a trip to Latin America, after which he informed us, "You know, you'd be surprised. They're all individual countries."

"Sure we made mistakes," he once said, "but point them out and we'll correct them. Let's not throw the baby out, though, with the dishes."

My favorite thing Reagan ever said is the following. The Lebanese foreign minister was giving him a half-hour lecture on all the political factions in Lebanon. *All* the political factions in Lebanon. You may imagine what this lecture sounded like. When the foreign minister concluded, Mr. Reagan approached him and said, "You know, your nose looks just like Danny Thomas's." Maybe this isn't a digression; I *am* talking about being out of things.

Being out of things involves a connection with nature. I mean a real connection with nature. We have of late, I mean of late in the last 25, 30, maybe 50 years, lost a connection with nature, and we are paying severe penalities for it.

There was a wonderful photograph I saw in a magazine a few years ago of a public demonstration by French farmers in Paris protesting against the Common Market, and they decided to make this a vivid protest by bringing in cows and sheep and slices—I forget what the technical term is—of wheat fields, so that the wheat fields could be recreated on the Champs Elysées. They put this stuff right in the middle of the city—an agrarian revolt. The police were ready for all sorts of trouble.

What happened instead was that couples started strolling through the wheat fields, and the police joined them, in a kind of visceral remembrance of something that existed in a buried life—Matthew Arnold's phrase—"the buried life." There were no clashes. The instant countryside bred companionship.

I am persuaded that the real force of the environmental movement, however other many good things will come of it, arises from a desire for our reconnection with nature. We can talk about cleaning the air, the water and oil spills, and so forth—all of which is needed. But I think the movement comes from somewhere hidden. We wish to remind ourselves of our primal connection with nature.

Being out of it involves living in the past. You remember in Thornton Wilder's play *Skin of Our Teeth* the fortune-teller says something like: "Your future? Anybody can tell you your future. I'll tell you your *past*." Live in the past. Find the past, find *your* past. You *can* go home again. Often finding the past involves cultivating a dream state. Again, that phrase of Arnold's, "the buried life," retrieving and occupying a state of reverie. "A state of reverie does not avoid reality," said Somerset Maugham, "it accedes to reality."

Mark Twain used to curse a lot. His wife wanted to cure him of the habit. One morning his collar button was lost or something, and Twain let fly with the usual barrage: Goddamn . . . blah, blah, blah. And his wife, Livy, wanted to show him how ugly such language sounded, so she repeated verbatim what her husband had just said: Goddamn . . . blah, blah, blah. Twain stepped back, looked affectionately at his wife and said, "Livy, you know the words, but you don't know the tune." Know the tune of your life. Be out of things.

Second antirule—Be slow. All I mean by that is to wait on experience. Wait way beyond the point that you think you ought to wait before your start to create some understanding of experience, much less to make some judgment about it. Going slow is anathema for journalists, of course, who are taught to get something in as fast as possible. But it's an anathema for citizens generally, too. We pick this up, perhaps, from journalism: the need to get something fast. Get it fast. Forget it fast. Move along.

Imagine the weekend in the Politburo when the Soviet Union was still the Soviet Union and all those guys gathered together in that place, while hundreds of thousands of people in the streets of Moscow were waiting for some revelation to come out of the meeting. And the Soviet leaders emerge from that weekend, and they say to the people: "Well, from now on you can vote for a party that isn't the Communist party." After seventy years, after a single weekend, they emerge and say, "Just kidding. We really weren't serious about this Communist thing. Go about your business."

What could it mean? Every headline noted the collapse of Communism, and journalists went through the facts that traced the collapse of Communism. But what was happening here was that people realized—and what could it have meant to realize this?—that they and their parents and perhaps *their* parents, too, had been living a lie. And it was now admitted that it was a lie. And what are you supposed to do when you live a lie? I don't mean the big lie, I mean the little lies that people told to one another. The competitions for personal advancement. The lurches toward individual achievement. Any of you who visited the Soviet Union saw signs in hospitals and schools: the teacher of the week, the best worker of the week, all that stuff to reinforce the lie. And then after a single weekend the leaders say, "Well, we really didn't mean this." Vaclav Havel, so honored by President Bush, wrote an essay called "The Power of the Powerless," or "The Power of Powerlessness," in which he describes a worker in Czechoslovakia who, every day, made sure that the sign "Workers of the World Unite" stood in his window, as if he had any idea of its meaning. As if the application of it had anything to do with his life.

There was, at the time that Richard and I were at Harvard, a terribly strange story of two high school seniors who had applied to Harvard from the same high school. Let's say their names were Jones and Smith. Smith was under great pressure from his parents to go to Harvard. Nonetheless, he was rejected. Jones got into Harvard and he also got into Yale and he decided that he wanted to go to Yale, so he wrote to Harvard and said "I'm sorry, I'm not coming." Wrote to Yale and said he was coming, and went off to Yale.

Smith, knowing that Jones had done this, then wrote another letter to Harvard under Jones's name and said, "I've changed my mind. I'm coming after all." And so, Smith, under the name Jones, entered Harvard. Ordinarily you have to live in a freshman dormitory—he figured a way that he didn't have to so that he wouldn't run into people he knew. He led a life in hiding under his false name. Everything was going along fairly well for Smith, now Jones, but there is a rule applying only to the first semester, that if you get a C or below in any subject, your parents are sent a letter informing them of this. Jones, *né* Smith, was doing pretty well at Harvard, except for one course in which he got a C. Anybody, as everybody knows, can do very well at Harvard. The trick is getting in—that's the second hardest thing. The first hardest thing is being thrown out.

· At any rate things were going swimmingly for our Smith, now under the name of Jones, but he got a C in one course and a note was sent home to his parents. Of course it wasn't sent home to *his* parents, it was sent home to the parents of the *real* Jones, who wrote back to Harvard saying, "We're dismayed to hear our son isn't doing too well at Harvard because he's doing quite well at Yale." Whereupon Smith/Jones was thrown out of Harvard. A minor irony in this story is that his name was expunged from the record, but of course it wasn't *his* name that was expunged from the record.

But what if he *hadn't* gotten the C, I've always wondered. That might have been the only time he could have been caught. And Smith as Jones would become Jones the sophomore. And Jones the junior. And Jones the senior. And Jones would enter law school. And Jones would get married to someone who might, if she chose to, adopt the name Jones. And their children would be called Jones and they would live a whole life named Jones. And he would die under the name Jones. And he would be buried in the cemetery, and written above his grave would be "Jones."

What does it mean to make decisions the accretion of which results in living a lie? If we knew that, we would know what happened all those decades under Communism, the meaning of those gulags, that art, those inventions, that shoe of Krushchev's.

When I was in what was then the Soviet Union, I was taken to Latvia. Every place a visitor went in the Soviet Union, someone was attached to him who had multiple functions. He was your translator. He was your guide. And he was a spy. It was all understood, and it was all good-natured. He was also a propagandist. "We will now visit a typical Latvian fisherman," he told me. The man had been prepared for this visit for months, you know, given new clothes, a new house. "We will just drop in on him."

So, we get to this guy's house and you can see he is practically shaking. He's not prepared for any of this stuff. And meanwhile I'm told how happy all the Latvians are to be Communists and how happy it is to be fishermen in this system because you have the privilege of donating all your fish to the community fishery. And, sure enough, I would dutifully ask questions of the fisherman about his life, and he would say: "Never better, never better. I love to go out there and catch these fish and give them all to the state."

Getting nowhere in the interview, I noticed a guitar in the corner and asked simply if he played, and would he play us a folk song. He started to play, and he had the most beautiful voice. He started to sing a folk song in Latvian. And then it happened. My translator-guide-spy began to sing also, to sing thirds harmony with the fisherman in an equally beautiful voice. And for one moment, the only true moment of the day, I could understand everything that was happening there. My accompanist was, after all, Latvian. He was home. The song had brought him home. But you had to wait.

Antirule #3: Write dead stories. The rule applies to readers as well as writers. Pay attention to the stories that people forget, that they say are over. Whenever something happens there is a closure, a verdict and a trial, something that says, "You will hear no more of this." Yet the stories that reverberate in our minds, in the aftereffects of our minds, are almost always the most significant.

You may remember a story that happened in a small town in the Midwest near Kansas City about twelve years ago. There was a bully in the town, I mean a really dangerous, bad-guy bully who raped women and beat up the men and was drunk all the time, and terrorized this small town. One day this guy is walking through town in the middle of the day, shots ring out, and the bully is dead. Cops come in and ask who did it. Beats me, says the town, didn't see a thing. Middle of the day, small town, everybody knew who shot this guy, but nobody saw a thing. Maybe there were several who shot him.

The cops give up. Federal agents come in, as in the Rodney King case. They decide, "Well, if we can't get anywhere with this as a murder case, we can decide that the man was deprived of his civil rights." There is a kind of logic to that. When you are killed, you really are deprived of your civil rights. Feds go in there, the town clams up just as it did before. Nope, didn't see a thing. Nothing.

For twelve years no one in that town has said a word in public about what happened on that Saturday afternoon. But imagine the story now. Now the dead man is no longer a bully. He's dead twelve years. And the town, meanwhile, has been living with a conspiracy, with the common knowledge that one or more among them is capable of murder. And this is a secret they cannot divulge. If you want a story, don't worry about the bully. Go into the town now, if you dare.

In New York a couple of years ago there was a terrible incident involving a man named Rodney Sumpter, who, being menaced by a homeless man in a subway—Rodney Sumpter was with his child—leapt upon the homeless man and beat him to death; beat his head against the subway platform. There was no indictment, and *that* case was over. It was in several ways a dead story. But why did that story reverberate in the minds of New Yorkers and in the minds of those who would read the story outside New York? Because it involved the inarticulate, unexpressed rage at the impotence people everywhere feel about homelessness. The admixture of fear and pity. Of wanting to do something to correct what you know is wrong, and not being able to. All the feelings that New Yorkers have as they step gingerly over the bodies of their fellow creatures on their way to work; they were in that story. Yet it was a dead story; there was no indictment. Nothing is ever over. The mind lives in aftereffects.

Antirule #4: Go to hell. What I mean by that is simply something you writers in the audience know already. You discover chaos inside you. It is useful. Use it. Nietzsche said, "You must have chaos within you to give birth to a dancing star." I mean discover real chaos. The kind of chaos that Huck Finn discovered when he decided to go to hell to do something honorable. Where I live there is chaos everywhere. I look out my window on Broadway and see chaos performing. What reverberates in me is the same chaos. Go to hell. It is useful.

Antirule #5. Distrust rational thought. We know the value of rational thought. We ought to be more in tune with the instruction of irrational thought, of intuition. We see public figures about whom we know something is terribly wrong, but we listen to the evidence and the words, and we decide to make definitions about those figures according to the externalities. You see Bud McFarland testify in the Iran-Contra investigation. You feel something is terribly wrong with him, and then something actually goes wrong; he tries to kill himself. Your intuition was right. Bess Myerson is picked up for shoplifting. All you had to do was trust your intuition. Oliver North with all that stolid talk, and that solid stance. Is there doubt in anybody's mind that he is crazy as a loon?

I work with some friends in my neighborhood with a homeless group. We do very little—put out a journal once a month consisting of the stories of their lives. We interview them, and then we write their stories, on the idea, which seems to work, that seeing their lives in print gives them a kind of credibility, puts them back on earth.

In one of these interviews I said to a woman named Betty, a woman in her sixties, "Betty, can I talk to you about your life?" She said, "Oh, I'd like to talk to you, Roger, but CBS is coming over later to interview me, so I don't know how much time I have. And you know how it is when you've been a former showgirl and Miss America and you've had all this celebrity and you've had a Hollywood screen test, and you've dated Joe DiMaggio. But if I have the time, I'll talk to you." So I wrote up what she told me, but I asked the psychiatrist in charge of the place if there was any harm in recording these fantasies. He said not if Betty believed them herself.

Two weeks before Betty died peacefully in her sleep a young woman came looking for her, who turned out to be her daughter, born in a mental institution in Texas where Betty had been a patient. The daughter in her dogged search for her mother had gone from state to state, and had finally come to our neighborhood and found her mother, and they were reunited. It was miraculous for the couple of weeks of life left to Betty.

The daughter also carried with her evidence that everything Betty had told me was true. She *had* been a showgirl in the Latin Quarter nightclub. She was not Miss America, but she was Miss Ohio, and she had gone to the Miss America contest. Another fact she *didn't* mention was that her brother was a pitcher for the Cincinnati Reds. She *did* date Joe DiMaggio, and she had a Hollywood screen test.

If I had been looking where I ought to have been looking, I would have believed all that about Betty, but I was trusting what seemed to be reasonable, rational thought. You see, Betty sang in the streets. If you listened to the voice, even through all that cigarette smoke, there was the truth about Betty—in her songs. Shelley said, "We need the power to imagine what we know." (That quotation, by the way, was taught to me this morning by Larry Goldstein, my closest friend.)

Antirule #6: Be beside the point. It's a variation of being out of things, but with a specific direction. It means literally choosing the other direction. I'm going to begin with a basketball anecdote, though I realize basketball is a painful subject to raise here at Michigan after the NCAA finals.

The basketball anecdote about looking the other way has to do with a back-court man at the University of Arkansas who was not doing so well, and he asked his coach what he was doing wrong. The coach said, "What do you do in practice?"

The kid answered, "I dribble and shoot, like most people."

The coach said, "In the next full scrimmage game, have somebody clock how much time you actually have your hands on the ball. That is, whether you're dribbling or you're shooting."

The kid did that, came back, and the coach asked, "How much time was it?" The kid was the point guard, so he would have his hands on the ball more time than other players. He reported that the time he handled the ball came to something over two minutes. A little over two minutes—out of forty. The player was shocked, of course. The coach asked, "What do you learn from that?"

The kid said, "I don't know."

The coach said, "Most of the game is played away from the ball."

In journalism, in the things that we watch, in the life we observe, most of the game is played away from the ball. Journalists are taught to be like heliotropic plants, to turn where the light is, or to turn where the noise is. But if you want to know about something, I mean really know about something, look away from the ball. If you want to know about poverty, don't look at a march on Washington, or at a tenement fire. Study the poor all the time. The poor are poor all the time.

Every time there is a natural diaster—the Ohio flood, the hurricane in Florida—people are missing the point by being on the point. So we are always told about these events in terms of the millions of dollars lost or how many people were injured, property damage, and so forth . . . when what we know to be the deeper truth, the inner life, the buried life of the story, is that we are helpless in nature still, and that nothing prepares us for certain events no matter how "advanced" we are. As we develop invention after invention, and sophistication after sophistication, these inexplicable uncontrollable things will always occur. *That* is the story of natural disasters.

Look away from the ball. Study people in repose, not people in crisis. There is a myth that exists among writers that behavior in the critical moment will reveal character. I do not believe it. I believe that behavior in the critical moment merely reveals behavior in the critical moment. And that people behave in aberrant ways in crises. But study people in repose, and you might have a chance of knowing what is going on inside their minds.

Antirule #7: Avoid the company of people. I regard that as an excellent general rule, but I will apply it to this talk as well. What I mean by this is to cultivate a useful privacy. There is so little privacy in our world, and again, as with the separation from nature, we are paying penalties for it. Rousseau said, "If I had to choose my place of birth, I would have chosen a state in which everyone knew everyone else so that neither the obscure tactics of vice nor the modesty of virtue could have escaped public scrutiny and judgment." Rousseau is what one would call in French a *tête* case. Who in his right mind would want a society where everything that one did or thought would be available to public scrutiny and judgment?

What purpose was served by revealing Arthur Ashe's AIDS? What good was served, except to provoke an extra amount of pain in a man who was going to die anyway, for those last months of his life? And it is not just that privacy is invaded in our time. Privacy is surrendered willingly—surrendered on Oprah, on Geraldo, on Donahue. I am always dumbstruck to watch the parents of children killed in a crossfire able to talk to a television reporter moments afterwards with all the aplomb of a seasoned television performer. They are ready to be public figures, ready to give out.

I don't really mean to advocate avoiding the company of people as much as I mean husbanding your time so that you are aware of the value of yourself without stumbling over into egocentricity or selfishness. I go back to Wordsworth. Coleridge was said to have visited Wordsworth, gone into the cottage, stayed four or five hours. They didn't say a word to each other. As Coleridge was walking out the door, he thanked Wordsworth for a perfect evening.

What privacy does is to develop certain valuable things in you. It develops a sense of language, of real language, not false language, not public language. For you, prize winners in these writing contests, the development of private language is essential. You will be misled. There will be temptations all the time to use some other word that is not your word.

So many words are used oddly today. I hear the word "fun" in the craziest contexts. A man works twenty years composing a dictionary of Zoroastrianism. Asked how the project went, he said "It was fun." An actor appears in a one-man play, *Pol Pot Tonight*. Says it was "fun," it was a lot of "fun."

There is a product advertised on late-night television in New

York called "Safe Ears." A woman steps forward to advertise gold-looking earrings that contain condoms inside. Condoms hidden in the earrings. Most inventive. The world has certainly come a long way from the Roy Rogers bullet ring I had as a boy, with its secret compartment, which contained nothing. Something else about "Safe Ears." They sell three to a set. Three earrings to a set. You'd think if your date was so constructed as to be able to wear three earrings, safe sex would be the least of her concerns. But the woman steps forward to say, "Safe ears are fabulous. And *fun.*"

Cultivate privacy because private thoughts are much more complicated than public thoughts. It has to do, again, with this chaos within you. Think of the way the mind is most of the time. This roiling of words. All this chaos which then comes out in some orderly fakery we call conversation. But the state of mind before that moment; that's the thing to cultivate. That is the private self.

Most of all, privacy, oddly enough, makes the best social sense. I think civilizations are made up of interacting privacies. That's where people really learn community; to be with one another. A sense of self, and then a sense of other, in that order.

The eighth antirule: "Betray your sources." I don't mean this the way it sounds. If somebody tells you a secret you don't say who it was. I mean something far colder. Every journalist deliberately betrays the people he or she interviews. The act is justified in the name of a larger truth, but it is still a betrayal.

The most extravagant experience I had with betrayal was with Richard Nixon. I interviewed him twice. The first time I put my tape recorder beside him. He looked at it—true story—and said, "Oh, that's one of those new tape recorders. They are so much better than the old tape recorders." I did not know if he was joking. I did not laugh. I did not say, "Oh, yes, Mr. President, these don't skip a minute." I did not say that.

I was interviewing him for a story I was doing on the anniversary of Hiroshima and I wanted to talk to somebody who had had his finger on or near the button more than anyone else, and Nixon qualified. The story came out; Nixon was delighted. I wasn't interested in Watergate for the story. I made no comments about his character or about his leaving office or anything. I was interested in Nixon as nuclear diplomat, and he was very knowledgeable on this subject. So we became pen pals in a sense. He would send me notes from time to time. I thought that this was a unique distinction until I discovered that he was sending hundreds of people in my profession notes, all for the same purpose—redeeming his name.

Then I was asked by *Time* to write a profile of Nixon. I did, and do, think he is the most interesting political character in my lifetime, and I was glad to write about him. I wrote a scathing profile. It was called "The Dark Comedian" and I just let fly with all the contempt that I held for what he did to the highest office in the country. Nixon flew off the handle, wrote to *Time* saying, "I will not give an interview to any organization in which Rosenblatt is working." His timing was poor, because in that particular summer I was working for *Time*, MacNeil/Lehrer, and CBS.

Of course, he didn't mean any of this. The thing that got him sore was the thought that I had betrayed him, and of course I had. In the interview he granted for this profile, I showed no sign that I was about to tell the world what I thought of Richard Nixon. I did my very best to let Nixon be Nixon, and to say all the things I wanted him to say, without misrepresenting what he was saying, in order to enact a work of obvious, blatant betrayal in the name of something else, of some other loyalty.

Yet did I understand Nixon? Do I understand Nixon now? No. It was and is all beyond me.

And so, I come to the ninth and last, and to me, the guiding antirule—Do not understand it. I do not mean pretend not to understand it and then create some other fiction within the fiction. I mean do not understand it. Retain the mystery.

I was watching the Academy Awards a couple of years ago. Typical ceremony: the most glittery people in the world, dressed to the nines. Dazzling. I had the remote control and I turned to the news, on which they showed the bodies lined up in that Bronx Happyland Social Club fire of the same year. The bodies were awaiting burial. I thought: How can I be seeing these two things almost simultaneously? Will they, said the mind trying to make connections, make a movie of the Happyland fire some day? Will it win an Academy Award?

I came back recently from a trip to the Sudan where I saw the worst place in the world. There is no second place. I've seen places where, physically, things were worse. But what makes Sudan the most heartbreaking place I have ever seen is that while people are dying from intratribal war, and the ethnic cleansing by the Moslems in the north of the Christians and animists in the south, while they are dying of all the diseases attributed to starvation and malnutrition, the thing that makes the Sudan the worst place I have ever seen is that nobody cares. Nobody is doing anything about it.

How can what is happening in the Sudan exist in the same world in which we, now, look at one another in this gracious hall, in which we take pleasure in one another's existence, wish one another the best? George Steiner in *Language and Silence* asks, "How could I be going to the movies and making love in New York at the same time that children were being dumped into the ovens in Auschwitz?" It is beyond us. I do not understand it. Do not understand it.

From that lack of understanding comes the kind of awe of experience out of which our work as writers could do a little good, could have its reverberations in other souls. Do not understand Rosebud.

When I was in high school, my father took me to the play *Inherit the Wind*. It starred Paul Muni playing the role of Clarence Darrow, and Ed Begley (Ed Begley, *Sr.*, you have to say now) in the role of William Jennings Bryan. And it introduced a new actor, Tony Randall, in the role of a character called Hornbeck who was to represent H.L. Mencken. You know the story of *Inherit the Wind*; it's the Scopes "monkey trial" in Tennessee where the teacher was tried for teaching evolution, and lost the case, but won the point.

I was sitting there with my father, having no knowledge that I would ever enter journalism, wanting to be a writer but not knowing how that was ever going to be achieved. In the middle of the play, the Bryan character has a stroke. He has a stroke because he is overwhelmed by the idea that he is defending the indefensible, and as eloquent as he is, he can't take it. And Hornbeck, the journalist, regards this as Darrow's triumph. Darrow has been brilliantly rational throughout on the matter of evolution, and the two of them, the journalist and Darrow, are on the stage together. The journalist gloats and says to Darrow, "Well, you really got him! You really made a fool of that Bible-beating bastard!"

And Darrow, heaving with contempt, looks at the journalist and says, "What could a man like you possibly know about a man like that?"

That is our question.

KATHLEEN NORRIS

DEGENERATES

PLOUGHSHARES

Not long ago I accompanied a Trappist abbot as he unlocked a door to the cloister and led me down a long corridor into a stone-walled room, the chapter house of his monastery, where some twenty monks were waiting for me to give a reading. Poetry does lead a person into some strange places. This wonderfully silent, hiddenaway place was not as alien to me as it might have been, however, as I've been living on the grounds of a Benedictine monastery for most of the last three years, and have steeped myself in the community's daily rhythm of prayer, work, and play.

Trappists are more silent than the Benedictines, far less likely to have work that draws them into the world outside the monastery. But the cumulative effect of the liturgy of the hours—at a bare minimum, morning, noon, and evening prayer, as well as the Eucharist—on one's psyche, the sense it gives a person of being immersed in the language of scripture, is much the same in any monastery. What has surprised me, in my time among monastic people, is how much their liturgy feeds my poetry; and also how much correspondence I've found between monastic practice and the discipline of writing.

Before I read a few poems of mine that had been inspired by the psalms (the mainstay of all monastic liturgy), I discussed some of those connections. I told the Trappists that I had come to see both writing and monasticism as vocations that require periods of apprenticeship and formation. Prodigies are common in mathematics, but extremely rare in literature, and, I added, "as far as I know, there are no prodigies in monastic life." This drew a laugh, as I thought it might.

Related to this, I said, was recognizing the dynamic nature of both disciplines; they are not so much subjects to be mastered as ways of life that require continual conversion. For example, no matter how much I've written or published, I always return to the blank page; and even more importantly, from a monastic point of view, I return to the blankness within, the fears, laziness, and cowardice that, without fail, will mess up whatever I'm currently writing and, in turn, require me to revise it. The spiritual dimension of this process is humility, not a quality often associated with writers, but lurking there, in our nagging sense of the need to revise. As I put it to the monks, when you realize that anything good you write comes *despite* your weaknesses, writing becomes a profoundly humbling activity. At this point one of the monks spoke up. "I find that there's a redemptive quality," he said, "just in sitting in front of that blank piece of paper."

This comment reflects an important aspect of monastic life, which has been described as "attentive waiting." I think it's also a fair description of the writing process. Once, when I was asked, "What is the main thing a poet does?" I was inspired to answer, "We wait." A spark is struck; an event inscribed with a message—*This is important, pay attention*—and a poet scatters a few words like seeds in a notebook. Months or even years later, those words bear fruit. The process requires both discipline and commitment, and its gifts come from both preparedness and grace, or what writers have traditionally called inspiration. As Bill Stafford wrote, with his usual simplicity, in a poem entitled "For People with Problems About How to Believe": "a quality of attention has been given to you:/when you turn your head the whole world/leans forward. It waits there thirsting/after its names, and you speak it all out/as it comes to you . . ."

"Listen" is the first word of St. Benedict's *Rule* for monasteries, and listening for the eruptions of grace into one's life— often from unlikely sources—is a "quality of attention" that both monastic living and the practice of writing tends to cultivate. I'm trained to listen when words and images begin to constellate. When I'm awakened at three a.m. by my inner voice telling me to look into an old notebook, or to get to work on a poem I'd abandoned years before, I do not turn over and go back to sleep. I obey, which is an active form of listening (the two words are related, etymologically).

Anyone who listens to the world, anyone who seeks the sacred in the ordinary events of life, has "problems about how to believe." Paradoxically, it helps that both prayer and poetry begin deep within a person, beyond the reach of language. The fourth-century desert monk, St. Anthony, said that perfect prayer was one you don't understand. Poets are used to discovering, years after a poem is written, what it's really about. And it's in the respect for the mystery and power of words that I find the most profound connections between the practice of writing and monastic life.

The *lectio divina* (loosely and inadequately translated as "prayerful reading") practiced by followers of Benedict, including Cistercians and Trappists as well as Benedictines, strikes me as similar to the practice of writing poetry, in that it is not an intellectual procedure so much as an existential one. Grounded in a meditative reading of scriptures, it soon becomes much more: a way of reading the world and one's place in it. To quote a fourth-century monk, it is a way of reading that "works the earth of the heart."

I should try telling friends who have a hard time comprehending why I like to spend so much time going to church with monks that I do so for the same reasons that I write: in order to let words work the earth of my heart. To sing, to read poetry aloud, and to have the poetry and the wild stories of scripture read to me. To respond with others, in blessed silence. That is a far more accurate description of morning or evening prayer in a monastery than what most people conjure up when they hear the word "church."

Monks have always recognized reading as a bodily experience, primarily oral. The ancients spoke of masticating the words of scripture in order to fully digest them. Monastic "church" reflects a whole-body religion, still in touch with its orality, its music. Both poetry and religion originate in the oral, and I suspect that they stray from those roots at their peril, becoming rigid, precious, academic, irrelevant. In the midst of today's revolution in "instant communication," I find it a blessing that monks still respect the slow way that words work on the human psyche. They take the time to sing, chant, and read the psalms aloud, often with a full minute of silence between them, in order to let the words sink in. The community I'm most familiar with keeps two minutes of silence after brief readings from scripture—in the time I've been with them, we've heard much of Isaiah, Job, Jeremiah, Acts, Romans, and Revelations read this way, as well as the entire books of Jonah, Ruth, and the Song of Songs—and it is astonishing how words will resonate in the vast space that our silence creates. It's not easy listening, or the hard-sell jargon of television evangelists; it's more like imbibing language—often powerfully poetic language—at full strength.

This style of reading and listening also allows fully for response, for one's own unruly thoughts to rise up out of the unconscious, sometimes in comical fashion. Once, at morning prayer during Easter season, when I heard that an angel in the book of Revelation said to John of Patmos, "Write what you see," my gut response was, "Easy for *you* to say." But when we ended a vespers reading with a passage from Job, "My lyre is turned to mourning, and my pipe to the voice of those who weep," I was awestruck, not only with the beauty of the words, but also with the way those words gave a new dimension to watching the nightly news later that evening, leading me to reflect on the communal role of the poet.

Poets and monks do have a communal role in American culture, although it alternately ignores, romanticizes, and despises them. In our relentlessly utilitarian society, structuring a life around writing is as crazy as structuring a life around prayer, yet that is what writers and monks *do*. Deep down, people seem glad to know that monks are praying, that poets are writing poems. This is what others want and expect of us, because if we do our job right, we will express things that others may feel, or know, but can't or won't say. At least this is what writers are told over and over again by their readers, and I suspect it's behind the boom in visits to monastic retreat houses. Maybe it is the useless silence of contemplation, that certain "quality of attention" that distinguishes both the poem and the prayer.

I regard monks and poets as the best degenerates in America. Both have a finely developed sense of the sacred potential in all things. (Think of Mary Oliver, or Galway Kinnell. Of Philip Levine or Denise Levertov. Joy Harjo, Lucille Clifton, Linda Hogan, Li-Young Lee, Gary Snyder.) In a world in which "meaningless" and "ritual" are taken to be synonymous, many desperately seek meaningful symbols in the empty rituals of drug use, pornography, shopping, sports. But the absurd practices of monks and poets are healthier. They value image and symbol over utilitarian purpose or the bottom line; they recognize the transformative power hiding in the simplest things. In a culture that excels at artifice, at creating controlled environments that serve a clear commercial purpose (shopping malls, amusement parks, chain motels), what poets do, what monks do, is useless. Worse than that, it's scary; it remains beyond consumerism's manipulation and control.

Not long ago I viewed an exhibition at the New York Public Library entitled "Degenerate Art" that consisted of artworks approved by Hitler's regime, along with art the Nazis had denounced. As I walked the galleries it struck me that the real issue was one of control. The meaning of the approved art was superficial, in that its images (usually rigidly representational) served a clear commercial and/or political purpose. The "degenerate" artworks, many crucifixes among them, were more often abstract, with multiple meanings, or even no meaning at all, in the conventional sense. This art—like the best poetry, and also good liturgy—allowed for a wide freedom of experience and interpretation on the part of the viewer.

Pat Robertson once declared that modern art was a plot to strip America of its vital resources. Using an abstract sculpture by Henry Moore as an example, he said that the material used could more properly have been used for a statue of George Washington. What do poets mean? Who needs them? Of what possible use are monastic people in the modern world? Are their lives degenerate in the same sense that modern art is—having no easily perceptible meaning, yet of ultimate value, concerned with ultimate meanings? Maybe monks and poets know, as Jesus did when a friend, in an extravagent, loving gesture, poured nard on his feet and washed them with her hair, that the symbolic act *matters*; that those who know the exact price of things, as Judas did, often don't know the true cost or value of anything.

MICHAEL NORMAN

A BOOK IN SEARCH OF
A BUZZ: THE MARKETING
OF A FIRST NOVEL

THE NEW YORK TIMES BOOK REVIEW

Put aside all your strict ideas about what is worthy and what is unworthy. . . . Just make it a matter of business.

—George Gissing, *"New Grub Street"* (1891)

It is a warm day in the early summer of 1992 and a young writer from the Old South is hustling down Fifth Avenue in Manhattan, late for a meeting with his editor. His first novel, still in manuscript, is nearly a year from the bookstore shelves, but the process of promoting it, and him, has already begun.

He walks south sweating in the sun, hope and history at his heels. He aims for something big. Not the Great American Novel, exactly—he has no ambition, yet, to encompass the culture, rewrite the idiom. Instead, he aims for something literary: a book to anchor a career, a road that might lead to a writing life.

Down Fifth Avenue he goes, then through the main entrance at No. 666, up to the 20th floor and over to an amiable receptionist.

"Hi," he says. "I'm here to see Nan Talese."

"Hello," says the amiable receptionist. "And you're . . . ?"

"Oh, I'm Mark Richard."

He is 36 years old, with shrewd eyes and a shock of dark hair, a sturdy man of medium height somewhat hobbled by congenitally bad hips. Late of Virginia and now of New York, he has worked as a fisherman, a photographer, a private-eye, a manager for a political candidate. He's lived high, dining at the table of well-to-do friends, and he's lived low, so strapped he's slept beside a highway.

At first glance, he seems poised for success. His short stories have appeared in Esquire, Harper's Magazine and The New Yorker, and in 1989 Knopf collected 10 of them in "The Ice at the Bottom of the World," which won the PEN/Hemingway prize and led to a Whiting Foundation grant. His editor, Nan A. Talese of Doubleday, publishes, among many others, Margaret Atwood and Pat Conroy, the former long a critical success, the latter a best seller. And his agent, Georges Borchardt, has counted among his many clients Beckett and Sartre, Jane Fonda and Tracy Kidder.

But in the catchpenny world of commercial publishing, where "value" frequently has meaning only at the bottom of a balance sheet, all this can add up to very little. In the counting rooms of modern American publishing houses, the past is measured in sales and returns, and Mark Richard's thin collection made almost no impression in the marketplace. So today he has come to his new publisher, Doubleday, hoping to find a way to make his next book—his first novel—sell.

Of course, no author or book is typical. But the story of Mark Richard (pronounced ree-SHARD) and "Fishboy" is instructive in illustrating the fate of a first novel. The author was selected as the focus of this essay not because he is the most promising writer of his generation, or because he is the season's young-man-about-fiction, but because he has an interesting writing style and because he had the forbearance to sit through more then 50 interviews spread across nearly two years.

Mark Richard is a late-20th-century writer, which is to say that like it or not, he takes a hand in selling his product. These days the most ardent apostles for art roll up their sleeves, hold their noses against the meretriciousness of the marketplace and practice a little economic determinism. Even Cormac McCarthy, Don DeLillo and William Gaddis—eminent novelists who are notoriously shy when it comes to publicity—have surrendered to the exigencies of modern publishing and agreed to be the subjects of magazine articles.

Some first novelists lend themselves to the hard sell. Such was the case with Donna Tartt and her 1992 book "The Secret History," a hefty campus novel that won its author commercial success and celebrity. But the publicity and marketing machine that put Ms. Tartt on the best-seller lists (and has so far, according to its publisher, netted over 200,000 copies in hard cover alone) will not grind nearly as hard for Mark Richard. "Fishboy" is not the sort of book to inspire gossipy feature stories. Narrow and oblique, it is an unexpected tale told in an unexpected way. What is more, the author does not have the kind of profile that suggests literary success. He attended Washington & Lee University, a small school in the South, not a well-known graduate-school writing program like that at the University of Iowa. He studied journalism, not the esthetic laws, as John Gardner called them, that writing programs purvey.

In the end, Mark Richard will discover what most authors discover: at some point, after all the angst and effort—the editor's grand plan, the publicist's pitch, the salesman's best show—the fate of any book, but especially a first novel, is often beyond reckoning.

"Fishboy" is a story—a myth, really—about a young grotesque, looking for redemption, who goes to sea on a trawler crewed by misfits and murderers. The plot is oblique, the characters bizarre, the language so rich it is sometimes impenetrable. Such a book is a tough sell, and not just to a general readership.

Long before it is sent out to fight for a place on the bookstore shelves, "Fishboy" will have to win friends inside the publishing house that releases it, especially among Doubleday's sales representatives, who pitch the company's list of titles to the nation's 30,000 bookstores. No sales rep has the time to tout every title on the list. Instead, a sales rep pushes the books he or she thinks will sell—or, sometimes, the ones that seem of personal interest. If Mark Richard's editor, Ms. Talese, can't convince Doubleday's sales force that "Fishboy" deserves at least a mention when they're out peddling the company's products, then the book—and the career that rides on it—could end up in the jaws of a pulp machine.

Most publishers divide their offerings into two main lists, fall and spring. Six to eight months in advance of each season, the sales force and marketing crew gather at a series of meetings to review the upcoming list; the decisions that are made at these sessions—closed to outsiders—can make or break a book. Major houses like Doubleday publish between 100 and 150 titles a season. Profit margins are too thin to promote aggressively each item on such a large list, so at their sales and marketing meetings the companies practice a kind of literary triage. They decide who gets the full treatment—the six-figure print run, the lavish book jacket, the pressure on the news media, the 10-city tour, the television interviews, the advertisements, the four-color posters and bookstore displays—and who is left to rely on luck.

The editors who are invited to attend the sales and marketing meetings are given only a few moments to present each of their books. "I'd say we get an average of 26 seconds to represent five years' worth of an author's work," said a senior editor at a major publishing house (one of many consulted for this essay who insisted on anonymity). And, said another editor, if an editor's pitch is flat or oblique, "if the sales force yawns or says, 'We don't get it,' then chances are there'll be no tour or promotion budget. Your little novel becomes just another couple of lines in the company's catalogue."

Sales people, of course, speak the language of commerce, not culture, so a clever editor tries to give a book the cachet of a best seller. "At sales conference you never bore the reps with a plot," said Gerald Howard, an editor at W.W. Norton. "The easiest way to present fiction to them is by analogy; you say, 'This book is a Chicano "Ordinary People" or a Yugoslavian "Joy Luck Club" or "Catcher in the Rye" displaced to California.' "

Then again, an editor can try pitching the author, not the book. Nan Talese has decided that the campaign for "Fishboy" will turn in large part on Mark Richard. The story of his eclectic life should make good copy for Doubleday's publicists and, as a former radio disk jockey, Mr. Richard acquits himself so well in front of a microphone that Ms. Talese plans to let him address the sales reps directly—by way of a videotape that will be sent to them with proof copies of the book.

And thus it is that Mr. Richard finds himself at the offices of his publisher this fine summer day, fussing in front of a camera as he prepares to tape a short pitch.

"Maybe," says Ms. Talese, doing a little coaching before the camera goes on, "maybe you can say, 'This is a ghost story,' so it has sort of a sense of mystery." (There is indeed a ghost in "Fishboy," but a ghost story it's not.)

The author is anxious, sweating through his polo shirt. "I want the reps to know that I'll do anything to make this book a success," he says. "Will they know who I am? Should I mention my first book?"

All at once the lights go on and the cameraman signals he's ready.

The author clears his throat:

" 'Fishboy' is the story of a discarded boy who has become a ghost. It is a story of murder and fratricide and patricide, but there also are some lighter moments and I hope even a love story thrown in. . . . I'm willing to go all across the country to give readings, to do whatever it takes to get this book out in front of the public. . . . I understand that you are the best at what you do. I would love to make this book such a success that the previous publisher will be very angry with themselves for letting this book go. Thank you, and it's nice to be with Doubleday."

"Great," says Ms. Talese.

"Very friendly," says the associate marketing director, John Pitts. "Very warm."

For his part, Mr. Richard seems uncomfortable. A postulant to literature, he has just painted his ambitiously unconventional work as conventional—yet another tale with sex and violence—just so he can win over his publisher's sales agents. (Much later, after a few beers, he will ask, "I wasn't too unctuous, was I?")

Now, however, back in the office of his editor, he encounters a more immediate problem.

"Did you bring the manuscript?" Ms. Talese asks.

The room grows quiet. He was supposed to have delivered his revision today.

"No," says Mr. Richard, clearly diffident. "But it's O.K. I know we're on deadline."

"I know you know," says Ms. Talese.

"It's going to be better," Mr. Richard goes on. "I'm telling you it's going to be a lot better."

"When will I see it?"

Mr. Richard shifts in his seat. "I'm, ah, going south on the 17th."

"I think," says Ms. Talese, "that you should leave "Fishboy" here—before you go."

"I need to turn up the volume."

"You need to work."

Doomsayers of American culture have been forecasting the death of serious literature since that day in the early 19th century when the Harper brothers opened their little shop in Manhattan and ushered in the era of modern American commercial publishing. True or not, it is painfully apparent today that technology, demographics and particularly the interest in increasing dividends and profits seen in the last two decades have had a profound impact on American literature. The world of letters has been changing, and these changes raise a number of disquieting questions:

Has the printed word lost its power to shape society? Who's driving modern culture—Toni Morrison and Alfred A. Knopf or the Beastie Boys and Bart Simpson? Is a great publisher still measured by a sense of taste and a willingness to defy convention, or only by its ability to survive in a marketplace where an average of 45,000 new titles a year—including perhaps some 4,000 works of fiction—compete for shelf space? And what about the modern editor? Is he or she nothing more than a bibliographic procurer, a deal maker who thinks of books not as culture but as a share of consumer spending? Or is the editor still the front-line critic, culling out the common and raising up the rare, helping us, as the 19th-century critic Margaret

Fuller put it, to "catch the contagion" of art? What kind of balance can be struck between literary fiction and commercial fiction? What is product and what is art? Can a book be both? Is it fair when the critic Denis Donoghue says that "a work of literature concentrates on being a work of literature at any cost"?

American publishers insist they "support" literary fiction, but their record suggests something else. Today, the big conglomerates that have spent the last 30 years buying up most of the country's major publishing houses want big books with big sales to justify their big investments—and books that need time to find their audience, books that might bolster a backlist a decade hence, tend to get lost in the process. This hunger for immediate sales, for best sellers, Thomas Whiteside says in his 1981 book "The Blockbuster Complex," has stripped away the veneer of gentility that once made the profession of publishing seem so noble. True, publishers have always aimed at the bottom line. (John Tebbel's 1987 history of American publishing, "Between Covers," is filled with tales of the mean and niggardly. As the 19th-century publisher Fletcher Harper told his contemporary George Palmer Putnam, after Putnam complained that Harper had pirated one of his editions, "Courtesy is courtesy and business is business.") But, inside the business and out, there used to be a sense that America's bookmen and bookwomen were the country's curators of culture.

No more. Now the voice from the editor's office is filled with censure and shame. "On the bad days," Gerald Howard wrote in an uncompromising essay in the summer 1989 issue of The American Scholar, "the days when another venerable American house is neutron-bombed by the mindless conglomerate . . . I decide that literature is the very last thing that publishing is about. I decide that publishing is about power and money and ego and sharp practice." Books are products, units, goods; this is a state of mind that corrodes culture. "There are houses these days where they are telling their editors not to edit, that it's not an efficient use of their time," said one veteran editor of literary novels. "You want those manuscripts to come in and get out there making money." Ted Solotaroff, who spent a career of several decades editing at three major publishing houses (most recently HarperCollins), has said there is a chill in the industry. And that chill has become a bit deeper just in the past month, with the announcements that Houghton Mifflin would close its Ticknor & Fields division and that Atheneum would no longer exist as a Macmillan imprint after this spring, and with the firing of half of Harcourt Brace's New York trade publishing personnel. "The conglomerateer," Mr. Solotaroff wrote in a 1987 article in The New Republic, "has bred an atmosphere of fear, cynicism, rapaciousness and ignorance."

Mark Richard is walking in his sleep.

Eleven months have passed. Through the summer and fall, the publisher has been busy. An artist designed an appealing deep blue cover and Nan Talese began to oversee a marketing and publicity plan for the book. Ms. Talese has approved lists of authors who might provide prepublication quotations, book critics to cajole, and booksellers to receive advance copies (called bound galleys, these are early proofs in paper covers, usually sent out months before publication in very small quantities but occasionally released en masse, as promotional "reading copies"). She has also signed off on lists of newspapers, magazines and radio stations that might give "Fishboy" space or play.

Meanwhile, Mr. Richard has struggled with the revisions— Ms. Talese had found sentences that went awry, gaps in the story, characters that weren't well explained—and he has been late in delivering them. "Every time I talked to Nan on the phone, I could hear her pencil tapping on the desk." Then he polished the galley proofs and met with Marly Rusoff, a vice president and associate publisher at Doubleday, to help plan a series of readings and promotional appearances.

Now, in early April 1993, "Fishboy" is on its way to the bookstores, and Mr. Richard is so nervous—"scared, really"—that he wakes up in the middle of the night standing by his desk or in front of his refrigerator. For the first time since he arrived in New York eight years ago, he has his own apartment. Spread out on his bed is a map, along with a travel schedule. In a month he'll be on the road, first on a publicity tour planned by Ms. Rusoff—a quick run through Miami, San Francisco, Seattle and Toronto—and then, starting the second week in June, on an automobile trip that he and Ms. Rusoff organized together: 28 signings and readings from Texas to Virginia. He can't, of course, drive his way onto the best-seller lists—"No one, including me, expects this book, an odd book, to have a broad appeal," he says—but he hopes to build an audience for his work, for this novel and the next, out on the road, town by town, bookstore by bookstore, one group of readers at a time. That, in any case, is the plan.

Sometimes a first novelist bolts from obscurity into the limelight: Ralph Ellison with "Invisible Man," Joseph Heller with "Catch 22," J.D. Salinger with "The Catcher in the Rye." Since critics know the mythology well, they are often attracted to first novels. "I've had first novels compared to Dante and Faulkner," said Jane von Mehren, the executive editor of Penguin Books. Prodigality aside, when a new voice gets noticed, she said, "that's exciting."

As literary truck, however, first novels find their way into print for other reasons. "The hope," said Ms. von Mehren, "is that the person will go on to sell 40,000 or 50,000 copies with their next book or the one after that." Such hope, on the part of publishers, represents a very small, very acceptable risk. Most first novels have advances against royalties that are less than $10,000 and print runs of 5,000 copies or fewer. The production costs of a first novel run roughly $2 a book. Publishers gamble a lot of these $2 chips, hoping one will hit. And some see this gambler's mentality as the undoing of the industry.

"The editor tells the author, 'We're crazy about your book and we want to publish you,' " says Ted Solotaroff. "Then, after publication, what happens in most cases is that *nothing* happens: no tour, no money for ads, virtually nothing. The mind set that involves acquiring a first novel is the fear that you may be missing something, the next Robert Stone or Ann Beattie."

These days, however, publishers are not a patient lot and tend to gamble on an author only once. "They want a sure thing," said Edward Burlingame, who for many years had his own imprint at HarperCollins, where he published, among others, Donald Barthelme, Colin Thubron, Roxana Robinson and Ron Hansen. "They don't have the courage to publish a book about which there's really a reason to be excited. If Joe Smith's first novel sells, say, only 6,000 copies, then the next time his editor goes to the publisher or marketing director, the reaction will be, 'Oh, my God, here comes Mary with another Joe Smith book.' "

No one knows how many people in America read serious literature. Last year Philip Roth estimated that "maybe there are 120,000" serious readers in America, and by readers he meant "people who when they are at work during the day think that after dinner tonight and after the kids are in bed, I'm going to read for two hours." Tom Jenks, the former associate fiction editor of Esquire, thinks about half that many people buy serious books. And Nan Talese is convinced that there are only 4,000 readers who "keep up with reviews of literary work, then will actually go into the store to buy the book." And what they do with it at home, she added, "only Heaven knows."

Such small numbers leave an ambitious unknown writer struggling against large odds. Publishers can afford the gamble, but authors can't—which explains Mark Richard's nocturnal strolls.

"I'm sure," he says, surveying his map, "in several places on the tour, I'm going to get there and only two people will show up for the reading—and one of them will be there for the wine and cheese."

The eyes are bright, the voice clipped, the conversation, as always, filled with recognizable names.

"I was with Mona Simpson the other night," says Nan Talese, "and she said that writing is about the soul and publishing is about the ego."

In fact, publishing is about profit, as Ms. Talese, a banker's daughter, well knows. For the last 30 years she's worked as an editor, at four houses. At Doubleday she has her own imprint (her name goes on the book's title page and on the spine), which, in effect, is like having a publishing house within a publishing house. She has some autonomy in acquiring books; below a certain sum, probably in the neighborhood of $150,000, she can offer advances without checking with the company president. She also oversees the design, marketing and publicity of each book she acquires. She publishes some 12 to 15 books a year; among them have been the fiction of Ian McEwan, Mary Morris, Gita Mehta, Robert MacNeil and three winners of Britain's Booker Prize, Ben Okri, Thomas Keneally and Barry Unsworth.

Bantam Doubleday Dell, which is owned by the German corporation Bertelsmann, is, according to a Publishers Weekly estimate of gross sales, the second largest publishing company in the United States. (Random House is the largest.) Part of Doubleday's success comes from its blockbuster authors, most notably John Grisham, whose law-firm melodramas exceed a million copies in their first printings and have sold over 4.5 million copies in hard cover alone. "We could make our operating expenses on just one of his books," said one Doubleday editor. As at other major publishers, commerce is in command at Doubleday. A few years ago Jack Hoeft, the chief executive officer of Bantam Doubleday Dell, told a room full of students at a summer publishing institute, "I pay editors to be able to smell out a book. 'But Jack,' some say, 'this is literature.' I say, 'How many will it sell?' "

The more publishers rely on formula fiction to fatten the bottom line, the less likely they are to commit resources to the rest of the list. About 15 years ago, Stanley Elkin was unhappy about Dutton's plans for his novel "The Living End." The catalogue described the book and listed the price, but there was no mention of an author tour or cooperative advertising. "The Living End," which John Irving reviewed in "The New York Times Book Review" and called "a fine and daring novel," was to be just another $2 chip. Mr. Elkin, a longtime and critically well-regarded novelist (who is, by the way, still published by Dutton), decided to exorcise his disappointment in a characteristically irreverent letter to his agent, Georges Borchardt:

"There's been an awful lot of talk about this being my breakthrough book," the author wrote. "(It even says that in the ad.)

Sure, I could sell upwards of 3,500 copies. (I can't stop being sarcastic, Georges, I'm afraid I'll hurt myself if I do.) I'm getting these failures vibes, Georges. I'm going to get more good reviews and nobody is going to make a penny. Dutton will be able to say, and probably will, how they done real good by literature, taking a chance on me. I seem to be good for the image, Georges, a feather in the cap of free enterprise, a kind of artsy loss leader. . . . Couldn't they at least have said something like WORD OF MOUTH AVAILABLE? These vibes, Georges, these vibes. And you want to know something? Having said all this, I don't even feel better."

Georges Borchardt became Mark Richard's agent after the young writer was sent to him by Esquire's Tom Jenks. Mr. Borchardt sent "Fishboy" to Nan Talese in the fall of 1991. She'd admired the author's earlier work, and after reading the manuscript, began to think about making an offer. "Fishboy" was then in its nascent form, "an experimental novel," she thought, "slim, difficult for a reader to grasp." She couldn't pay much for just one book, but when the author told her he had another novel in the works and enough stories for a second collection, Ms. Talese put together a deal: about $120,000 (no one will say for sure) for the hard-cover and paperback rights to all three books. (When all is said and done, if Mr. Richard's annual income for the length of the contract is $15,000, he'll be doing better than most journeyman writers.)

In the late summer of 1992, "Fishboy" was presented to the Doubleday sales force. (Along with proof copies, Doubleday sends its sales reps a videotape on which editors—sometimes along with authors—introduce their books for the coming season.) Ms. Talese tried to convince them that "Fishboy" was "really a phantasmagoric dream and you're carried along by the beauty of the language." Many, however, were not convinced. They sent back word that they found the book too difficult to read. "That's fine," Ms. Talese replied, "it's not for everyone, but I believe it will get tremendous press coverage and attention because critics like to discover someone new." And then she announced that she was thinking of a first printing of 10,000 copies, many more than the customary number for a first novel, a clear signal to the sales reps that she considered "Fishboy" more than just another $2 gamble.

The marketing campaign for "Fishboy" began a year ago this month, four months in advance of publication. Nan Talese mailed bound galleys to 1,100 independent bookstores, places that had been identified across the years as good outlets for literary fiction. She hoped the work would speak for itself, though she included a letter extolling the author's virtues, his unusual background and her conviction that the work would get good reviews.

Before reviews appear in the popular press, the industry's trade publication, Publishers Weekly, and its major previewing rival, Kirkus Reviews, offer their opinions. Both sources are read by bookstore owners, librarians, newspaper book editors and arts editors across the country. A good review in both can prompt the stores to file larger advance orders. The reviews in Kirkus are consistently more captious than those in Publishers Weekly. If "Fishboy" could win plaudits in Kirkus, then it might break out early, as they say in the industry, and take on a buzz.

The review appeared in the March 1 issue: "The promise of Richard's story collection is only fitfully apparent in his surrealistic first novel. . . . The transition from short story to novel has proven difficult for Richard, and his incantatory style, thrilling at the start, looks too effortful over the long haul."

Orders were slow, so Ms. Talese dispatched a second letter to her 1,100 independents:

"It is not often one reads a manuscript and has the instinct that it is the work of a young writer who will be significant in American letters. I remember when editors said that of Cormac McCarthy in the 1950's. I saw that in the work of Mark Richard. . . . The figures registered in our computer show that all independents have ordered only one or at most two copies of "Fishboy." I fear that if you do not have more than that when the reviews appear readers will not find "Fishboy" and we know they rarely return later. I hope Richard will not have to wait 25 years as McCarthy did."

As a marketing conceit, it was both clever and ironic: it traded on the reputation of a man who takes little part in publishing except to write his highly acclaimed books and it implied, without any evidence whatsoever, that a buzz had already begun.

It is now the first week in May, the official publication date. The major reviews—from The New York Times, The Washington Post, The Los Angeles Times and The Chicago Tribune—ought to appear soon. The critics, of course, might dislike "Fishboy"—or, worse, simply ignore it. But at least it is in the stores, on the shelves.

Nan Talese is sitting at her desk, staring at an elegant arrangement of tulips in a crystal vase. "Publishing literary novels is like sailing a small craft," she is saying. "Either you catch the wind or you have to paddle very hard."

READER BY READER
AND TOWN BY TOWN, A NEW NOVELIST
BUILDS A FOLLOWING

"Art must be practiced as a trade, at all events in our time.
This is the age of trade."   —George Gissing, " New Grub Street" (1891)

When Marly Rusoff is lucky, a book sells itself. When she's not, a handle can be hard to come by.

"Well, I think that Mark Richard is going to be remembered as one of the most celebrated writers of his generation." She sighs, "And that's not a publicist's hype." Then she winces. "It's difficult," says Doubleday's vice president and associate publisher. "When you say he's part Melville, part King James Bible, part Faulkner, you feel like an idiot. It's hard to describe."

Perhaps she should be oblique, she suggests, especially this week, a week in early May 1993, just before the book is published. Waiting for the approbation or opprobrium of the critics, the prudent publicist affects a certain uncertainty. "Mark Richard may be called the Joseph Conrad of our day," she says. "Who knows?" And then she smiles.

Ms. Rusoff learned the business from the selling floor up.

The daughter of a bookbinder, she owned a bookstore in Minneapolis, then went to work as a sales representative for Simon & Schuster, crisscrossing the cold brown hills of South Dakota with boxes of books in the trunk of her car. She came to New York and worked in the publicity department at Houghton Mifflin, then in 1990 moved to Doubleday, where she now creates the "publishing plan" for 25 to 30 books a year. In a trade of tin-pot reputations where hype is the order of the day, she is spoken of with respect. She won't oversell a book, they say; she doesn't try to pass off a second fiddle as a concertmeister.

Today she's groping for words. The book that she's trying to sell, "Fishboy," by Mark Richard, a first novel, has a thin story, almost no plot and dense language that requires close reading. The narrator is a ghost who tells his life story, recounting a dark fable about an abandoned child, more fish than human, reborn in a swamp, who goes to sea in the company of a crew of cutthroats and grotesques. Such work is hardly what Hollywood would call "high concept." And, like all literary fiction, it will have to fight for a place on the bookstore shelves.

The audience for such fiction, "serious readers," as Philip Roth calls them, is tiny: perhaps 120,000, says Mr. Roth; more likely, say others, much less. In this marginal market, if a first novel sells 10,000 or 15,000 copies, that is considered a victory. The writers of literary fiction sometimes "break out" early with a "big book" that appeals to a general audience, but for the most part they build their reputations slowly, book by book, reader by reader.

On the surface, Mark Richard would appear to have certain advantages. His publisher, Doubleday, a division of Bantam Doubleday Dell, which is owned by the German corporation Bertelsmann, is one of the largest, oldest and most successful concerns in the industry. His agent is the well-respected Georges Borchardt. His editor is Nan A. Talese, who, under her own imprint, publishes both critical and popular successes, among them Margaret Atwood and Pat Conroy.

Mark Richard (pronounced ree-SHARD), 37 years old, has been working for some time to position himself. He came to

New York in 1985 and in the eight years since then, his short stories have appeared in major publications like Esquire and The New Yorker. Along the way, some of his stories were collected and published by Alfred A. Knopf in "The Ice at the Bottom of the World," which won the PEN/Hemingway prize and led to a Whiting Foundation grant.

Hungry for success, Mr. Richard is also willing to do just about anything to help sell his first novel. He and Ms. Rusoff have talked about a four-city publicity jaunt to be followed by a driving tour of the South, with signings and readings at 28 bookstores from Texas to Virginia.

For the moment, however, all plans wait.

Next week is the book's official publication date—in effect, when the company formally releases its product to the critics and the public. Without the reviewers' warranty—or, in its absence, widespread word-of-mouth or interest generated by feature articles in major magazines and newspapers—"Fishboy" will have little chance.

Ms. Rusoff has spent a good deal of time, on the telephone or by letter, trying to convince the editors of the major newspaper book review sections—The New York Times, The Washington Post, The Chicago Tribune, The Los Angeles Times, The Philadelphia Inquirer, Newsday—that "Fishboy" was worth a look. (At one point, she was calling the book a "fever-dream" and the author "kin to Garcia Marquez.") Now, a week away from publication, she's worried. "In the past," she says, looking down at the novel's deep blue cover, "I've seen books like this get trashed."

Every year for the last 10 years, American publishers have released an average of 45,000 new titles. Roughly 10 percent of these are fiction—including mysteries, melodramas, romances, military sagas, thrillers and so on. Many are derivative, written to formula—a different kind of "Presumed Innocent," another "Hunt for Red October."

Richard Eder, the Pulitzer Prize-winning book critic for The Los Angeles Times and Newsday, whose reviews are available nationwide on the Los Angeles Times Syndicate, figures that he looks at maybe 200 first novels a year. Every week, a load of books and bound galleys is delivered to his Boston office. He arranges them in piles on the floor, then sits down among them to browse. He reads here, he reads there. If a sentence catches his eye, he keeps reading. Twice a week, he writes about something he's read—usually, but not always, a work of fiction. His reviews reach an audience of between three and four million people.

One day last spring, "Fishboy" arrived at Mr. Eder's apartment. He pulled the proof copy from its cardboard mailing envelope and put it in a pile of seven or eight others. His method of culling is, well, metaphorical: "I taste them, I sniff them, I lift them up. There's a kind of smell about a book I'm not going to review." Like most critics, he looks for literary staples: a Norman Mailer, a John Updike. Absent a known commodity, he takes a "cursory sniff" at new products. Here he indulges his tastes. He does not like Southern Gothic fiction or American domestic realism—"which includes a lot of good, tidy literature"—or anything over 1,000 pages long. He "loves" examples of magic realism, "but I don't think it works that often, so I look for them." And thus he turned to "Fishboy."

Mr. Eder knew that the author had won a Whiting grant, which "was kind of like a friend saying, 'This guy is worth a look.' " So he opened the bound galleys and started to read: "I began as a boy, as a human-being boy, a boy who fled to sea, a boy with a whistling lisp and the silken-tipped fingers of another class. A boy . . . thrown from a car into a side-road swamp. A child born again there, slithering out of the sack. . . ."

Mr. Eder put the galleys down. "The first two or three pages were indecipherable." But he did not toss "Fishboy" away. He rarely judges a novel by its opening pages because "God knows, if Theodore Dreiser were on my floor and I read the first 50 pages, I wouldn't have reviewed him." He picked the galleys up again; he read about an ax fight, a mermaid, a helmsman turned inside out and a mate who hated the cook so much that he killed him. Then he turned to his computer and wrote an 800-word review:

"Richard's novel is a trifle . . . a hefty dose of spirits. The fumes occasionally overpower it, and the author's heady images stagger grandiosely. . . . Its hallucinatory ins and outs read like a particularly laborious recipe from the magic-realism cookbook. . . . There is something downright plucky and resourceful about the young narrator. He is an altered state Huck Finn. What he lacks is a river. . . . Richard has written an essentially literary adventure. His hero floats feistily—but on a book, not a raft."

What Mr. Eder intended was, as he later explained, "a mixed review." He admired the bold effort, the author's mythic echoes and literary allusions, but, essentially, Mr. Eder thought "Fishboy" had failed. "Huck Finn" without a "river" was clearly a metaphor for the book's chief weakness: its lack of a clear story. "Fishboy," he said in an interview, "floated around in a fog."

Mr. Eder's review, the first major review of Mark Richard's book, appeared in Newsday and The Los Angeles Times on May 6, 1993. And in New York the people at Doubleday were hardly downcast.

Marly Rusoff is on the telephone. "We're having a frantic day, but I want to refer you to Richard Eder's review. It's a really fun review. It's given me a much lighter heart about the book. He calls it 'an altered state Huck Finn.' So it's, as we've been saying, an American classic. He gives it a good review, but what I love about it is, it makes the book sound like so much fun. I've always been a little shy about talking about how much fun the book is because you have an idiot, a dead sheriff, two convicts, a murder, so this gives me the courage to tell people what a terrifically fun book this is."

Ms. Rusoff's reading of Richard Eder's review could be taken as an example of what the longtime editor Ted Solotaroff has termed the "cognitive dissonance" that makes American publishing sometimes seem like never-never land. Was Ms. Rusoff trying to wrap a technical failure in the cloak of a critical success? Or was she simply looking for material to help with the handle, the pitch—and Mr. Eder's review had the kind of "buzzy lines" she'd been hoping for?

"Now I can talk about it as 'an altered state Huck Finn.' You pick up things along the way. With a first novel, you have to have some endorsement beyond yours and a couple of the author's friends'. You have to build up a bunch of material. Now I can probably get some momentum from this. I've read positive reviews that are so boring you'd never consider spending $25 on the book. A selling review is a review that people might talk about. It goes beyond appearing in print; it becomes part of conversation. And word-of-mouth is really what works in the end. 'Altered state Huck Finn'—yes, that's something people will talk about."

Tonight Mark Richard's friend Pearson Marx is throwing a party for "Fishboy" in her posh Upper East Side apartment. It is a catered affair with champagne and smoked fish, ham and turkey. Doubleday is represented by Nan Talese (sporting a black beret), Marly Rusoff (a tentative smile) and various young and attractive supernumeraries. An assembly of the author's friends are here, as well as his mother and sister. David Hirshey, the deputy editor at Esquire, is in attendance, standing in a circle of literary youngbloods clustered around Gay Talese, Ms. Talese's husband.

Some book parties are promotional stunts; the publishing house asks its well-known authors to lend their cachet to a newcomer and invites the press to watch as everyone walks around offering congratulations and rubbing elbows. Other parties, like this one, are simply part of the tradition of celebrating someone's work. Tonight's affair is private (the author asked the only reporter in the room to leave his notebook at home), a small break from the serious business, a few moments when "Fishboy" is nothing but a book.

Back at work, Marly Rusoff is trolling. She's been faxing Mr. Eder's review to feature editors and radio and television producers. The author, she's been telling them, is good copy—a teenager from Virginia who became the youngest disk jockey in the country, a college boy who went to sea on fishing boats, a writer in the Southern tradition who has made a myth that's fun to read.

Now and then she gets a nibble—National Public Radio, which attracts a significant book-buying audience, wants to know more—but no one will commit to an interview. Mr. Eder's review is not nearly enough to create the "buzz" that flowers into the "phenomenon" that demands attention. Everyone seems to be waiting—waiting for The New York Times.

The New York Times Book Review does not always make or break a book. But, say book publicists, its influence is such that critics and editors across the country regularly follow its lead. More than 8,000 books and bound galleys are sent to the Book Review every year; only about 2,500 titles end up being featured in its pages. The packages arrive at the Book Review's gray offices in waist-high rolling mail bins. Staff workers toss out anything judged inappropriate for review (romance novels, genre westerns, game books, how-to books, textbooks and so on)— the sorts of titles the Book Review has decided not to cover or, say its editors, books that its readers don't expect to find in its pages. The survivors, about 100 titles a week, are divided among eight preview editors who screen books and bound galleys, make assignments and shepherd reviews into print.

The previewers record their impressions for the master files. Some of their comments cut to the quick. "Deeply dry," said one, about a book exploring military strategy in the Middle East. "No, deadly dry." Others are more prosaic: "This semi-memoir" about the Warsaw ghetto "is more a document than a book for a general audience." Occasionally, a previewer has some fun: "A veddy British journalist (now a freelance television producer) has veddy interesting (and sometimes veddy troubling) adventures wandering around the islands of the South Pacific. She becomes veddy concerned about the despoliation of paradise—but not veddy concerned about the neglected state of her own prose."

Every Thursday morning, the eight preview editors gather around an eighth-floor conference table with Rebecca Sinkler, Marvin Siegel and Robert Harris, the editor, deputy editor and assistant editor of the Book Review. The preview editors present the books they think are worthy, then make suggestions—from a wide-ranging group of scholars, novelists, journalists, historians, editors and experts in various fields—about who might write the review that will appear in print.

"We fall on their suggestions and try to tear them apart," said Ms. Sinkler. The editors, she said, aim for "lively and informed matches of reviewer and book." They also try to avoid conflicts of interest, even deeply hidden ones: "We might say Y can't review X because she was sleeping with X's agent's first husband." And there are all kinds of other questions. "If you have a book that's sheer misogyny, do you give it to a radical feminist? No."

When the bound galleys of "Fishboy" arrived at The New York Times, the previewer was ambivalent: "Richard's collection of short stories was an uneven, bleakly modernist, sometimes chillingly effective piece of work. His new novel, a sort of absurdist nautical fairy tale (which the publisher, alas, is calling a reinvention of the sea language and myths found in Melville and Conrad), is a similarly mixed bag. A young boy hangs about a strange, female-populated fishing station, scarfing oysters and yearning for the sea. Strange boats come and go. He is involved in what might be a murder. He is taken aboard a boat. He sees strange things. He returns. Sometimes these encounters are described in an interesting way, in vivid images. But the point of it all often seems lost in the posturing."

That Thursday the consensus around the conference table was that—because of the first reading of the book itself and the competition from other, seemingly stronger titles—"Fishboy" did not warrant a full review. It was assigned to a freelance journalist, Margot Mifflin, who had written regularly for the Book Review for several years and was known to have a taste for modern fiction. She was asked to write what is known as a "brief," a 200- to 300-word paragraph for the In Short page.

On occasion, reviewers have such a strong reaction to a book that they ask their editors for more space. Sometimes they get it, sometimes they don't; sometimes there's space, sometimes the reviewer is off the mark. Ms. Mifflin told the previewer who had made the assignment that she loved the book. The editors had come to trust her judgment, they said. They knew she was not simply angling for a byline.

Ms. Sinkler took a hard look at the book and, in the end, decided that "Fishboy" was the kind of work "on which reasonable people could disagree"; it also appeared to have a quality she admired—it seemed "ambitious," the kind of writing that takes chances. So she was persuaded to "bump it up" to a 600-word review that ran on the bottom of page 7 on May 16.

The posturing modernist was now, in Ms. Mifflin's words, a writer with a "seemingly fathomless imagination" who "has folded a host of exquisitely rendered tales into a stunning novel."

"I'll take that, yes-sir-ee-bob, I'll take that any day of the week."

His agent, Georges Borchardt, has just called to read from a copy of the Book Review and Mr. Richard, who is packing for a quick publicity trip, is ebullient. "Georges says the most important thing is to get noticed. And I want the book to get noticed. I'm not trying to put it in every home, but I do want to shove it from shore and get it sailing on its own."

The next day he leaves for a short four-city publicity tour— Miami, San Francisco, Seattle, Toronto. Most of the 8,000 copies from the first printing have been shipped to the stores. Now all the author has to do is persuade readers to buy them.

Mr. Richard will not sell hundreds at each stop. There will be no queues in the streets outside bookstores, no clamoring for his signature on the title page. In fact, the spot sales on tour count for little. Literary fiction is hand-sold slowly across time and the hand that matters most is the bookseller's. So the smart author tries to meet as many clerks and managers and bookstore owners as he or she can, hoping that when someone wanders up to the register "looking for a good book," the bookseller will recommend him.

The trip took eight days. In Miami, he gave a reading and answered questions at Mitchell Kaplan's store Books & Books. For the most part, it is the independently owned bookstores

(16,765 of them in the United States) and not the large chain stores (12,853) that take a chance on new work.

The literary reading, a cross between abject salesmanship and performance art, is an old form of cultural conversation, but it can serve the modern author in many ways. Serious fiction needs a following to survive and often the 20 or 30 people who attend a reading at a bookstore become fans of the writer for life.

Any reading turns on the personality of the author. Some can't emote, others can't stop. "I've done a thousand author readings, and I've found that talent and humility are not first cousins," said Meg O'Brien, who interviewed Mr. Richard in Miami for her show "Cover to Cover" on WLRN, a public radio station. "But Mark said all the right things. Every one of those 20 people there fell in love with him."

Mark Richard has been writing, off and on, since childhood. When he reached puberty, his voice dropped dramatically, and at age 13 he went to work as a disk jockey. After high school, he studied journalism at Washington & Lee University in Virginia, but a professor who took an interest in his work started to push him toward literature—Poe and Dickens, Faulkner, Fitzgerald and Twain. Mr. Richard left school for a while, worked on fishing boats along the Eastern Seaboard, then returned, finished his degree and in the years that followed bounced from one job to another: photographer, Xerox machine operator, envelope stuffer, newspaperman. He moved to Virginia Beach, lived in a "nasty place" at the edge of a honky-tonk strip and divided his nights between typewriter and a spot at the bar at a gin mill called the Thunderbird Lounge.

Now and then, Mr. Richard would send his work to New York, to Esquire magazine, where it would end up in a slush pile in Tom Jenks's office. "But the stories always popped out," said Mr. Jenks, who was then the magazine's associate fiction editor. "They were filled with yearning and longing." The writer had talent, but little technique and no discipline. "Sometimes I'd work on his manuscripts and send them back," Mr. Jenks said, "but he was always resistant to revising them. Instead I'd get four more stories."

In 1985, on a vacation to North Carolina's Outer Banks, Mr. Jenks finally met the author. At one point that day, as Mr. Richard remembers it, Mr. Jenks offered some advice: "Tom said, 'You want to play hardball fiction? You've got to come to New York.' " The industry was in New York, and so was a large community of fellow travelers. He needed to meet editors and mix with other authors, Mr. Jenks told him; he needed to become serious about his work. Six months later, Mr. Jenks got a call at his desk in Manhattan. "I went around to the Old Town Bar on 18th Street off Broadway and there he was," said Mr. Jenks. "He had on Maui shorts, a T-shirt and sandals. He said, 'Here I am. What do I do now?' "

Mr. Richard went on to publish a few stories in Esquire and other magazines, but the fees were modest and in the years that followed he lived hand to mouth, often on the largess of friends. At one point he was so impoverished that he was eating the baby food in the apartment where he was house-sitting. About that time, two editors from Esquire invited him to lunch. As Mr. Jenks tells the story, one of them "noticed that Mark only ate half of his sandwich and wrapped the other half up to take with him. They said, 'That's ridiculous. We don't treat our writers like that,' and the magazine arranged for him to get an advance on his next story."

Along the way, on Mr. Jenks's advice, Mr. Richard had taken a writing course with Gordon Lish, an influential editor at Knopf who offers expensive tutorials and often places the work of his students in The Quarterly, his small literary magazine. After the course, Mr. Lish offered Mr. Richard a contract for a collection of short stories, "The Ice at the Bottom of the World." (Mr. Richard will not talk about the terms of the contract, but it was probably a modest one.) Later, with Mr. Jenks's help, he picked up an agent, Georges Borchardt.

Mr. Richard started "Fishboy" a few years after he came to New York. He'd just read "Far Tortuga" by Peter Matthiessen, a novel that inspired him to experiment with a story, written in dialect, about a Caribbean fisherman. Soon he dropped the dialect and changed the locale. But the story wasn't working, so he kept rewriting it. Gradually, a character called Fishboy emerged: "He was a minor character at first, but he was always the one saying something interesting. He said, 'I began as a boy, a human-being boy,' which implied to me that he ended up as something else. But I didn't know what." Fishboy took over the story, and by 1991 the story had evolved into a novel.

At that point, unhappy with the way Knopf had handled his story collection, Mr. Richard began to think about switching publishers. Meanwhile, at a party, he met Nan Talese. She'd read his collection and admired his work. He told her about "Fishboy" and some other projects. A short time later, Ms. Talese called his agent, Mr. Borchardt. After reading the manuscript of "Fishboy" and hearing about Mr. Richard's plans, she offered a three-book contract.

Miami's reading in a small room at Books & Books was packed, but in San Francisco only a handful of people filled the seats. In Seattle, the number grew to 50; then, in Toronto at an arts festival, there were 100. Mr. Richard came home happy, but spent. Who, he wondered, was buying his book? His first night back in his apartment, he walked in his sleep and woke up in his living room.

On Monday, Ms. Talese called with just the right tonic: they were going back to press, she said, from the initial print run of 8,000, only 150 books were left in the warehouse and she was about to order a second printing of 2,500. And there was more. The author had been booked on National Public Radio, the "Fresh Air" show—2 million regular listeners at 150 stations around the country, an audience, according to the network's market research, that includes a large number of educated book buyers.

It was Ms. Rusoff who had wangled the gig. The show's host, Terry Gross, rarely interviews fledgling novelists. They tend toward shop talk, says one of the producers, Amy Salit, and nothing can kill a radio show quicker than a disquisition on intertextual analysis. "But Marly called us so many times," she said. "She was so persistent. She sent us reviews. Then Terry read the book and the writing was good. And his personal experience tied into it, so there was something interesting to talk about."

A month after the show, Mr. Richard began a 28-bookstore tour through the South. He flew to Texas, borrowed a 1979 Cadillac Sedan de Ville from an old friend, Dolphin Overton, and set out to sell his book.

As it turned out, he was not the only author to take to the open road last summer. Paul Kafka, the author of "Love Enter" from Houghton Mifflin, visited 62 cities as he logged 18,000 miles in a 1983 Oldsmobile station wagon. And it is likely that others were touring the hinterlands as well.

"They know if they're not out there peddling, the book won't get the attention it deserves," said Leigh Haber, vice president and director of publicity and advertising at Harcourt Brace. "Writers are no longer content to sit by while publishers market their books."

Marly Rusoff had worked with Mr. Richard to plan a trip. (The cost of the two trips, plus postcards, fliers, T-shirts and the like, as well as the cost of local "co-op" ads to promote the readings, and finally, 1,100 galley copies sent to independent bookstores across the country—in short, the cost of promoting "Fishboy"—came to about $12,000 or $1 a book, which is the industry standard.) They set the schedule, then tried to drum up publicity for each reading by calling ahead to the local newspaper, and to radio and television stations near each bookstore. By the time he was ready to leave, they had managed to marry a number of readings to interviews.

His route took him roughly from Austin, Tex., to Washington. Here and there, he paused to make a few notes, an ad hoc journal of life on the road:

"Out of Kingsville, 72,740 miles on speedometer. . . . Visit to chain-saw art store. . . . Old fat woman abuses child roughhousing pet dog. . . . Tequila on screened porch. . . .

"Good crowd at Europa Books in Austin. Invited to University of Texas to see rare book room, 'Ulysses' manuscript. . . .

"Stopped in Waco at the What-a-Burger for directions to David Koresh compound. Got T-shirt. . . .

"Thunderstorm busted reading at Borders in Dallas. Went on call-in talk show. Came after two white supremacists. . . . This guy says, 'I want to know, this Fishboy, is he a fish or a boy? I jus' wish he'd make up his mind'. . . .

"Lake Charles, La. Stayed with Uncle James and Aunt Kitten. Saw alligators in game preserve and stepped on two snakes. . . ."

It is late June, and as Mr. Richard nears Wilmington, N.C. (76,359 miles on the speedometer), Ms. Talese sends him a message. "Warehouse empty," it says. "Going into third printing." He is delighted that 2,500 more copies of his book will be coming off the presses but tired, melancholy even. At the beginning of the summer, he had said, "I'll do anything to push this into the stores." Now he is finding the whole business a little depressing: "You go to these bookstores, find the owners are still hung over from the person they were doing the reading with the night before. At one place a guy asked me, 'When are we going to see your next novel?' I said, 'The way the money's going, sooner than expected.' "

He decides to stay in a down-at-the-heels hotel at Wrightsville Beach outside Wilmington. He needs some time to "decompress," he says, to soak in the surf and stare at the saw grass and myrtle along the dunes. That night, however, as the Cadillac turns into the parking lot of the Galleria Shopping Plaza and stops in front of Bristol Books, he is still restless. "Bet there will be between three and five people here tonight," he says.

The manager, his wife and four smiling clerks welcome Mr. Richard warmly, not a crapulent eye in the bunch. "Fishboy" and "The Ice at the Bottom of the World" are stacked neatly on a cart by the cash register. The manager steers the author to the front of the room, and soon the air is filled with his story.

A dozen people have settled down to listen, but a tall man with a beard and, apparently, an appetite decides to wander the stacks. Each swing takes him past the refreshment table. He looks at a book on astronomy and wolfs down four cookies; he fingers a book on health and gobbles two pieces of cheese. When the reading is finished, he stops his grazing and wanders over to the cart that holds Mr. Richard's books. He picks up a copy of "Fishboy," eyes the price ($19.95) and puts it back. Then he sees "The Ice at the Bottom of the World" in paperback ($7.95). He takes up the book, finishes off a cracker, and gives the book to Mr. Richard to sign.

After closing, the clerks check the totals: 14 copies of "Fishboy" and 8 copies of "The Ice at the Bottom of the World." For a brief moment, Mark Richard is a best seller.

And on he went through North Carolina. At McIntyres Books in Pittsboro, the reading was packed. He did well in Manteo too, then went to Norfolk, Va. ("I appeared on a television talk show with two anchors who had no idea who I was. On a commercial break, the woman turned to me and said, 'Is this a book about children?' ") Williamsburg was next, then Richmond, Washington and, finally, home.

"Maybe I won't have to do this with the next book," he said, as the fall and his 38th birthday approached. "I really want to go hide somewhere and just do work. I'm done."

But "Fishboy" wasn't. Mr. Richard gave a reading in Iowa City, then went on an assignment for Esquire, then returned to Virginia for some work with the BBC and some more book promotion. The reviews continued right through September, and in mid-November he read in South Carolina at a national meeting of state arts directors.

Ms. Rusoff calculates that Doubleday has sold, to date, 11,700 copies of "Fishboy" out of the 13,000 that were printed. Mr. Richard's little book has had a good "sell-through," as they say in the trade. In other words, it is being read. And this June, when Anchor Books publishes "Fishboy" in paperback, his readership is likely to grow.

His agent was "pleased," but cautious. Mr. Richard was "pointed in the right direction," but he still had a lot of work ahead of him, said Georges Borchardt. "After all, he's only written two books."

His publicist was "extremely" pleased. "If it's not the beginning of a successful career," Ms. Rusoff said with a wink, "then it's the beginning of a cult."

His editor was characteristically ebullient. With "literary first fiction," Ms. Talese said, "huge numbers are not as important as committed readers."

It appeared to be a case of commerce and culture serving each other. The company probably made a little money and brought a promising writer into its fold. For his part, the author found a home and began to woo an audience for his work.

The example of Mark Richard and "Fishboy" would delight a cultural deconstructionist: its conclusions are inconclusive and contradictory.

Critics in the industry say that for every "Fishboy," there are probably dozens of failures—books that get no reviews, that don't even sell out their first printings. And many editors worry, with good reason, that the economics of the business and the unchecked cupidity of the conglomerateers have turned American publishing into a vast counting house that has long since lost the spirit of art and ideas. "The heads of publishing companies have never been literary idealists," said Edward Burlingame, who for many years had his own imprint at Harper-Collins. "They wanted to make money, but they wanted respect, to contribute to the culture. Now it's, 'What's the profit?' "

Boosters in the industry dismiss the requiems and wax romantic about the creative spirit. They insist that in a quiet corner of many houses there is at least one editor agitating for literature. The optimists have faith that no matter how avaricious the age, literature will endure. "Good writers," said Deborah Futter, an editor at Doubleday, "will keep writing even if success eludes them because they feel compelled to write."

That may be true, or it may be what editors tell themselves before they send yet another first novel out to the stores.

Mark Richard is working on a second novel now—"Babyhead," a political satire set in the South. Like most writers, he is not inclined to discuss a work in progress. All he will say is that compared with "Fishboy," it is "more grounded." One wonders: Is he still as bold, as adventurous when he's turning out his sentences? Or has a hard summer hustling his book persuaded him to stick his nose in the wind before he sits down to write?

PAPER TRIALS

THE NEW YORKER

For people who make their livings as writers, the routine messages of everyday life have to be put together with some care. You don't want to leave rough drafts lying around. I've known novelists for whom the prospect of composing a note asking that a son or daughter be excused from gym that day can bring on a serious case of writer's block.

I was reminded of this recently when our car had to be left on city streets for a few days, and, attempting to benefit from the experience of a couple of trips in the past to AAAA Aardvark Auto-Glass Repair, I took on the task of composing a sign to inform potential pillagers that it contained nothing of value. Hours later, my wife happened to ask me to do some little chore around the house and I heard myself saying, "I can't right now. I'm on the fourth draft of this car sign."

There was no reason for her to be surprised. She has seen me stuck badly on an R.S.V.P. In fact, a routine piece of social communication can be particularly knotty for writers, since they habitually try to express themselves in ways that are not overly familiar. This is why a biographer who seems capable of producing a twelve-hundred-page Volume I in fairly short order can often be inexcusably late with, say, a simple thank-you note. Reading over what he's put on paper, he'll say to himself, "I can't believe that I wrote anything as lame as 'Thanks for a wonderful weekend.'" Then he'll put aside the entire thank-you-note project until a fresher phrase comes to mind. A few weeks later, while the draft is still marinating on the writer's desk, the weekend's hostess feels confirmed in her impression—an impression that began to surface with the wine-spilling incident on Saturday night—that the biographer is a boor or a yahoo.

What my fourth draft of the car sign said was "No Radio." I thought that was spare and to the point, without extraneous language. I came to it from "No Radio or Any Other Valuables," which I decided, after some reflection, protested too much.

"What do you think?" I asked my wife, handing her the sign.

"It's O.K.," my wife said. "I saw some ready-made signs for car windows at the hardware store, and that's what one of them said, so I guess it's what people think is effective."

"You saw the same sign—worded in just that way?"

"I'm not saying you plagiarized it from the hardware store."

"Actually, I haven't been in there in some time," I said.

"It's really O.K.," my wife said. " 'No Radio' is fine."

It's fine if you're satisfied to be writing at the same level as some gorilla at the sign factory. Thinking I needed fresh ideas, I phoned my older daughter, who lives just around the corner. "What would be a good sign to put in the car to discourage crackheads from smashing the window so they can get at six cents in change on the floor and the spare fan belt and an old pair of pliers?" I asked.

My daughter, a survivor of one of those earnest and progressive nursery schools in the Village, said, "How about 'Use Words Not Hands'?" This was a reference to what the teachers at her nursery school were constantly saying as the little monsters attacked one another with any weapon available. At one point, we all began to wonder exactly what the words for sneaking up behind another kid and pulling her hair might be.

It wouldn't surprise me at all if that hair puller had turned to a life of petty crime. Much as I enjoyed contemplating the look on his face when he spotted his nursery-school slogan on a car he was about to break into, I decided that the impact of "Use Words Not Hands" rested on the sort of allusion that an editor would criticize as "too inside."

The next draft was a complete departure—more of a new approach, really, than just another draft. It said, "There Is Nothing of Value Here." Upon reflection, I decided that it sounded too philosophical. I could picture a car thief who came upon it turning to his partner in crime and saying, "Talk about pretentious!" So now I'm sort of stuck. Meanwhile, the car's on the street. It is not completely without protection. An old shirt cardboard taped onto the back window bears the words "Sign in Preparation."

WILLIAM H. GASS

ANYWHERE BUT KANSAS

THE IOWA REVIEW

I was nearly ten when my parents gave me a chemistry set for Christmas. It came in a handsome wooden box and contained a rack for test tubes, as well as niches where vials of powerful powders might be kept. There was a little packet of sensitive paper (litmus, I think), a knobbed glass rod, the obligatory manual, a metal loop for suspending a test tube over a flame, a conversion table (ounces into spoons), and suitably exciting poison labels. Dreams flew out of that box when its lid was lifted: dreams of bombs and poisons, of plots described in disappearing ink, of odors distressful to the weak. I set up a small lab in the basement and there I performed my experiments. "Performed" was the right word. "Experiment" was not. For I didn't follow the booklet where it led, or listen to its lectures. I slopped about, blending yellow with white and obtaining brown, mixing crystals with powders and getting dust, combining liquids with solids and making mud.

Later, in high school, I would take chemistry the way I took spring tonics and swallowed headache pills. Although I broke beakers and popped little pieces of potassium into puddles of water to watch the water fly, I did occasionally manage to obey tutorial instructions as well, repeating experiments which others had long ago undertaken. My predecessors had asked their questions of Nature with genuine curiosity, and waited, like an eager suitor, her reply. My method displayed a different spirit, which was to fudge my procedures in order to obtain the result already written in the chemmy books. I was not being taught to experiment, or even to repeat experiments. I was being taught to cheat.

An experiment, I would learn much later, when I studied the philosophy of science in graduate school, had to arise from a real dissatisfaction with existing knowledge. There was a gap to be filled, a fracture to be repaired, an opening to be made. Nature's interrogator had to know how to ask the correct question, and to state it so clearly that the answer would be, in effect, an unambiguous "yes" or "no," and not a noddy wobble. Every experiment required a protected environment and an entirely objective frame of mind. The results should be quantifiable, and the process repeatable. Every successful repetition spoke favorably for the quality of the first occasion. Furthermore, experiments were never carried out against the rules, but were performed, like surgery, always well within them, otherwise they would not be recognized as experiments at all.

What is generally called "experimentation" in the arts, more nearly resembles my ignorant and youthful self-indulgent mess-making. I was acting out a fantasy, not learning anything about chemistry, and while every smelly substance I concocted had to have been made according to chemistry's laws, I did not know those laws, nor could I have learned them from anything I was doing. And how many botches have been excused by calling them the results of the experimental spirit? We have to imagine an artist wondering what would happen if she were to do this, try that, perform a play in silence, omit the letter "e" in three pages of French prose, construct a world of clothes-hanger wire, color walls with cow manure. Having found out, though, then what?

A good experiment is as perfect and complete as the Parthenon, but the word, in popular speech, is derogatory, as if the experiment were going to be on the audience. Experiments, moreover, even if elegant and crucial, are admired for their results—the "yes" or "no" they receive—and (except for specialists) not for their procedures. We don't want to read interrogations, we want to read results.

Critics, patrons, academicians, characteristically insecure

and immature beneath their arrogant demeanors, are devoted to rules and definitions of decorum. Scarcely has an innovative form, a daring method, a different point of view, established itself than its codification begins: it must be given a catchy name (and labeled "experimental" perhaps, at least avant-garde, or something even trendier such as "existential," "absurd," "meta-fictional," "minimal," "surreal," "post-mod"); next, its superficial qualities are catalogued (it looks to the future in this respect, remains unchanged in that, returns to the past right here, but seems, at another point, content with the status quo); its cultural links are then explored and evaluated (does it reveal the sorry *Geist* of the *zeit*? does it express malaise? is it symptomatic of some social sickness? is it toughly feminist? is it resolutely gay?); finally it will be given a fresh critical vocabulary, a new jargon to fit this latemost fad like a cowboy boot pulled over a golfing shoe. Since, and sadly, by the relentless use of commandments and plenty of otiose rhetoric, the latest craze can be put in place as quickly as an ugly tract gets built; it is therefore repeatedly necessary for writers to shake the system by breaking its rules, ridiculing its lingo, and disdaining whatever is in intellectual fashion. To follow fashion is to play the pup.

Many fictions which appear to be "experimental" are actually demonstrations. When Galileo dropped his proofs from Pisa's tower, the proof was purely in the seeing. To demonstrate an equal fall for both a lead and paper ball, he'd have had to put Pisa's tower in a vacuum tube and monitor the competitive descent of his samples with instruments more precise than any he had at hand. But that was not the point: the point was the persuasion of the eye and the subversion of a backward principle. If Doctor Johnson claims you can't write a satisfactory poem about a coal mine, the poet is, of course, called upon to write it. Disgracing one more rule won't dissuade everybody of the view that art is made by recipe, because the constitutionally constipated will begin drawing up additional regs at once; but it will encourage the intelligent suspicion that neither by breaking nor abiding is quality achieved.

So "subversive" is often a good name for some of these fictions. Between my muck-about basement days and the discipline provided by my high school class, I enjoyed an interlude as a bomber. With sulfur from my then neglected set, a little potassium nitrate purchased from the pharmacist, and charcoal scraped from any charred board, I discovered that I could make gun powder. By filling pill capsules also obtained at the drug store with my gray mix, and slamming the whole thing with a stone, I could make a very satisfactory bang. It provided me with an exhilarating sense of power. It wasn't long before I was coating wet string with my concoction in order to make a fuse. However, I was open to experiment: sometimes I wet the string and sometimes I made a paste and sometimes I soaked the string in the grainy mixture. Then a toilet tube packed with paper and powder was set off with a sound so violent it shouted of my success.

"Make it new," Ezra Pound commanded, and "innovative" is a good name for some kinds of fiction; however, most newness is new in all the same old ways: falsely, as products are said to be new by virtue of minuscule and trivial additions; or vapidly, when the touted differences are pointless; or opportunistic, when alterations are made simply in order to profit from perceived improvements; or if applied like a brand, and meant simply to mark a moment, place, or person off from others, and give it its own identity however dopey.

You may be the first to open a play with the word *merde;* or the first to write of America because you discovered it; or the first to detail the production of ball bearings; or be brave enough to say straight out that, actually, the emperor's new clothes are tacky; or be accounted a pioneer because no one had described, before you, how it is to die of a bad disposition. Perhaps your poem on the taste of sperm will cause another sort of sensation. However, innovation that comes to something is nearly always formal. It is the expression of style at the level of narrative structure and fictional strategy. When we describe a writer's way of writing as individual and unique, we are referring to qualities it is often impossible and always unwise to imitate—Beckett is simply Beckett, Proust Proust—but original as their voices may be, they are not, just for that, innovative, because innovative implies the beginning of a new direction, whereas the style of late James (which I have the good taste to admire) has realized its completion and signifies an end.

The style of *Finnegans Wake* was certainly new and inimitable, but it was the cyclical structure of the work which was innovative; it was the polyphony of the text, the principle of the portmanteau, the landscape of the dream, the text's extraordinary musicality, which provided that wealth of stimulating possibilities for other writers.

There is something to be said for just getting away from it all. Writers begin as readers of a driven and desperate kind. Over the hills and far away, Lady Castlemain is meeting her beau beneath a blooming . . . what? . . . chestnut tree; Horatio Le Paige is pitching his last game, the bases are jammed, his arm is sore, the crowd is on his case, the catcher has called for an illegal pitch, which may be his only way out; Baron Pimple has caught Miss Tweeze without her duenna. Readers begin by wanting to be anywhere but here, anywhere but Kansas, and, when those readers begin writing, a good many of them will want to write anything except what they've been reading, not because some of what they read wasn't wonderful, for once upon an unhappy time it took them anywhere but Kansas, but because such writing had become its own Kansas now, and represented dullness and repression and the damnably indifferent status quo. Anything if it's not normal narrative . . . anything but characters given sunken cheeks and a hard stare, yes, better the Tin Woodsman, better the Bert Lahr lion, but also anything other than the predictable plots and routine scenes, neat outcomes, and conventional values . . . anything but Oz. Transportive fictions make sure of that. Their originality may be secondary to their denial of everyday; their subversive qualities secondary to their profound desire to be anywhere else, anywhere that hasn't Aunt Em, anywhere not over that sentimental rainbow, anywhere so long as it's not to a sequel.

Many times metafictions, because they caressed themselves so publicly, behaved more like manifestos than stories. They were more "explanatory" than "experimental." Instead of showing that something could be done by doing it, they became tutorial, emphasizing technique; teaching the reader how to read; admonishing him for his traditional bourgeois expectations; and directing his attention to art instead of nature, to the reality of the work instead of the reality of the world. That has always been a lesson more than hard to learn, for most people prefer to duck the difficult tedia of daily life, and ask that their experience of the wider world be filtered through layers of sensational detail and false feeling—hence neither living right nor reading well.

Exploding toilet paper tubes had been such a noisy success, I moved on to lead pipe. Into a piece I had found which was about six inches long and half an inch in diameter, I packed plenty of powder, tamping it down with the wooden handle of a small screwdriver, and then closing up both ends with thin, minutely folded, layers of cardboard. Set off by fuse alongside a neighbor's house where I stuck one end in some soft ground like a flare, it exploded with a smoky roar that could be heard for blocks, and fragments of pipe flew everywhere, a large shard penetrating the wall of my friend's front room. I ran as if riding the wind. I believed I heard sirens—police after me? firemen to the house? my father rising toward the higher elevations of his rage? Ah, we do like to fancy our books are bombs, but bombs, we need to remember, in order to make a great show— do their damage, prove a point, teach some slow wit a lesson— have to blow themselves to bits and pieces first.

When learning to play any instrument well, to wrestle, lift weights, dance, sing, write, it is wise to exercise. Try describing a hat in such a way the reader will realize its wearer has just had her dog run over. Practice putting your life into the present tense where you presumably lived it. Do dialogue—let's say— between a hobo and a high-class hooker, then between an ambulance chaser and a guy who sells scorecards at the ballpark— let's say—about the meaning of money. Between pints, get the arch of the dart down pat. Shoot foul shots day in and rim out. Pick a sentence at random from a randomly selected book, and another from another volume also chosen by chance; then write a paragraph which will be a reasonable bridge between them. And it does get easier to do what you have done, sing what you've so often sung; it gets so easy, sometimes, that what was once a challenge passes over into thoughtless routine. So the bar must be raised a few notches, one's handicap increased, the stakes trebled, tie both hands behind your back. Refuse the blindfold, refuse the final cigarette, refuse the proffered pizza. Do dialogue in dialect: a Welshman and a Scot arguing about an onion. Hardest of all: start over.

Of course, if you feel you have mastered at least some of your medium, you can improvise—take its risks and enjoy its pleasures. Now you trust yourself to go the right way like a roach to the kitchen, as if by instinct: taking off from an idle word, a casual phrase, a small exchange between disillusioned lovers, a notion about narrative time you got while reading Bergson, an item in the morning paper; then letting the music lead, a surprising association rule, or a buried meaning rise raw and green and virile as a weed, until the rhythm of the sentence settles in, the idea begins to unfold like a flower, time finds itself without hands, a character begins to speak in an unfamiliar tongue, and the shape of the scene is in front of you— nothing to it—you modify the metaphor, vary the normal flow of feeling . . . yes, it is certainly lovely, the facility between give and go, the rapport you have with your material, ease of flow . . . yet one person's grateful pee is not another's—that's a law about all calls of nature—accordingly, the improviser must be careful to make his modulations, like those riffy moments in music, so splendid they shall not seem contrived, and the best way to do that is to contrive them.

I rather prefer . . . the exploratory, although the word suggests surgery, and as a label is no more suited to the totality of its subject than "innovative," "subversive," or "experimental" are.

The explorer sees in front of him an unknown territory, an unmapped terrain, or he imagines there must be somewhere a new route to the Indies, another polar star, gorgons alive and well amid jungle-covered ruins, mountain views and river sources grander than the Nile's, lost tribes, treasure, or another, better, way of life; because he is searching, not inventing; he is trying to find what is already there: regions of life as neglected as his own history, themes as far from general attention as a cavern at the bottom of the sea, structures as astounding as those which show up stained in tissue slices. Explorational fiction records an often painful and disappointing journey, possibly of discovery, possibly of empty sailing; yet never toward what may lie out of sight in the self, since that is what improvisation discloses, but of what lies still unappreciated in the landscape of literature—implications unperceived, conclusions undrawn, directions everyone has failed to follow. The spirit of the explorer may be indeed to scalpel society and show its rotting organs, nor is every implication nice as toast with tea; however the key to this kind of fiction is that the chest, which the existence of the key suggests, must be (or be believed to be) there in six feet of sand beneath the bolt-scarred tree. In that sense, exploration is the work of a realist, however fanciful that reality may seem to those encountering it for the first time.

Maybe we can pun our way to another genre, inasmuch as labels seem to matter more than their jar. The prefix "ex-" apparently has to be there, since we already have the "explanatory," the "experimental" and "exploratory," as well as the sweat from "exercise." Nevertheless, we ought not to be tied tamely to the past. How about "innoversive fiction"? I like the "metamusical" myself. "Excremental" belongs to Joyce. "Minnovative" describes a movement whose small moment has come and gone. "Exploramental" makes me think of "florabunda," though I do fancy "postcynical" and could easily find a use for "metafutile." Remember when all we had to worry about were the Yellow Press, Blue Movies, and Black Humor?

I could see a plume of gray smoke when I looked back toward my imagined pursuers, and my legs grew longer through every lope (I had experimented, I had made my exclamation point, and I was now being taught), nor did I begin to gasp for breath and feel my blood beating hard in my head, until I had run right out of my neighborhood and saw a strange little shop and strange houses of one story, strange streets lined with shallow ditches, lots of transplanted Christmas trees, a strange black boat-tailed bird, strange absence of lamps, and felt I had found a country where every noun began with "strange" and "and" was its only connective . . . my boom had blown me farther than the pieces of its pipe . . . to a strange, yes . . . to a strange strange lampless land.

WILLIAM GOLDMAN

BUTCH CASSIDY AND THE NAZI DENTIST

WILLIAM GOLDMAN: FIVE SCREENPLAYS

Movies are centrally, crucially, primarily about one thing only: story.

This is not to say I prefer *Die Hard* to *The Seventh Seal.* But you had better give a shit about that Knight's adventures, his chess battle with Death, had better want him to win, had better be locked into his travels, or the movie is just another exercise in style that we can't remember if we saw or not.

Movies must tell a compelling story or they stop existing in our minds. Stanley Kubrick once said this: "A good story is a miracle." By good story he meant, oh, maybe something with an interesting premise that develops logically and builds to a satisfying and surprising climax.

Do you know how hard that is?

It just *kills* us, people who try to tell stories to survive. Maybe once, maybe two or three times in a lifetime, we get away with it, have the experience of riding confidently atop our material, not praying we can skill our way clear of the falseness, the tricks we hope work so you won't turn away from us with the moviegoer's equivalent of scorn, which is boredom.

I've gotten away with it a few times. Once with a movie titled *Butch Cassidy and the Sundance Kid,* which I'll discuss a little here. (Once with a movie titled *The Princess Bride,* which I won't.) I'm not attributing quality to either of them—I would never do that to anything I've written—but I can look at those two and say I don't give a fuck what you think, these are *mine*.

BUTCH: YOU MUST KILL ALL YOUR DARLINGS

Butch was their story first—these two guys, traveling together for years and decades over countries and continents, finally going down, wildly outnumbered, in Bolivia. They had done what F. Scott said you couldn't do, be American and have a second act in life, because when they fell they were legends again, as famous in South America in 1911 as they had been in their great days in the Old West nearing the turn of the twentieth century.

I was moved when I first read about them, always will be. Have no idea really why. Today, their journey is familiar. When I began, maybe ten people alive had the least idea who they were. When a great success happens—and this movie was certainly that—the most gratifying aspect of it for me is that what I thought was a glorious piece of narrative turns out to be the same for people around the world. It is, if you will, a validation of my sense of story.

One of the great true Cassidy stories was when he was young and in jail in Wyoming, I think it was, and he came up for parole, and the governor met with him and said, "I'll parole you if you'll promise to go straight."

And Butch thought a moment, and then he said: "I can't do that."

In a stunned silence, he went on, "But I'll make a deal with you: If you'll let me out, I promise never to work in Wyoming again."

And the governor *took the deal.*

And Butch never robbed in Wyoming again.

Even today, that's probably the best character introduction I've ever come across. When I was researching the story, reading whatever I could find, I *knew* this was how we would meet Butch. And that kind of building block is essential when you're stumbling through material, trying to get a grip on the best way for *you* to tell this particular story. The entire posse chase, almost half an hour of screen time, was only writable for me because I knew the Sundance Kid couldn't swim, something I'd read was true of a lot of western figures of that period. I don't know how it is for others, but building up confidence is the single hardest battle I face every day of my life.

Anyway, I had this wondrous governor anecdote.

And it fell out of the movie. (It's included in the prequel, *Butch and Sundance: The Early Days*, which Allan Burns wrote and Richard Lester directed, a nice movie that I suggest you rent because I know you haven't seen it because *nobody* saw it when it was in release.)

It works there because they were kids when that movie takes place. But I couldn't use it because it was off the spine. The movie I wrote was about these two legends who become legends all over again in a different country. I had no time to get young Butch arrested, jailed, and then offered pardon. And no governor with a sniff at reelection is going to release the most famous outlaw of his time. Maybe you can figure out a way to fit it in. I sure wanted to, and I sure couldn't. Faulkner said this: In writing, you must kill all your darlings. I'm not sure I totally subscribe to that, but I do believe that you had damn well better be willing to.

A brief word about what follows.

The standard screenplay form is not only unreadable, it is something far worse, it is *wrong*. All those capital letters and numbers that stop our eye and destroy any chance at narrative flow have nothing to do with writing. They are for the other technicians when the movie is actually in production so they will know what scenes they are doing that day. "Oh, look, guys, we're shooting scenes 104, 106, and 109 today." I have never used them; hate them, always will.

I try to make my screenplays as readable an experience as I can, for a good and greedy reason—I want the executives who read them and who have the power to green-light a flick to say, "Hey, this wasn't such a bad read, *I can make money out of it.*"

Truism: We all want the movies we write to get made.

The screenplay is a limited form, as the sonnet is limited, as plays are limited, and as the epic poem and the novel are not.

We cannot ramble. We are hemmed in by length. We do not handle aging well. If we attempt philosophical dialogue, we empty theaters. In fact, *any* dialogue that doesn't push us along is suspect.

If a character tries at length to tell us who he is, if he just stands there and talks, there is no law on earth that says we have to sit there and listen. And we won't. We can get popcorn, take a pee, snooze, whisper, leave. We can do any number of things, but the one thing we won't do is listen.

It gets harder and harder today to put new twists on old twists, which is a great part of the screenwriter's task. We do it as skillfully and hopefully as we can. But that damn audience is watching us. Teenagers today see more movies in a year—at theaters, on tape, on the tube—than anyone of my generation saw in the first twenty years of life. We have an audience today that is more knowledgeable than any audience has ever been. One of the great early movie hits was simply of a cow eating grass. I don't think Mr. Paramount would green-light that today.

This is a moment from the *Butch Cassidy* screenplay. At the end, they are trapped and out of ammunition. Butch has to run to get more while Sundance covers him. They are surrounded by a lot of Bolivian policemen, who are shooting at them.

cut to
BUTCH, streaking, diving again, then up, and the bullets landing around him aren't even close as
cut to
SUNDANCE, whirling and spinning, continuing to fire and
cut to
SEVERAL POLICEMEN, dropping for safety behind the wall and
cut to
BUTCH, really moving now, dodging, diving, up again and
cut to
SUNDANCE, flinging away one gun, grabbing another from his holster, continuing to turn and fire and
cut to
TWO POLICEMAN, falling wounded to the ground and

cut to

BUTCH, letting out a notch, then launching into another dive forward and

cut to

SUNDANCE, whirling, but you never know which way he's going to spin and

cut to

THE HEAD POLICEMAN, cursing, forced to drop for safety behind the wall and

cut to

BUTCH, racing to the mules, and then he is there, grabbing at the near mule for ammunition and

cut to

SUNDANCE, throwing the second gun away, reaching into his holster for another, continuing to spin and fire and

cut to

BUTCH, and he has the ammunition now and

cut to

ANOTHER POLICEMAN, screaming as he falls and

cut to

BUTCH, his arms loaded, tearing away from the mules, and they're still not even coming close to him as they fire, and the mules are behind him now as he runs and cuts and cuts again going full out and

cut to

THE HEAD POLICEMAN, cursing incoherently at what is happening and

cut to

SUNDANCE, whirling faster than ever and

cut to

BUTCH, dodging and cutting, and as a pattern of bullets rips into his body, he somersaults and lies there, blood pouring and

cut to

SUNDANCE, running toward him and

cut to

ALL THE POLICEMEN, rising up from behind the wall now, firing and

cut to
SUNDANCE as he falls.

You can say that is not Shakespearean, and I would agree with you. You can say a lot of unenthusiastic things about it, and I would probably agree with you. But there is one thing I can say about it that you cannot disagree with and that is this: *It's all one sentence.*
Twenty cuts.
Three hundred words.
Why did I do that? Look, that's a famous action scene. But it wasn't a famous scene when I wrote it. It was the first movie original of my life. I was in new and strange terrain. That's the peak of my story. All those years of research, of trying to figure just what the story should be, that's all climaxing here. I was killing my heroes, for Chrissakes—*and I didn't fucking want you looking away.*
When I write a screenplay, more than anything else I want this: I want to control your eyes.
And this time, I think, I managed to pull it off. Which is the best that a screenwriter can do, even if it doesn't exactly earn you immortality. Not long ago, I was having dinner alone before a Knicks game at Quatorze Bis, my favorite French bistro, when one of the waiters came over. The staff there is mostly young— writers, actors. This guy said he had just seen a movie I wrote, *The Princess Bride,* and was saying how much he liked it, and, of course, I was pleased, and I thanked him and said it was one of my two favorites, that and *Butch.*
He kind of looked at me.
"*Butch Cassidy,*" I said.
Glass.
"*Butch Cassidy and the Sundance Kid.* It's a western."
"I don't know that one," he said.
After my initial shock, I realized there was no reason he should know it—it came out before he was born. We sneak into people's memories for only a very short time—no one gets to settle in. Every movie, no matter how it is received initially, is but a blip on the screen. As, alas, are we all. . . .

MARATHON MAN: REVISITING DR. MENGELE

I once ended a novel with the notion that "life was material—everything was material, you just had to live long enough to see how to use it." I believed that then, still do, and it is certainly true of a scene I wrote in Manhattan in 1973, but that began life thirty-five years sooner, in the town of Evanston, in the state of Illinois.

That being when I first encountered Meyer Cohn (not his real name).

A handsome man, a good and loving father, pillar of the community, hail-fellow-well-met, all that shit. I didn't care, I hated him. Because I was eight years old, and though it may seem petty for one human to dislike another over something as trivial as this, so be it. The son of a bitch scared me. *Hurt* me. Made me scream. Made me cry.

Cohn, need I add, was a dentist.

Who did not believe in novocaine.

Half a century after I escaped him, I can still see him in his white jacket, his knee on my chest (believe it), doing these awful things. He explained the knee to my mother by saying that I had a very strong tongue and needed to be firmly held down. We lived in a neighboring small town, and I used to beg not to go back, fake the most amazing ailments. Didn't work. (Anybody under forty won't know this, but the only thing in the universe that has improved on our watch is dentistry.) Eventually, my family found a fellow close to home, and Cohn took his place in memory.

Flash-forward to 1973, and I am writing a novel—a thriller. Now, in a thriller you start with the villain. I started with Josef Mengele, the most intellectually startling of the Nazis (an M.D. *plus* a Ph.D.). And I knew this: I needed to get him to America. But why in the world would he come? Mengele, when I began fiddling with this story, was either alive in South America or had been alive in South America, choose one. Living secretly or palatially. I chose palatially.

But this was one of the brilliant minds of his generation. Why would he be so dumb as to risk his world to visit America? I was reading the papers one day when the answer came. An

American doctor, in Cleveland I think, had begun doing a revolutionary operation—heart-sleeve surgery—and people were streaming in from all over the world. Mengele would be among the needy.

I have always had an unerring brilliance when it comes to narrative, and here was just another brilliant example. Mengele would come to Cleveland for surgery. Mengele *had* to come to America, the reasoning was rock solid. I had scored another coup.

One day, I was just walking around—I get a lot of ideas just walking around—when reality thudded home. *Schmuck*, what kind of a villain is he if he's so fucking frail he needs *heart surgery? Asshole*, what kind of a thriller do you have if the villain is already *dying? Ahhhhhhhh.*

I don't know if it's true for other writers, but for me, when a piece of material becomes urgent, there is only a certain window of time in which it can be put down. If that passes, the window shuts, the material is dead, often forever. I had never tried a spy thriller, owned the standard lack of confidence, and felt a certain sense of panic setting in.

Then I read an article about how some Nazi leaders had accumulated great fortunes by knocking the teeth out of their prisoners and melting the gold down, or taking jewels from their colons, where desperate men and women had been hiding their valuables for centuries. It all fell in place. The name, Szell, I chose from the great conductor—just saying it made me feel sadistic. The reason for visiting—to get his diamonds. The only man he trusted—his father—the man who had been in charge of the fortune in America, is killed in a car crash in the opening.

So Szell has to come. A doctor, a monster, a Nazi, but I wanted worse, I wanted more—so bless you, Meyer Cohn, because Szell became one afternoon, suddenly and forever, a dentist. I had my villain. And I knew he had to torture someone because I remembered the pressure from my childhood, being helpless in the chair with that knee forcing me down, unmindful of my pain.

Babe, the hero (Dustin Hoffman in the flick; Olivier played the dentist), appeared because I had become fascinated with this notion: What if someone close to you was something totally different from what you thought? In the story, Hoffman thinks his brother (Roy Scheider) is a businessman, whereas the reality is that the man is a spy—who has been involved with the Nazi, Szell.

Once I had that, the rest was essentially mixing and matching, figuring out the surprises, hoping they would work. (You never know. I don't, anyway. Same is true of screenplay writing. Each time out is just as scary. I wish it weren't so, but there it is.) So now I had my torturer, my method, and my victim, and early on in the novel I gave Babe a toothache. At the time I was building this into the book, I went to see my gum guy, a wonderful periodontist, a joy. He never hurts people, plays Bach on the radio, is fascinated with restaurants, as am I.

We are talking of a genuinely kind and decent human being.

He asks what I am writing, and when I am about to leave, I tell him and mention that Babe has a cavity and what I am about to do to him—

and—

and—

and I will never forget the look that dropped onto his face.

"Oh, no," he said quietly, his eyes all dreamy. "No, Bill. Forget the cavity. You want pain. You want genuine, unforgettable pain. You want pain that would make you want to die. Bill, listen to me—*have him drill into a healthy tooth.*"

On and on this sweet man went, talking to me of the glory of anguish, of how it would be impossible to keep any secrets if someone were drilling into a fine, strapping tooth. I have rarely been more frightened. Here this sweet fellow I'd known for twenty years was Jekyll-Hyding as I watched. He wouldn't stop. The level of agony would be unsurpassable. Death would be preferable. The memory of being destroyed in the chair would never leave you. . . .

He's still my gum guy. But now I get nervous when we're alone.

In 1992, years after the book and the movie, I was in Los Angeles when I got a twinge of pain that I knew meant root canal. I chose to ignore it, hoped it would stay bearable until the end of the week, when I could get back to New York.

It didn't. I asked around, got a specialist, went to see him. This fellow worked in an office of specialists—a long railroad car of root-canal guys. I sat in the chair; he started to work.

And to chat. "What brings you to Los Angeles?" he starts, and I already know the—you should pardon the expression—drill. When asked, I either lie and say I sell corn futures or tell the truth. Which is no fun because I am *waaay* too old to be giving my credits, which is how this scenario usually ends. I decide to buy time.

"Business."

"And what kind of business might that be?"

The crossroads question. I go for it. "I'm a writer."

"What kind of writing is it that you do?"

Pause. "Books and movies."

"*Hmmm.* Interesting." And now the most hated question of all. "What movies have you written that I might have seen?" (Often, they haven't seen any.)

I am totally in his power, understand. Tilted way back. He is a big man and seems bigger looming over me. To hell with it, I decide. Go for the gold.

"*Marathon Man.* Both the book and the movie."

Pause.

The information registers. Every dentist on both sides of the Iron Curtain knows *Marathon Man.* "Excuse me," he says. He is gone, but after a while he comes back, gently works at my mouth until he is done. I thank him. Get up to go.

And as I walk into the hallway, I see this whole corridor of dentists, all of them staring at me from their cubicles. He had told them all whom he was punishing. I was not used to the attention. All these men, staring at me. I was, within the confines of that suite, famous.

Everyone in the movie business is a star fucker. Never happened like that to me before, never since. But right then, at last, I was twinkling. . . .

MISERY: WARREN BEATTY SAVES THE DAY

I got a call from Rob Reiner saying he was interested in this book by Stephen King and wondering if I would read it. He became interested when Andy Scheinman, Reiner's producer, read it on a plane and wondered who owned the movie rights. The book had been published for a while, was a number-one novel, standard for King.

They found out it hadn't been sold—not for any lack of offers but because King wouldn't sell it. He has disliked most of the movies made from his work and didn't want *Misery*, perhaps his favorite, Hollywooded up.

Reiner called him, and they talked. Now, one of the movies made from his fiction that King *did* like was *Stand by Me*, which Reiner directed. The conversation ended with King saying, sure, he would sell it, but he would have to be paid a lot of money and Reiner would have to agree to either produce or direct it.

Reiner, who had no intention of directing, agreed. He would produce. He called me. I read *Misery*. I had read enough of King to know this: Of all the phenoms who have appeared in the past decades, King is the stylist. If he ever chooses to leave the world that has made him the most successful writer in memory, he won't break a sweat. The man can write anything, he is that gifted.

Misery is about a famous author who has a terrible car crash during a blizzard and is rescued by a nurse. Who turns out to be his number-one fan. Who also turns out to be very crazy. And who keeps him prisoner in her out-of-the-way Colorado home. It all ends badly for them both (worse for her). I was having a fine old time reading it. I'm a novelist, too, so I identified with Paul Sheldon, who is not just trapped with a nut but also trapped by his own fear of losing success. And Annie Wilkes, the nurse/prison guard, is one of King's best creations.

When I do an adaptation, I have to be kicked by the source material. One of the ways I work is to read that material again and again. And if I don't like it a lot going in, that becomes too awful. I wasn't sure halfway through if I would write the movie, but I was enjoying the hell out of the novel.

Then, on page 191, the hobbling scene began.

Paul Sheldon has managed to get out of the bedroom in his wheelchair. He has gotten back in time to have fooled

Annie Wilkes. That was more than a little important to him because Annie was not the kind of lady you wanted real mad at you.

Except, secretly, she does know, and in the next fifteen pages, takes action.

I remember thinking, Jesus, what in the world will she do? Annie has a volcanic temper. What's in her head? She talks to Paul about his behavior, and then she eventually works her way around to the Kimberly diamond mines and asks him how he thinks they treat workers there who steal the merchandise. Paul says, "I don't know, kill them, I suppose." And Annie says, "Oh, no, they hobble them."

And then, all for the need of love, she takes a propane torch and an ax and cuts his feet off and says, "Now you're hobbled" when the deed is done.

I could not fucking believe it.

I mean, I knew she wasn't going to tickle him with a peacock feather, but I never dreamed such behavior was possible. And I knew I had to write the movie. That scene would linger in audiences' memories as I knew it would linger in mine.

The next half-year or so is taken up with various versions of the screenplay, and I work with Reiner and Scheinman, the best producers I have ever known for scripts. We finally have a version they okay, and we go director hunting. Our first choice is George Roy Hill, and he says *yes.* Nirvana.

Then Hill calls and says he is changing his mind. We all meet. And Hill, who has *never* in his life done anything like this, explains: "I was up all night, and I just could not hear myself saying 'Action' on that scene. I just haven't got the sensibility to do that scene."

"*What scene?*" (I am in agony—I desperately want him to do it. He is tough, acerbic, brilliant, snarly, passionate.)

"The lopping scene."

What madness is this? What lopping scene?

"The scene where she lops his feet off."

"George, how can you be so wrong? That is not a *lopping* scene, that is a *hobbling* scene. And it is great, and it is the reason I took this movie, and she only does it out of love."

"Goldman, *she lops his fucking feet off,*" he says. "And I can't direct that."

"It's the best scene in the movie when she *hobbles* him. It's a character scene, for Chrissakes."

He would not budge. And, of course, since it was the most important scene and the best scene, it had to stay. A sad, sad farewell. We were about to send the script to Barry Levinson when Rob said, "To hell with it, I'll direct it myself."

And so the lopping-scene poll came into my life.

Because Hill has a brilliant movie mind and you must pay attention. Rob had no problem directing the scene. But what if George was right? I, of course, scoffed—the *hobbling* scene was a character scene, unlike anything yet filmed, and it was great, and it was the reason I took the picture, and it had to stay.

Still, we asked people. A poll was taken at Castle Rock, informally, of anyone who had read the script. Rob would keep me abreast in New York. "A good day for the hobblers today—three secretaries said leave it alone." That wasn't exactly verbatim, but you get the idea.

Enter Warren Beatty. Beatty understands the workings of the town I think better than anyone. He has been a force for thirty-five years and has been in an *amazing* number of flops, and whenever his career seems a tad shaky, he produces a wonderful movie or directs a wonderful movie and is safe for another half-decade.

For a short while, Beatty was interested in playing Paul. Rob and Andy met with him a lot, and I spent a day there when the lopping scene came up. Beatty's point was this: He had no trouble losing his feet at the ankles. But know that if you did that, the guy would be crippled for life and would be a loser.

I said nonsense, it was a great scene, a character scene, the reason I took the movie, and it had to stay as it was. Casting continued. I went on vacation as we were about to start, and while I was gone, Rob and Andy wanted to take a final pass at the script, and I was delighted. They wanted it shorter, tighter, tauter, and they're expert editors. When I got back, I read what they had done.

It was shorter, tighter, tauter—

But the lopping scene was gone, replaced with what you saw in the movie—she breaks his ankles with a sledgehammer.

I *screeeeamed*. I got on the phone with Rob and Andy and told them they had ruined the picture, that is was a great and memorable scene they had changed, it was the reason I had taken the job. I was incoherent (they are friends, they expect that), but I made my point. They just wouldn't buy it. The lopping scene was gone now and forever, replaced by the ankle-breaking scene. I hated it, but there it was.

I am a wise and experienced hand at this stuff, and I *know* when I am right.

And you know what?

I was *wrong*. It became instantly clear when we screened the movie. What they had done—it was exactly the same scene except for the punishment—worked wonderfully and was absolutely horrific enough. If we had gone the way I wanted, it would have been too much. The audience would have hated Kathy and, in time, hated us.

If I had been in charge, *Misery* would have been this film you might have heard of but would never have gone to see. Because people who had seen it would have told you to stay away. What makes a movie a hit is not the star and not the advertising but this: word of mouth. In the movie business, as in real life, we all need all the help we can get. And we need it every step of the way.

STEPHEN SPENDER

MY LIFE IS MINE;
IT IS NOT DAVID LEAVITT'S

THE NEW YORK TIMES BOOK REVIEW

In a few weeks my autobiography "World Within World," first
published in 1951, will be reappearing in American bookstores.
"World Within World," an account largely of the years between
the great wars, was started in 1947, when I was 38 years old,
and completed in 1950. I am now 85, old enough to see new
controversies surrounding my book, controversies that have involved the issue of plagiarism, the nature of biography and the
treatment of homosexuality in literature. I have been forced to
consider whether I would have wanted to rewrite portions of my
book to take advantage of changed political, social and literary
attitudes. However, except for a new introduction, I have decided to keep the text of "World Within World" exactly as it
was in 1950.

The occasion for a surge of interest in "World Within
World," particularly in the United States, is that last year a
young American writer, David Leavitt, published a novel,
"While England Sleeps," closely derived in plot and text from
about 30 pages of my autobiography, concerning my relationship with a man I call Jimmy Younger.

My book describes how after my marriage to Inez Pearn, my
friend, who was also my former lover, joined the International
Brigade and fought in the Spanish Civil War. At first Jimmy
was enthusiastic (although he did write to me complaining that
some of his fellow recruits were from a "gang of Glasgow razor-
slashers"). But his later letters reflected his disillusion with the

Communist Party and his horror of combat, which he experienced at the bloody battle of Jarama in 1937. He deserted, was captured and sent to prison. I felt responsible for him—"someone I loved had gone into this war as a result of my influence"—and having gone to Spain, I tried to save him from being shot as a deserter. I obtained a promise from the commissars of the brigade that Jimmy would be transferred to noncombatant duty. But when the Franco offensive against Madrid was renewed, all available men had to be rushed to the front.

Jimmy again deserted and took refuge with a woman in Valencia who promised to get him a berth as a crew member aboard a ship leaving Spain, but who instead handed him over to the brigade police. I used my influence to see the brigade authorities and was given the opportunity to dine with the "comrades" who were to be Jimmy's judges, including a young Polish intellectual, and to argue in Jimmy's defense. He was finally released from the brigade on my evidence to them of his ill health, and he returned safely to England.

With names changed (Jimmy to Edward, etc.), this is almost exactly transcribed in Mr. Leavitt's novel of last year. There's even a Polish judge and mention of a "razor-slashing gang." He does make some changes; in his version Edward-Jimmy is smuggled onto a ship, where he dies in the manner of the hero's bathetic death in Frederic William Farrar's Victorian novel "Eric: Or, Little by Little," which in the early part of this century was in all small boys' libraries.

Mr. Leavitt subsequently wrote an article for The New York Times Magazine entitled "Did I Plagiarize His Life?" The answer to his question is that plagiarism of a life is not at issue. It is plagiarism of the work, since plagiarism is defined by the Oxford English Dictionary as "the wrongful appropriation or purloining, and publication as one's own, of the ideas, or the expression of the ideas (literary, artistic, musical, mechanical, etc.) of another."

Mr. Leavitt did not observe in his acknowledgments that "World Within World" was an important source, extensively used, in "While England Sleeps." He confirmed the fact only after the reviewer for The Washington Post, Bernard Knox, a distinguished classicist and himself a veteran of the Spanish Civil War, immediately detected it. Therefore Mr. Leavitt may have hoped that his appropriations would remain undetected. Indeed, he seems to consider it a piece of great hard luck that I should ever have heard of the existence of his book, and explained in reply that he "had originally composed" an acknowledgment, "but had been advised by an in-house lawyer at Viking to omit the reference." He has tried to maintain that he used "the facts" of my life rather than my book itself. However, as the English writer James Fenton pointed out in his review in The Independent, "What is being tampered with here is an achieved literary work"; he advised Mr. Leavitt to withdraw "While England Sleeps." "An author has a right to chuck his own book in the bin," Mr. Fenton wrote. "That's what I would do. Quickly."

Since this more honorable course of action was not taken, I brought a suit charging infringement of copyright. Before my case could be heard in the High Court in London, Mr. Leavitt and his publishers, Viking Penguin, settled the case by legally undertaking to withdraw his novel worldwide, including America, pulp thousands of existing copies, and pay all legal costs. In this way it was acknowledged that my detailed lists of strikingly similar passages given in affidavit were no "legal fiction," as Mr. Leavitt now wishes it to be seen, and that far more than "facts" had been taken: literary structure, character development, dialogue and plot had been lifted as well. By the wisdom of his lawyers, Mr. Leavitt was spared an appearance in court, and many authors who had watched the developments were glad that the outcome demonstrated the effectiveness of copyright protection.

Mr. Leavitt should not have felt aggrieved, however, for his situation was in no way that of the biographers he regards as comparable, whose subjects are dead or out of copyright, whose research is thorough and who use their own words; or that of a novelist who uses his or her own material. He would have you believe otherwise: "When writing historical fiction about a period in which one did not live, however, one obviously has to look into the past—to eavesdrop on history itself.''

No one would disagree with him there, but doing so surely does not mean finding some past person's autobiography and presenting a great part of it as one's own current fiction. In his essay, Mr. Leavitt cites Susan Sontag's use in her novel "The Volcano Lover" of Lady Hamilton, and Mary Renault's account of Alexander the Great in "The Persian Boy," neither subject an autobiographer, both long dead and out of copyright. For her novel "Regeneration," Pat Barker may or may not have had access to copyright material of Siegfried Sassoon, who is also dead, but none of these three took someone else's creative work and in their fiction presented plot, characters and dialogue as their own.

Although American and British law equally defend an author's copyright in the general principles described, British law also extends to the author's moral right not to have his work "adapted," distorted or trivialized. Therefore, Mr. Leavitt's fantasy accretions to my autobiography, which I find pornographic, certainly do not correspond to my experience or to my idea of literature, and also arguably contravene the copyright law by adaptation, given the extensive use of my words, characters and plot.

Moreover, even had I ever been disposed to write such scenes, they could not, in 1951, have found a publisher. In his essay, Mr. Leavitt seems as astonishingly unaware of the legal position of homosexuals in England before the law was reformed as his novel showed him to be of the history and geography of the Spanish Civil War and the poverty that prevailed in 1937. Wartime Barcelona, unforgettably described by George Orwell in "Homage to Catalonia," was far from the glittering 1990-ish tourists' playground of "While England Sleeps." The many such historical errors of his 1993 book prompt me to offer him, and possibly also some of his contemporaries, a little necessary background.

In the late 1920's and 30's, England seemed dominated by reactionaries and imperialists. One of their weapons was censorship. There was, it is true, no official Governmental censorship for literature (though there was a British Board of Film

Censors), but any member of the public who considered a book to be obscene or pornographic could appeal to a magistrate's court to have it banned on those grounds. Many instances showed that such a plaintiff was almost certain to win his case. James Joyce's "Ulysses," D. H. Lawrence's "Lady Chatterley's Lover" and Radclyffe Hall's lesbian novel "The Well of Loneliness" were all banned.

This was a time when publishers would write to authors who seemed to have overstepped the line dividing the publishable from the obscene, explaining that such-or-such a scene had to be cut out of a novel if it were to appear without fear of prosecution. It was not a frivolous demand. As Noel Annan recounts in "Our Age," even as late as the 1950's, under a reactionary Home Secretary and Director of Public Prosecutions, many reputable publishers were prosecuted, just as arrests of homosexuals, which often were followed by imprisonments, rose from an average of 800 annually before the war to 2,300 in 1953. Homosexual acts remained a criminal offense until the 1960's, so that people identified as homosexuals could be imprisoned, and writers who wrote about them could be prosecuted for obscenity. "The Well of Loneliness" was suppressed in this way, because such novels of overt homosexuality certainly fell into the category of obscenity. It was not until the liberalizing Home Secretary, Roy Jenkins, introduced reforms that became law, successfully tested in the famous Lady Chatterley case of 1960, that writers no longer chafed under such constraints.

Authors of the 1990's like Mr. Leavitt, who are entirely free to exploit a wave of popular interest, would do well to understand that writers as recently as the 1950's ran considerable risks of being prosecuted under both these intolerant laws. It was for this reason that in 1950, while prepared to take the risk for myself, I gave my former lover the pseudonym Jimmy Younger in "World Within World." My autobiography was received in 1951 as ahead of its time in its frankness, admired as such by some reviewers, attacked by others for what was seen as excessive candor.

But it will be clear to any reader of the book that between Jimmy and myself there had been a love relationship. We had lived together, sharing a flat in London and traveling abroad between 1934 and 1936. After those years we separated, though we always kept in touch with each other. Early in the Spanish Civil War and soon after my marriage, Jimmy Younger joined the International Brigade.

Mr. Leavitt, in his essay, wrote that the theme of his book, "if it belongs to anyone, belongs to E. M. Forster, who wrote in his famous essay 'What I Believe' " that "if I had to choose between betraying my country and betraying my friend, I hope I should have the guts to betray my country.' " Mr. Leavitt added: "It seems to me crucial, in reading these sentences, to remember that Forster was homosexual, since for gay men and lesbians the choice between cause and friend is rarely abstract; indeed, particularly in the age of AIDS, it is often viscerally real."

It is surprising to a member of my generation that sometimes young people today cannot imagine the intense urgency with which antifascist youth responded in 1937 to the probability of Hitler's prison state gaining total domination of Europe. The idealistic volunteers in the International Brigade felt that far from betraying their country, they would preserve its freedom by fighting to prevent, as they believed, the greater catastrophe of a world war.

Their altruistic decisions to die if necessary for deliverance from an evil tyranny have nothing in common with the involuntary suffering of a plague, heroic though victims of AIDS undoubtedly are. The choice Mr. Leavitt quoted from Forster cannot apply to them. It puzzles me how seldom it is perceived that Forster's choice is dubious. One has only to think of the Cambridge spies to realize that in betraying their country they were inevitably also betraying their friends, many of whom were unable to forgive them. Public treachery and private deception cannot so easily be disentangled.

Jimmy had now become far more religiously left-wing than I, surprising in that his relaxed, pleasure-loving nature seemed ill suited to Communist puritanism. I thought his going to Spain was a reaction to my marriage. I was particularly worried because, although when we first met he had recently been a

Guardsman, I did not believe he had the character to be a volunteer in a "ragtag army," as Louis MacNeice, in his poem "Autumn Journal," described the Spanish militia.

Perhaps I blamed myself too much. Reading now through letters to me from Christopher Isherwood at the time, I find one sent from Brussels, where Christopher was then living, written a day after he had been visited by Jimmy, accompanied by his friend Giles Romilly (Winston Churchill's nephew), who also had joined the International Brigade and who was to distinguish himself in the battle of Boadilla. Christopher wrote on Dec. 27, 1936:

"I think Christmas was a success, and they enjoyed themselves and didn't worry too much. I suppose when they get to Paris and are among all the others, it won't be so bad, anyhow. [Jimmy] certainly was very cheerful, in the full armor and spirit of the party line. What a blessing religion is. Poor Giles got bouts of being mildly scared; but we had a lot of fun in the boîtes, in the true Foreign Legion manner. He was chiefly upset because, last night, he lost his ring, given him by his mother, and, not unnaturally, felt that this was a bad omen.

"You can set your mind absolutely at rest about one thing: [Jimmy] is not going to Spain on account of your marriage. And he's not feeling badly about it any more. I am absolutely certain of this, because we had a conversation when we were very drunk, and the way he said it was really convincing. No doubt you know this anyhow: but it's worth telling you, as an outsider."

In appropriating for his own novelistic purposes this Spanish episode from my book, Mr. Leavitt added a new, distorting dimension to "World Within World" by introducing into the story of an upper-class English writer and his working-class friend lubricious accounts of homosexual lovemaking between them. This left me wondering: if the laws regarding obscenity had been different when I wrote "World Within World," would I have added scenes describing sexual acts?

The answer, I am sure, is no. In our own lives, living among other people, we are aware, of course, of their love affairs, heterosexual or homosexual. But we do not know, nor, I think, want to know about their sexual acts. Knowledge of what people do when they are in bed together may be true, but it is not true to what we know or wish to know about them.

In part that's one reason why I resent my biography being mixed up with David Leavitt's pornography. I still feel that if he wanted to write about his sexual fantasies, he should write about them being his, not mine, for by his use of my copyrighted book, his central narrator was made clearly identifiable.

Predictably, when Mr. Leavitt wrote "Did I Plagiarize His Life?" he said he found such objections of mine "particularly galling." "Yes, the novel was sexually explicit—exuberantly so; yes, it described in frank language the erotic evolution of a gay relationship," Mr. Leavitt wrote with evident self-congratulation, adding, "But if 'While England Sleeps' was pornographic, so were most of the novels by John Updike." Someone should point out to Mr. Leavitt that it is no parallel whatever to claim affinity with John Updike, who, after all, uses his own material, honestly, and with incomparable style.

What is pornography anyway? W. H. Auden defined it by saying that if read by 12 people, a passage is pornographic if a majority of them would be sexually excited by it. It may be that such a readership exists, responsive to Mr. Leavitt's dozen or so explicit scenes, and that his writing is appreciated. But what he sees as "exuberant" a great number of readers, of all sexual identities, found tediously repetitive and unesthetic; "The boys are at it like rabbits" was Rhoda Koenig's comment in New York magazine. And the wry joke of Richard Dyer in The Boston Globe, that Mr. Leavitt's mother "should have washed his mouth out with soap," hardly suggests readers captivated by the exuberance of romantic love. So although his intention may very well have been to represent sexual love in a compelling way, one is tempted to quote a satirical phrase of Randall Jarrell's: "It's ugly . . . but is it Art?"

Writing in The New York Times, presumably of Mr. Leavitt's motives, James Atlas maintained, "By writing frankly about matters that Mr. Spender was prevented from addressing, he would strike a blow for sexual freedom, affirm what the older writer could only intimate—the validity of romantic and sexual love between men." Apparently, some members of Mr. Leavitt's 90's generation see themselves as valiantly doing battle to present the validity of a form of love, which, nevertheless, has been extolled throughout the ages.

The apparent assumption of Mr. Leavitt and his supporters— that it is somehow mandatory for a writer to avoid the charge of hypocrisy by introducing explicit sex scenes, possibly suppressing his esthetic judgment in so doing—seems to me as intolerant as the attitudes toward the gay community about which they justly complain. The freedom of writers to develop their creative gifts as they judge best cannot be served by being required to accept this assumption.

Christopher Isherwood opens his revisionist autobiographical "Christopher and His Kind" in 1977 with the delighted admission that to him in the pre-Hitler 30's BERLIN MEANT BOYS! But while taking advantage of the freedom he now enjoyed to say this, he did not use that freedom to describe physical acts between him and his lovers. Why not? He would surely have done so had he thought such confessions really revealing. But I believe he thought that such confessions would not contribute to his development of his characters.

That does not mean, of course, that writers should not describe such acts, if they are revealing of character. (I myself wrote as early as 1930 a novel called "The Temple," describing a walking tour down the valley of the Rhine by a young Englishman and two young Germans. Because of a scene of sexual relations between two of the characters, the book remained unpublished until the late 80's.) But arguing that to describe them explicitly is some kind of virtue, and not to describe them is some form of self-censorship, is simply perverse.

The sex scene that is not revealing of the character described—in contrast, say, to the last section of James Joyce's "Ulysses," which is truly revealing of the character of Molly Bloom—often tells us more about the interests of the writer and the reader than it does about the subject. Modern "tell all" biographies sometimes read like conspiracies between writer and reader to betray the subject into being, as it were, hijacked to the confessional.

One has the feeling that neither writer nor reader would ever dream of making such confessions about himself or herself. Thus the subject's human failings always appear as revelations of characteristics in regard to which biographer and reader are innocent spectators. In contemporary biography I often feel that in fairness there ought to be a law whereby, in an appendix, all the failings and vices of the biographer, and by extension the reader, should be set down. As Baudelaire put it as the end of the long confessional introductory poem to his "Fleurs du Mal": *"Hypocrite lecteur, mon semblable, mon frère"* (Hypocrite reader, my double, my brother).

LEE UPTON

THE CLOSEST WORK

FIELD

When Louise Bogan wrote of lingering childhood memories she remarked that "such memories, compounded of bewilderment and ignorance and fear, . . . we must always keep in our hearts. We can never forget them because we cannot understand them, and because they are of no use." Perhaps only in the conventional sense was she referring to the "use" that we make of certain memories; perhaps we feel ourselves to be used by memories, particularly those that, once dormant, rise before us with surprising new strength.

When I entered grammar school I did not know the alphabet, and I was perhaps very slow to learn to read. But once I began to read it was as if I were within the room of the book, entering without having heard the door open before me or close behind me. To be absorbed: the phrase has a specific resonance for me, for it was as if I had been admitted wholly into reading and writing. Repeatedly I would read the often mediocre books that we were given in grade school, discovering that speed and concentration determine certain effects. And when I went on to study books that were beyond my capacity I felt a sense of gratitude, as if the books sent me forward into the wonderfully strange.

Reading and writing, done with pages less than an arm's length away, were activities accomplished in a small space removed from the more hazardous bewilderments of childhood.

Otherwise, outside of the book and the papers on my desk, I experienced a sensation of stopping short—a zone, a range of distance—that I avoided and feared.

Then, so much of the world was unreliable. How long it would take me to learn to tell time, to play games on the playground. In some situations, I simply could not understand what other children seemed to understand easily. I accepted my own bewilderment as inevitable, and I came to rely on my reading and my writing. Poems, what little I knew of them, were the best sort of matter for the intense reading I depended upon, and they offered intimations of a way of being that much of the world refused me. Poetry was an efflorescence, an inky apparition. Poets were their words. They were the matter of their books. Somehow, I believed, poems materialized after the poets' deaths. I came home from school with words written on my hands as if my words were my skin.

A vague air of insult traveled about the mid-Michigan farm community in which I was raised. To write poetry meant to affront insult through presumption, for poetry was the most presumptuous thing to which I had been introduced. It repudiated our slights and elevated our value. And it came to me, often enough even in its doggerel form, as the most particularly impossible thing around me.

A year before I secretly pledged myself to poetry, a photographer taking my picture (I am a seven-year-old in my First Communion dress) remarks: "One of her eyes droops." I am not offended but feel grateful for his close attention. In the photograph I am seriously trying to be Mary the Mother of God. Because my prayer book has been forgotten, I am staring at a blank sheet of paper at the level of my breastbone. The paper is folded to resemble a book.

By the time it is discovered that I cannot see writing on the blackboard at school, not even from the front row, that I cannot read the numerals on the clock on the wall, that I have panicked secretly when attempting to recognize the faces of my playmates as they ran about on the playground, I am nine years old. I have learned to read and to write and have promised myself a secret and seemingly impossible ambition—and all this has been conditioned by my being a child like many others, simply enough, commonly enough, a myopic child.

A preoccupation with perception and scale—a sensitivity to distances: these emerge in some measure in my poetry from my experience with early work close to the page. If I prefer to repeal certainties, if often the work seems to draw up short before diverse panels of meaning, it is because I would duplicate an atmosphere of both absorption and resistance. To point to the subjectivity of any vision, to move from opacity to contingent moments of clarity: these have been customary for me.

My repetition of the sensation of working close to the page, of looking up from miniature figures into vague distances, occurs in my poetry as an endeavor that is marked by repetition. In the very act of repeating a sensation from the past I am inevitably touching the pulse of much poetry, for of course many poetries are devoted to repetition, most commonly repetition of word, of phrase, of sound, of image, of conception. In turn the poem lives through repetition; it is measured by its ability to lure readers to repeat the poem over an individual life and over the lives of generations. The poem *bears* repetition and may grow from the poet's compulsion to repeat, paradoxically, because it does not repeat itself twice in the same way. In our individual lives the poem continues to reveal to us new filaments of meaning as if we may only partially see, only partially hear, the poem in each reading. "The words of a dead man / are modified in the guts of the living," Auden wrote, his imagery suggesting that it is the body that consumes the poem, the body that modifies it for us.

The drive to repeat in the poet—the compulsion emerging from latent sources in the memory and in bodily sensation and, often enough, in the conscious will to intervene in repetitive patterns of language—is in turn affected by the desire to reveal a phantom at the borders of consciousness. The unnamed force that we recognize in some poems (I think immediately of Emily Dickinson's spiritual intimations) issues a ghost light, flickering and dissolving but providing us with a glimpse of other orders. However briefly, a sense of immense depths and incredible breadths is ours. This sensation of freedom may repeat itself while we write poems and while we read the poems of others—perhaps if we are patient, if we are determined to see and to listen most fully, to allow our fallible senses to move against their limits.

As a child, when I at last wore glasses, it became clear to me that by having my near-sightedness corrected I also gained new vulnerabilities. The feelings of other people suddenly seemed unbearably close, as if I were being violated in some inchoate manner. To see clearly meant it was now possible to feel in a new way and thus to experience others' repugnance or irritation or dismay. There were more colors in people's faces, and the colors took on sharper edges. Yet it was difficult to make any edges appear around myself. When I became a teenager I disliked wearing glasses and tried at times, miserably, to go without them—out of vanity and out of the self-protection that young people so often desire.

The temptation to look away from what has the potential to harm is a common temptation that the poet must labor to overcome. The poet must make felt and seen what we would instinctively avoid. Louise Bogan writes of an experience of this order in "A Tale," a very early poem which she reprinted in most of her collections. In a desolate landscape a young person encounters the monstrous: "something dreadful and another / Look quietly upon each other." These two unknown monstrous beings are locked together by their gazes as if to see, however "quietly," means to risk identification and, in such sustained proximity, paralysis. As her autobiographical prose informs us, Bogan was blind for two days in childhood as a result of apparently repressed trauma, most likely involving violence and her mother. She writes of the return of her vision: "I remember my sight coming back, by seeing the flat forked light of the gas flame, in its etched glass shade, suddenly appearing beside the bureau. What had I seen? I shall never know." Surely the recesses of her poetry, her attention to invisibilities, her extreme challenge to conventional comprehension, to "making sense," were profoundly influenced by such an early experience.

My own problems with sight were surely in no way tragic but common and correctable. I was fortunate to have been given the experience of the contingency of vision. It is perhaps good to know something of how inevitably we adapt ourselves to the strangeness of even a small and frequently experienced difference. To realize at a relatively early age how resistant the world was to understanding is not, perhaps, poor training for anyone who would write poetry. It guarantees that one sees the world as if one lingers at the edges of the gulf between one's self-knowledge and the world's knowledge of selves. The poetries that I come to most often are recalcitrant to measure and sensitive to the margins of experience.

In the small compass of the personal, I have been referring to vision, but I wish now to discuss the speech that may seem necessary in response to another sort of sensory boundary. If proximity, being close to the page and finding there a quality of intimacy, has been significant for me (as it has been for many others) still other proximities affect my work. I am interested in thinking at the edges of perception, thinking of the poem at the boundaries of comprehensibility. I mentioned, earlier, the ghost light, the abraded perception, that one finds in certain poetries as if the poem must not only point to the senses but show the labyrinthine ways in which the senses meet their limits. I have had the fortune to be close to a life in which understanding was shown to be no guarantee of value and in which compressed, uncommon language was not only respected but desired.

Among my most memorable experiences were those of repetition in which I must be careful to speak distinctly and to repeat myself. As my father's ability to hear became poor, he taught himself to watch faces intently, to move his lips with our lips as we spoke to him. To be heard by him meant that all of us in our family must weigh our words. This speaking required a rapid foreshortening. We reduced our remarks to make them pointed and to make repetition somehow easier for ourselves.

In his partial deafness, my father cared for words deeply, especially those that were memorable and odd, whatever words might resist our enemies. He would have been pleased with very little, I believe now, but I felt then that he wanted something from his children toward which he could immediately respond. He wanted a stubborn quirkiness of sentiment that answered his own sense of the stubborn quirkiness of things. It was characteristic of him to most admire people who worked hard (just as he did as a farmer) and yet he was most fond of remarks that reflected, however difficult it was to make such remarks, an irreverent ebullience, a relief from care and labor.

At times I would be tired even before I spoke to him, as if it would be too much of an effort for me to repeat myself and to make words strong enough for him. I was ashamed, then, because he was so obviously patient with me. I knew too that speaking with him could be a wonderful event—his face reflecting a tender surprise and a stoic foreknowledge of the ways of the world. Yet it was also somehow a painful event, as if too much feeling threatened to fill me at once. To be listened to with such hope, from someone so eager for laughter, eager for the jarring dislocations of meaning that create laughter: How fortunate I was, and how readily his fullest responses made whatever was anaesthetized and reluctant to feel within me break open and thaw painfully.

In my early work a tone of voice may be heard that is, I have only recently come to realize, derived from a training in inflection and repetition that I received from my father, when even the most innocent words bore the potential to baffle and harm—or to meet the undisguised yearning in his face.

It is a commonplace to speak of the sensuous nature of much poetry. Yet some of us seek the sensuous which reflects blight, a pock mark, and erosion. The senses reveal shifts, decay, limitations, for the senses live while we live. They may abandon us as they respond to time and to trauma. To chart the contours that perception may afford us has been of particular interest to me in my earlier work, for the body does not give the same message to us all. To finger the contours of sensory abridgement, to press at the nature of the seen and the heard—these are possibilities that may, for some of us, at least for some time, prove sustaining. One gains, inevitably, a sense of one's boundaries. And one gains the hope of trespassing against such limits, to know better the range of a common struggle.

ANNETTE GRANT

ONE SONG, START TO FINISH: A MUSIC LESSON

THE NEW YORK TIMES MAGAZINE

In "Merrily We Roll Along," Stephen Sondheim posed the question: "Which comes first generally—the words or the music?" And answered: "Generally the contract." When we asked him the same question he was less cynical: "Words first, always the words."

Many aficionados of the Broadway musical consider Sondheim the best living songwriter—complex, urbane and witty. He has had plenty of practice, having composed maybe 400 songs, most of them for his 15 stage productions, but also for movies—songs for Madonna in "Dick Tracy"—and for television ("Evening Primrose"). And now he's headed for Broadway again with a new show, "Passion," his third collaboration with the writer and director James Lapine.

The story has been on Sondheim's mind since 1981, when he saw the movie "Passione d'Amore," directed by Ettore Scola and based on an epistolary novel called "Fosca," written in 1869. In it, Fosca, an ugly and sickly woman, falls in love with a handsome army captain, Giorgio, who in turn loves and is loved by a beautiful married woman, Clara. Fosca throws herself at Giorgio, who is repelled. She entreats him to write her a letter, a love letter, which she dictates. The letter-in-song acts as a centerpiece of the one-act, 1-hour-50-minute show.

" 'Passion' has about 20 musical scenes and songs that reappear and develop through variations," says Sondheim. "Structurally, it's most like 'Sweeney Todd,' and like 'Sweeney' I was attracted to it immediately."

Sondheim, who says he has a kind of "puzzle mind," claims to be a slow writer (he and Lapine began "Passion" in the summer of '92), though he can move fast when he has to ("Send in the Clowns" was written in two nights). He works at home, in a study lined with records. There he rounds up his pencils ("Blackwing 602, the best—soft lead, six-sided so they won't roll away and *wonderful* erasers"), his legal pads (he prefers pads with 28 lines on each page, the easier to write between them), his rhyming dictionary (Clement Wood, 1936), his thesaurus (Roget's 19th edition) and begins. In the fullness of time, after many drafts—all saved, annotated, boxed and filed—a song is born. Here he tells us how he does it.

1. A CUE FROM THE SCRIPT

Sondheim considers a page of James Lapine's script. Lapine has written out the text of Fosca's letter, to give Sondheim a blueprint for the song, which is tricky and crucial. The lovesick Fosca is dictating the love letter to Giorgio that she wishes he would write to her. It is the fullest expression of the musical's theme: if only he could see her inner beauty instead of her outward ugliness, he would love her in return. Since Sondheim writes the songs chronologically, this is the seventh or eighth one he has taken on, depending on how you count. "Writing everything in order lets you keep adjusting the tone you want and avoid overlapping," he says. He has, of course, written many songs that have been inserted into shows at the last minute, but it's always hard to make them seem perfectly integrated.

Sondheim looks at the script both for inspiration and specific lines to lift. He crosses out one sentence ("Please forgive me Fosca for not saying this sooner, for not recognizing your kindness"), "because it doesn't fit the emotional tone of the rest of the scene." He plays with musical conceits at the piano, but doesn't yet have a specific tune in mind.

2. DREAMING SOLUTIONS

Sondheim has a further conversation with Lapine and makes notes on a yellow pad. He analyzes Fosca's message: "She's meaning that hate can be turned into love." The lines "I wanted to see you in the light" and "I wanted to forget you," culled from these conversations, will appear in the final draft of the song as "But now I see you in a different light," and "I wish I could forget you," as do several other thoughts that will make it in more condensed form. ("You've shown me feelings I didn't know I had. If you die, there will be a hole.") Even in his notes, Sondheim has begun to write in song bites rather than in straight prose.

The process of writing the lyrics and music for this song takes a week of working 8 to 12 hours a day. Sondheim starts around noon. Throughout the process he is often stumped and depressed. He shares the work with no one but Lapine. Much, he says, gets solved in dreams. "Maybe not specifically, but whatever sleep does to the subconscious lets ideas bubble up."

3. AN OUTLINE

Sondheim outlines the whole ballad, looking for its shape and not worrying about specific words and rhymes. "This is stream of consciousness and free association. I note principal points I want to make, and then check the ones I definitely mean to keep," he says. These include "I wish I could forget you" and "I know I've upset you." In fact, almost all the ideas that appear in the final lyrics turn up on this page. "I've wanted you to go away, but if you did, it would pain me; should you die tomorrow, your love will live on in me; your love is so pure that it has made me see you in a different light; I was blind, but now I see." Sondheim says that "getting the outline is half the battle, and that goes for musical outlines, too." And he sticks to it, "probably not because I'm so disciplined, but because I'm a very organized person."

4. GETTING RHYTHM

In an early version of the lyrics, Sondheim starts setting sentences from Lapine's script into abbreviated lines: "I know that I've been cruel/I know (see) I've been unkind." He says: "I'm trying to keep to a traditional format. I start with short phrases, looking for a rhythm, a song form. It stops being a speech, a recitative—something I hate—and takes on a beat." Notation on the top of the pad shows that he favors a major key at this point.

Meanwhile, he has been at the piano working on the music, which he says is more time-consuming—writing each bar, recopying it—than lyrics. He has already composed earlier sections of the score and knows that the sweeping musical scheme is "lyrical and rhapsodic and lush." The whole production is about "love and passion and the music has to reflect that tone." To capture this he relies on some signature touches to enhance the tonal color—modal harmonies and more chromaticism (a dissonant saturation of notes) than he has used since "Sweeney Todd."

5. 'CRUEL' BECOMES 'UNKIND'

Sondheim does a musical sketch with the rhythm da-da-DUM. He tries a canon (a repeating form): "Fosca speaks, Giorgio repeats after her, 'There are times (there are times)/I've been cruel (I've been cruel).' But that's unwieldy for a whole song. I abandon the idea." He also rejects the word "cruel" because it's hard to rhyme with anything but "fool," which is fine for a comedy, but inappropriate for "Passion." He substitutes "unkind," which is easy to rhyme. "No words are absolutely taboo," he says, "but generally I keep the language straight forward and simple." The word "feeling," which appears in notes, is also discarded. "I don't use any participles here because they tend to soften. They're good for flow, but I want this song to have strength."

6. AN UPSIDE-DOWN MELODY

Keeping to the style of a drama that is composed through instead of having show-stopper set pieces, Sondheim also experiments with a melody that is an upside-down version ("to give an opposite point of view") of a theme he wrote for Fosca's first stage entry. He calls it the "Fosca motif."

7. A BREAKTHROUGH MOMENT

Then he turns it right-side-up again, adds one note, and pencils in a partial lyric, "forget you," from his original outline. This is a breakthrough moment, because the melody, a simple, yearning, seven-note theme, and the rhyme scheme (forget you, met you, upset you) now meet like a handshake. Sondheim also tucks the rhyme inside the line, a subtlety he likes. He now thinks "a minor key is more suitable, because Fosca"—the ugly one—"has been in a minor key all along, while Clara"—the beautiful one—"has been in a major one, although I don't necessarily hold with the notion that major is always happy and minor is always sad." Fosca's aria remains unnamed because the show intentionally has no breakout numbers.

He doodles an arpeggio accompaniment also based on earlier Fosca themes. This is one of his favorite activities because he has now written enough music to enjoy "just fiddling around." The result, which uses rapidly changing harmonies and rippling chords to suggest emotions welling up, helps Sondheim delineate a character who is agitated, feverish and impassioned.

8. REASONS AND RHYMES

Rhyme time. Working with "I wish I could forget you" and "I wish you'd leave my mind," Sondheim scribbles "et" and "ind" rhymes in the margin, among them "regret, beset, abet, offset, threat, let, met" and "designed, behind, maligned, combined, defined, bind, find." He also needs "some kind of refrain, one that can be repeated and developed without being exhausted." He chooses "That doesn't mean I love you/I wish that I could love you," which serves to emphasize Fosca's self-awareness: she *knows* that Giorgio doesn't love her, though she desperately wants him to. But Sondheim isn't entirely happy with it and may still change it before opening night.

Sondheim now works on the whole song, each section on a different yellow pad. In the "release" (the center part) he shows Fosca's obsessively romantic vision of what could be: "A different kind of love/Like none I've ever known . . . a love that's made of stone." He says, pleased: "I move into a brighter key, a major key. I really have it both ways in this song." He wants the music to soar and wonders if the 15-member orchestra (with only four violins) in the pit can sound like 25.

9. INTO THE COMPUTER

Sondheim moves to the computer. "After two quatrains, it's neater, easier to read. Also, I'm ready to go really fast, print out, revise, print out, revise, sometimes three versions in a day." He rewrites extensively in the margins. The rhymes begin to fall into place—"known/stone/alone," "breath/death," "knife/life." He varies the length of lines and reappearance of rhymes "to keep it from being boring, predictable. An old trick, but it works."

10. FINISHING TOUCHES

Even after copying out the music, Sondheim continues to revise, scribbling new passages and rubbing out old ones as he thinks of new harmonies and rhythms to make the section more vivid and seductive. "In the end, I erase the page number, 6, to show that it is discarded, and recopy the changes on the real page 6." After the score is finished he discovers that the singer cast as Fosca has a lower voice than he thought. Rewrite? Hardly. He instructs the music copyist to move her music "all down by a major third."

The lyrics are also finished, but are they? A new version of the final three lines, which appear in fragments in early notes, is penciled into the final score. Where did it come from? Sondheim shrugs. "I don't really remember. Maybe there wasn't room on the paper, or it was on the back of a page. But even if I didn't write it down exactly, I always intended it that way."

> The finished song:
>
> *But there you are and there you will stay.*
> *I wish I could forget you,*
> *Erase you from my mind.*
> *But ever since I met you,*
> *I find*
> *I cannot leave the thought of you behind.*

That doesn't mean I love you,
I wish that I could love you.

I know that I've upset you.
I know I've been unkind.
I wanted you to vanish from sight,
But now I see you in a different light.

And though I cannot love you,
I wish that I could love you.

For now I'm seeing love
Like none I've ever known,
A love as pure as breath,
As permanent as death,
Implacable as stone.
A love that, like a knife,
Has cut into a life
I wanted left alone.

A love I may regret,
But one I can't forget.

I don't know how I let you
So far inside my mind,
But there you are and there you will stay.
How could I ever wish you away?
I see now I was blind.

And should you die tomorrow,
Another thing I see:
Your love will live in me.

Coda: As it turns out, Fosca's aria will be reprised in the last scene of the show, though Sondheim says it "probably hadn't been decided when I started." The audience is left with Fosca's last note and a chord that trails away, unresolved, ambivalent—*very* Sondheim.

NANCY WILLARD

WHAT WE WRITE ABOUT WHEN WE WRITE ABOUT LOVE

THE WRITER

The first book I ever wanted to steal was a slim blue paperback called *Tales of French Love and Passion*. It showed a woman in a low-cut gown and elbow-length gloves eyeing a man with a goatee and moustache: the devil, I supposed, or one of his minions. Because the devil wore a striped polo shirt and a beret, I assumed he was on vacation—a cruise, perhaps. The woman was giving him a sly smile; she had one arm raised, as if she were waving at someone just out of the picture.

I was twelve, going on sixteen. Every summer my mother and sister and I moved from Ann Arbor, Michigan, to a ramshackle cottage sixty miles away, in the sleepy settlement of Stoney Lake. My father, who was teaching summer school, drove to Stoney Lake every Friday after his last class, and on Sunday he drove the family car back to Ann Arbor.

All week long the old men of Stoney Lake went fishing and the young men went to work in town or at the gravel pit across the lake, and the mothers and grandmothers sat on their front porches and watched the dust rise and fall in the dirt road, and gossiped in Italian, and so the air hung heavy with their secrets. Only our house felt as dull as a convent.

Thank God for my mother's younger sister, Nell, who chose to spend the first month of her summer vacation with us and whose *Tales of French Love and Passion* showed me what I was missing. She kept the book on the nightstand, next to her

Madame DuBarry Beauty Box, and her favorite story, "Room Eleven," was no secret; when I picked up that slim blue volume, it obligingly opened to p. 33:

> She picked all her lovers from the army and kept them three years, the time of their sojourn in the garrison. In short, she not only had love, she had sense. . . . She gave the preference to men of calm allurement, like herself, but they must be handsome. She also wished them to have had no previous entanglements, any passion having the power to leave traces, or that had made any trouble. Because the man whose loves are mentioned is never a very discreet man.
>
> After having decided upon the one she would love for the three years of his regulation sojourn, it only remained to throw down the gauntlet.
>
> —From *Stories of Love and Passion: A Collection of Complete Short Stories Chosen from the Works of Guy de Maupassant*

Not for her second-graders at Northville Elementary did Nell pluck her eyebrows, oil her eyelashes, and rouge her cheeks. She was young, pretty, and thrice divorced. When she scanned the *Oxford Weekly,* she was appalled to find that God hosted all the regular social events announced in its pages; even square dancing was held in the basement of the Methodist church. The only gatherings that escaped His watchful eye were auctions.

The auctions always took place on somebody's front lawn. On one hot Sunday in July, we stood in the crowd that milled around the front yard opposite the high school, listening to the auctioneer's patter and laughing at his jokes.

Nell bid on whatever looked like a bargain. Who knows why we suddenly want what we don't need? When an upright piano was pushed into view and the auctioneer shouted, "What am I bid for this piano?" my mother bid ten dollars.

"Ten dollars!" sneered the auctioneer. "Madam, I'd buy it myself for ten dollars if I had a place to put it. Look at the work on this thing."

"Do it play?" called a voice from the back of the crowd.

"Play? Play?" The auctioneer touched middle C. "Can

anyone here give us a demonstration?''

Nell was on the platform in an instant. She pulled up a kitchen chair, and she played ''You Are My Sunshine'' and ''Four Leaf Clover,'' then eased into the rippling improvisation she used to quiet her second-graders.

''Twenty!'' shouted the voice in the back.

''Twenty-five!'' shouted my mother.

''Twenty-five going once, twenty-five going twice—''

The auctioneer paused. The silence was deafening.

''All done at twenty-five!''

''My God,'' whispered Mother, ''where will we put a piano?''

While the auctioneer's assistant was smoothing Mother's five-dollar bills and tucking them into the cashbox, Nell was talking to one of the movers, a man whose sweat-soaked shirt stuck to his back in ragged patches. He was the only mover with black hair, and it fell around his eyes in tight curls. Nell signaled to my mother.

''His name is Lou Lubbock,'' she said. ''For two dollars, he'll move the piano on his pick-up truck.''

By the time Mother had counted her change, Lou had rolled the piano up a ramp into the back of the red pick-up and was sitting in the cab beside a man whose face we couldn't see.

''Did you tell him where we live?'' asked my mother.

''I told him to follow us,'' said Nell.

''You did?'' exclaimed Mother. ''Who's that old gentleman with him?''

''His father.''

The piano, which had looked almost diminutive among wardrobes and breakfronts at the auction, appeared monstrous when Lou tried to bring it through the front door of the cottage. Mother cast anxious glances at Lou Lubbock's father. He did not look as though he'd ever moved anything heavier than a telephone book.

''Won't go through the front door,'' he remarked, as the two men set the piano on the grass.

''I guess we'll have to take it back to the auction,'' said Mother. She sounded relieved.

"What doesn't go through the door goes through the window," said Lou. "Trust me."

With the practiced hand of a burglar, he pried out the top half of the big window in the living room and pushed his father through. Then he lifted the front end of the piano, letting it straddle the sill.

There was a sudden thud, and all at once the piano was standing in the living room as if it had always been there. As Lou Lubbock took his leave, somewhere between our front door and his truck, he invited Nell to go roller skating.

That summer Nell kept company with the piano mover and I read *Tales of French Love and Passion* and mooned around the visible borders of their passion like a twelve-year-old voyeur. But when school started in September and our teacher asked us to write about what we did on our vacation, did I write about Aunt Nell and the piano mover? No. I wrote about the lake, the fish, and the turtles. What I learned about love that summer sank out of sight but not out of mind. Like so many visitors from the invisible world, those memories come unannounced and never when I call them.

Writers believe they choose the stories they want to write, but this is an illusion. Our stories choose us, and they are as patient and sure as the heroine in that tale I found on my aunt's nightstand. Not until ninth grade did I meet it again when I happened to check out of the school library a modest gray hardcover called *The Complete Stories of Guy de Maupassant*. As I reread it with astonishment and awe, the longing that had infused the summer of the piano mover washed over me. I wanted to write a love story. And de Maupassant made it look so easy.

There are two ways of beginning such a story. The first lets you know right away that you're reading a love story. The second does not; indeed, it takes pains to hide its true intent. A beginning of the first kind can make you feel you're eavesdropping on a telephone with a party line. Here is the opening of John Updike's "Love Song for a Moog Synthesizer":

She was good in bed. She went to church. Her I.Q. was 145. She repeated herself. Nothing fit; it frightened him.

Yet Tod wanted to hang on, to hang on to the bits and pieces, which perhaps were not truly pieces but islands, which a little lowering sea level would reveal to be rises on a sunken continent, peaks of a subaqueous range, secretly one, a world.

—From *Problems and Other Stories,* by John Updike (Alfred A. Knopf)

What Updike gives us is a close-up: the raw surface of the lover's confusion as he picks over the bits and pieces of a relationship, puzzling over them, gathering them into the lap of a long sentence, trying to understand love through the sum of its parts.

Now turn the telescope of the lover's vision around. The moment you step back and put a little distance between you and the characters, you have space to examine their motives, as Alice Walker does hers in the opening sentence of her story, "The Lover": "Her husband had wanted a child and so she gave him one as a gift, because she liked her husband and admired him greatly."

No writer can surpass Isaac Babel for opening sentences that perfectly balance distance with immediacy. Take the beginning of a story called "First Love," which, by its very title, announces its subject—a dangerous practice for the novice writer:

When I was ten years old, I fell in love with a woman called Galina. Her surname was Rubtsov. Her husband, an officer, went off to the Russo-Japanese War and returned in October, 1905. He brought a great many trunks back with him. These trunks, which weighed nearly half a ton, contained Chinese souvenirs such as screens and costly weapons. Kuzma the yardman used to tell us that Rubtsov had bought all these things with money he had embezzled while serving in the engineer corps of the Manchurian Army.

—From *The Collected Stories,* edited and translated by Walter Morison (Criterion Books)

Though Babel's impassioned opening sentence seems to give the whole story away, he follows it, not with a description of Galina, but with three purely factual statements: her name, her husband's occupation, and what he brought home from the war. The last sentence in the paragraph turns from fact to rumor and gives us a little of the husband's character through the eyes of the yardman. The husband is a crook. Babel knows that part of telling a story well is holding back and that Chekhov's advice on writing about grief also applies to writing about love:

> When you . . . wish to move your reader to pity, try to be colder. It will give a kind of backdrop to . . . grief, make it stand out more. . . . Yes, be cold. . . .
>
> —From *Chekhov*, by Henri Troyat (Ballantine Books)

Why am I seeking advice from Chekhov? Because Nell's story is knocking at a locked door in the back of my mind, and I can't find the key to let it out. The key is the right voice to tell it. Should the teller be a twelve-year-old child, narrating the events with an innocent eye? Or the child, grown up now, looking back? Should I tell it in the voice of my mother, looking askance? Or should I hand the story over to Aunt Nell, who is not looking at all but stepping headlong into love?

Here's one possible way into the story:

> The piano went for twenty-five dollars, plus three dollars extra if you wanted the auctioneer's assistant to move it. Nell asked him if he would move it for two as she and her sister were short of cash. Watching him push it up the ramp into his pick-up truck she thought, I could run away with that man.

The instant I've written these lines, I know I'm lying. It was not love at first sight. Every evening Lou Lubbock called for Nell in his pick-up truck, and every night I dozed but did not fall asleep until two in the morning, when his truck clattered down the dirt road to our house, and Nell let herself in through the kitchen door, and my mother tiptoed downstairs in her nightgown. Together my mother and Nell sat in front of the empty fireplace and went over the day, piece by piece. A hole in the floor under my bed gave me a clear view of the living room. If I pressed my ear to the hole, I could catch most of their conversation. It might go something like this:

Mother: So where did he take you?
Nell: We went roller skating.
Mother: Oh, you love roller skating.
Nell: Not with him. He's a terrible skater. All he wants to do is eat.
Mother: Where'd you eat?
Nell: He took me to the Harvest Table.
Mother: That's a nice restaurant.
Nell: But he chews with his mouth full. And he always has dirt under his nails. I said to him, "Lou, just because you work on cars all day doesn't mean you can't wash up afterwards."
Mother: Why do you go out with him?
Nell: Because he's there.

Oh, he was certainly there. Though he was always on her mind, she made it clear to us that she would leave him at the end of the summer. Even she would never have called what passed between them love.

Who knows better than Chekhov the power of love that begins with mild curiosity and ends with obsession? In "The Lady With the Pet Dog," a man has an affair with a woman he meets at a resort hotel, expecting to forget her when the affair ends, as he has forgotten other women. In a single paragraph, Chekhov shows us the lover's inability to forget:

A month or so would pass and the image of Anna Sergeyevna, it seemed to him, would become misty in his memory, and only from time to time he would dream of her with her touching smile as he dreamed of others. But more than a month went by, winter came into its own, and everything was still clear in his memory as though he had departed from Anna Sergeyevna only yesterday. And his memories glowed more and more vividly. In the street he followed the women with his eyes, looking for someone who resembled her.

—From *The Portable Chekhov*, edited by Avrahm Yarmolinsky (Viking)

To tell Nell's story the way it happened, I need the kind of beginning that doesn't appear to be part of a love story at all. Take, for example, the opening of Rachel Ingalls' "Faces of Madness."

> Four other boys in William's class shared his name. At home he was Will. At school someone else was called Will; two were Bill, and one went under a middle name. Only William was given the full, formal version.
>
> —From *The Literary Lover,* edited by Larry Dark (Viking Penguin)

Nothing in the opening hints at how the main character, William, will spend his life and fortune looking for the woman his parents prevented him from marrying.

After the summer ended, Nell rarely mentioned Lou Lubbock. A week before Christmas, one of the women who lived in the cottage next door called to say Lou's truck had skidded on a patch of ice and flipped over on him. "He was trapped for six hours before he died," she added. "Thank God he was alone when it happened."

That winter when Nell came to visit on weekends, I could feel the ghost of Lou Lubbock listening, invisible and helpless, as she told the story of how she'd met her first husband in the Laundromat. She'd just put two quarters into the dryer.

> "I went to get a Coke from the machine, and he snuck over and opened the door of the dryer and threw all his stuff in with mine. When we tried to sort it out, my bra was hooked around his undershirt. One thing sort of led to another."

Now let me interrupt myself with a story which I hope will illuminate the problem facing any writer who has ever set out to write a love story. Three years after the summer of Nell and the piano mover, my sister, who was living in a sorority house in Ann Arbor, accepted the fraternity pin of the boy she was dating, and called home, four blocks away, to announce the good news.

"I've been 'pinned'!"

I was fifteen and thought the choice of words was unfortunate;

it made me think of wrestlers on a mat, of butterflies skewered under labels. But to those wiser than I, it meant she was one step away from being engaged. It also meant that on a Monday night in the middle of May the whole fraternity would assemble under her window and serenade her. Of course my mother and father and I were not invited. But she explained that if we brought binoculars and hid behind the trees or in the bushes that flourished in the front yard of the First Presbyterian Church across the street, we could get a good view of the whole ceremony.

On the appointed evening, my mother and father concealed themselves behind two large oaks, and I tucked myself into a honeysuckle bush between the church and the parking lot, with its single car, and waited for the show to begin. The fragrance of honeysuckle filled me with a nameless sorrow. Because I had the worst view, my mother had entrusted me with the binoculars. The sorority house was dark save for a single upstairs window, at which my sister stood, holding a candle so that love could find her. Presently I heard the clatter of footsteps in the distance. What appeared to be a well-trained army of salesmen was marching toward my sister's light, two by two, on the opposite side of the street. They assembled under her window, and after a small silence—during which I could almost hear the squeak of a pitchpipe—they burst into song.

A love song, no doubt. I've forgotten the words. In the middle of it, the young man paying court to my sister held up something large and lobed—his heart, I thought, till it lit up and through the binoculars I saw it was a model of his fraternity pin. Was it my fear of the dark that made me turn the binoculars away from my sister to the parking lot? What did it matter that I had the worst view of the pinning ceremony? I had an extraordinary view of the couple necking in the car in the parking lot.

Writing a love story is a little like finding yourself with a pair of binoculars in your hand, caught between passion and scruples, ceremony and sex. If you err too far in either direction, you can end up on the side of pornography or romance. The difference between a love story and a romance is one of intent. When you write a romance, you carefully follow where many have trod, so that your readers can recognize the genre through its conventions. But in a love story, you try to show love as if your characters had just invented it. Follow your characters, and they will give you the story, but you can't tell ahead of time exactly where they'll lead you. Rousseau's advice for writing a love letter is also useful for writing a story: ". . . you ought to begin without knowing what you mean to say, and to finish without knowing what you have written."

Love has its roots in the particular and the ordinary. Surely one of the writer's greatest challenges is to show how imagination can transform an ordinary human being into one whose absence turns day into night, heaven into hell, happiness into an abyss. Weather, light, fragrance, memory and loneliness have more to do with the alchemy of love than beauty or grace; Maurice Chevalier once remarked that "many a man has fallen in love with a girl in a light so dim he would not have chosen a suit by it." For showing that alchemy, I know of few writers who can surpass Thomas Mann in this passage from "Tonio Kroger":

> Strange how things come about! He had seen her a thousand times; then one evening he saw her again; saw her in a certain light, talking with a friend in a certain saucy way, laughing and tossing her head; saw her lift her arm and smooth her hair back with her schoolgirl hand, that was by no means particularly fine or slender, in such a way that the thin white sleeve slipped down from her elbow; heard her speak a word or two, a quite indifferent phrase, but with a certain intonation, with a warm ring in her voice; and his heart throbbed with ecstasy. . . .
>
> —From *Death in Venice and Seven Other Stories*.
> Translated by H. T. Lowe-Porter (Vintage Books)

We are in love, and love what vanishes; isn't that why the sight of a thin white sleeve slipping down a girl's arm can break someone's heart? While lovers lie in each other's arms, the world is singing an older tune: "Golden lads and girls all must / As chimney-sweepers, come to dust."

But though the teller vanishes, the tale does not. Several years ago when I started to work on a novel called *Sister Water,* the voices of women—in the living room at two in the morning— these voices I thought I'd forgotten did not forget me. As I wrote the chapter in which the main character receives word that her husband has been killed in a car accident, I knew what Aunt Nell would say,

"Death is so ordinary," she whispers. "Write about love."

JUSTIN KAPLAN

A CULTURE OF BIOGRAPHY

THE YALE REVIEW

Woody and Mia, Charles, Camilla, and Diana (also known as Squidgy), Joey and Amy, O. J. and Nicole, Hillary and Bill, John and Lorena, Oprah and Roseanne, Tonya and Nancy: a list like this shucks and adds every fifteen minutes. We enjoy a nonstop transitory first-name intimacy with a great deal of secondhand experience. We blur the difference between news, entertainment, scandal, and trivia. The broadsheet *New York Times* and the tabloid *Weekly World News* often serve up the same dish, although the presentation differs. Issues and ideas don't shape daily discourse—celebrity, personality, and anecdote do. We've become a culture of biography.

Biography as we know it is largely an Anglo-American phenomenon. Other societies draw a stricter line than we do between public and private arenas, between the work and the life. They don't share our obsession with childhood and adolescence, "creativity" and "identity," the quirkiness and singularities of private lives. We assume we have a right to know everything about other people. This includes knowing what they "do" in bed—with whom and with what—even though it can be argued that this may have only a strained connection with what they do out in the world. By current standards, biographies without voyeuristic, erotic thrills are like ballpark hot dogs without mustard. For a society that feeds on packaged information and instantaneous celebrity, the notion of privacy is almost as anachronistic as the buttonhook. Although legally moot, the distinction between public figures who are fair game for comment and private people who think they shouldn't be—between the individual's "right to privacy" and the public's "need" to know—has been blurring for centuries. "The business of the biographer," said Samuel Johnson, "is to lead the thoughts into domestic privacies, and display the minute details of daily life." Coleridge complained about an "Age of Personality . . . of literary and political gossiping, when the meanest insects are worshipped with a sort of Egyptian superstition."

It's become a commonplace to speak of a "golden age" of English-language biography that had its beginnings with Johnson and James Boswell in the eighteenth century, produced notable work in the nineteenth (J. G. Lockhart's Walter Scott and J. A. Froude's Thomas Carlyle, for example), and was reinvigorated in the twentieth by Lytton Strachey, who celebrated biography as "the most delicate and humane of all the branches of the art of writing." By now biography has become our version of folk epic, a tribal exercise in which we tell and interpret the stories of lives that seem to hold some degree of at least passing fascination. The curiosity biography satisfies is as natural and self-justified as breathing.

"All the lonely people—where do they all come from?" We inhabit a culture of loneliness and disengagement, of eroded loyalties and divided communities. But at the same time, and largely through the instrumentality of television, we've come to devalue solitude, mistaking it for loneliness, and have lost whatever ability we once had to endure, respect, and profit from it. Whatever its excesses and limitations, biography is an antidote for loneliness and a restorative of solitude. It shapes the way we frame experience through narrative and character, the way we look at history and other people.

Perhaps it's a reaction against what is often cited as the glumness, grotesquerie, and psychic isolationism of much serious contemporary fiction. But biography at its best emulates—perhaps anachronistically—the imaginative world of the great classic novels: *Madame Bovary, Vanity Fair, David Copperfield, War and Peace, Huckleberry Finn, Remembrance of Things Past.* I'm thinking of biographies like Strachey's *Queen Victoria*, Henri

Troyat's *Tolstoy*, Robert Caro's *The Power Broker*, the life of New York City's master builder, Robert Moses. We share in the lives of their protagonists, something we rarely do when we read today's novels and short stories. Good biography exercises what C. Wright Mills called "the sociological imagination"; it explores the intersection of history, society, and individual experience. It renders individual character in the round, tells a generously contexted story that has a beginning, middle, and end, and may even suggest a degree of social continuity and personal responsibility. And good biography does this without moralizing. To the extent that it judges, it does so, as Walt Whitman said of poetry, "not as the judge judges but as the sun falling around a helpless thing."

Along with a torrent of new and reprinted biography published each year there's been a remarkable proliferation of books, lectures, symposia, academic conferences, essays, and literary journals *about* biography—its theory, practice, history, and generic self-awareness. The books are titled *Telling Lives, Extraordinary Lives, Shaping Lives, Writing Lives,* and similar variations on the theme. Strachey made fun of fat two-volume biographies, but he himself is the subject of a two-volume, 1229-page biography; Boswell, of a wall of Boswelliana. "Life Likenesses: The Seductions of Biography," a 1993 conference at Harvard, offered topics like "Postmodern Biography as Witness to History" and "Celebrity and Bisexuality." ("There's almost an eroticism about biography," said one panelist. "We want to know the real story.") Such concentrated focus on the genre is a fairly recent development in our culture of biography. I wonder if the theory and practice, the function and future, of fiction or poetry or history are getting anywhere near the same share of attention. I wonder, too, whether such subtilizing refinement and self-consciousness in theory (combined, in practice, with more sensationalism and less seriousness) may not be signs that biography is entering its "silver age."

At the low end of the biography status scale are *People* magazine, the supermarket tabloids, and TV programs like *Hard Copy, Inside Edition,* and *A Current Affair*—all in all, an inexhaustible slop bucket of inside stories about the rich, famous, and dysfunctional. Biographies of movie and rock stars and of athletes are a little higher on the scale. Then come the collected works of Kitty Kelley, the Saddam Hussein of privacy invasion. Symptomatic of the impacted condition of biography, a writer named George Carpozzi, Jr., has even written Ms. Kelley's and titled it *Poison Pen* (he's also "done" Jacqueline Kennedy, Gary Cooper, and John Wayne). There wasn't much left of Nancy Reagan after Ms. Kelley finished with her (in *Nancy Reagan: The Unauthorized Biography*) except a mound of beak and feathers. I almost admire Ms. Kelley for her scouring thoroughness and her eye for unsavory detail. What she gives us by way of biography is pretty much what the culture asks for and deserves. Her critics claim that her books are essentially drive-by shootings, but they're biographies all the same, just as novels by Danielle Steel and Barbara Taylor Bradford are novels no matter what Flaubert or Virginia Woolf might think.

David McCullough's thoroughly engrossing account of Harry Truman figured conspicuously in the 1992 presidential campaign. Both candidates and both parties cited McCullough's book for their purposes. David Brock's *The Real Anita Hill: The Untold Story* also made news. A reviewer in the *Nation* argued that it reflected "a journalistic standard so low that no reputable publishing house should have touched it." For quite a while, however, *The Real Anita Hill* rode high on the best-seller lists. In an op-ed piece in the *New York Times,* the surviving children of Joseph and Rose Kennedy denounced Nigel Hamilton's *JFK: Reckless Youth* as "a grotesque portrait of our parents." They said their "earliest . . . memories [were] of exchanging goodnight kisses with Mother and Dad every night." Six months later, as the *New York Times* reported, the Kennedy children were apparently "gearing up" to go after Joe McGinniss for his biography of Senator Edward M. Kennedy, *The Last Brother,* which was then about to be published. As it turned out, there was no need for the Kennedys to do anything about this book, an innovative subgenre of biography that McGinniss eventually identified as a "rumination." The critical response to *The Last Brother* suggests that McGinniss not only shot himself in the foot but followed the senator's example and drove off the bridge. Its sole interest, said one reviewer, lay in the questions it inadvertently raised about "the wiles of the publishing industry" and the nature of "America's voyeuristic marketplace." The resulting furor and ethical breast-beating may have had less to do with the book itself than with our own alarm about the addictiveness of biography and the extent to which it rules our lives.

As for "literary biographies" that generate news beyond the book pages, recall Ian Hamilton's aborted work on J. D. Salinger. To block its publication, Salinger, a celebrated recluse who hadn't submitted to an interview in years, came out of hiding in Cornish, New Hampshire, and, under vigorous questioning, testified at length in a New York lawyer's office. His remarkably revealing deposition went public immediately and at considerable cost to his privacy but he prevailed: Hamilton, who had innocently (to take the most tolerant view) set out to write a literary biography called *J. D. Salinger, A Life,* had to retreat to the legal hidey-hole of a barebones account published under the title *The Search for J. D. Salinger.* This was a "metabiography": its subject was not Salinger but, in the tradition of A. J. A. Symons's brilliant *Quest for Corvo,* the problems involved in writing about Salinger.

The hot center of Diane Middlebrook's biography of the poet Anne Sexton was not the poetry but transcripts of hours and hours of Sexton's sessions with one of her psychoanalysts. This caused an uproar over medical and literary ethics, confidentiality, and the privacy of the dead as well as the living. The same degree of inflamed public attention has also been bestowed less on the work than on the life and suicide of Sylvia Plath, the subject of about half a dozen biographies and Janet Malcolm's adroitly self-serving account, *The Silent Woman: Sylvia Plath and Ted Hughes.* Ms. Malcolm analyzed the traffic among Plath's biographers, taken singly and as a group; Plath's husband and sister-in-law, the custodians of her posthumous reputation and literary estate; and Malcolm herself, who plunges into a slough of contention and comes out of it washed whiter than snow. Her own roles as prosecutor, judge, and jury excepted, she sees this long-running imbroglio as an allegory of "subjects" (and readers) victimized by a corrupt narrative convention. Biography, she writes, "is the medium through which the remaining secrets of the famous dead are taken from them and dumped out in full view of the world. The biographer at work, indeed, is like the professional burglar, breaking into a house, rifling through certain drawers that he has good reason to think contain the jewelry and the money, and triumphantly bearing his loot away."

The thrust and imagery of Malcolm's fulmination inevitably call up Henry James's *The Aspern Papers*. Sly and manipulative, but rather thick all the same, the narrator (or anti-hero, or even villain) of this brimstone-and-hellfire fiction about biography lies his way into the Venetian palazzo of an aged woman. He wants what she's got: the private papers of her one-time lover, a famous dead author named Jeffrey Aspern. He plays on the old woman's penury and on the vulnerability of her "plain, dingy, elderly" niece, whom he leads to believe that after her aunt's death he may marry for her dowry—the Aspern papers. In one of the several climaxes of this ferocious fable, the old woman discovers the biographer about to break into her secretary. "I never shall forget," he says, "the tone in which . . . she hissed out passionately, furiously: 'Ah, you publishing scoundrel!' " The old woman dies; the niece burns the papers; the narrator's "chagrin" at their loss is "almost intolerable."

Resentment of "publishing scoundrels" was nothing new when Henry James published his story. The "golden age of biography" had added a new terror to death: "the journeymen of letters" (Strachey's phrase) who followed the physician, clergyman, and undertaker into the house of lamentation. "Biographies are murder," said Henry Adams. "They belittle the victim and the assassin equally." He regarded his masterful autobiography, *The Education of Henry Adams,* as "a shield of protection in the grave," a preemptive move in which he "took his life" in his own way in order to prevent biographers from taking it in theirs. (An unavailing tactic, as it turned out: Henry Adams dead is a thriving industry for American biographers and scholars.) In the same hope of fending off biographers, Charles Dickens made a bonfire of his private papers and invited his children to roast potatoes and onions in the embers. Walt

Whitman, Henry James, and other writers followed Dickens's example to such an extent that our view of the landscape of nineteenth-century literature is partially obscured by the smoke rising from these archival pyres, which is not to say that the biographers have been deterred from doing their work.

Closer to our time, the writer Germaine Greer has described biography as "rape . . . an unpardonable crime against self-hood." Others say that biography is voyeuristic, invasionary, exploitative, a wild-goose chase: its methods are obsolete, its premises shaky, its promises of unmediated reporting alto-gether fraudulent, and its end product just a pile of paper and a collection of gossip. Biography, says Roland Barthes, is "a novel that dare not speak its name." Julian Barnes, author of *Flaubert's Parrot,* says biography can be compared to a net— "a collection of holes tied together with strings," those holes containing half-truths, untruths, evasions, and incongruities. The reality of the life slips away like a greased piglet, a flown bird. The book the author creates, Proust wrote in *Contre Saint-Beuve,* "is the product of a different *self* from the self we manifest in our habits, in our social life, in our vices. . . . What one be-stows on private life . . . is the product of a quite superficial self, not of the innermost self which one can only recover by putting aside the world and the self that frequents the world."

Still others decry the elitism and phallocentrism of conven-tional biography, its implicit gospel of success, devaluation of autonomous "texts," and market-driven tendency to produce narratives that highlight fetishism, kinkiness, addiction, alco-holism, incest, violence, abuse, and suicide. *Pathography*—a term introduced by Sigmund Freud in his study of Leonardo da Vinci and recently recycled by Joyce Carol Oates—denotes life-accounts that make you wonder how their subjects man-aged to get out of bed in the morning, much less write novels or poems, paint pictures, compose music, become leaders, make money, or do any other part of the world's work. Going public with pain is now a literary convention as well as a social impera-tive, and one could easily infer an entire society of victims, co-dependents, and candidates for a universal twelve-step program.

The biographer might be described as a hermit crab inhabiting the shell of another's life or as a jockey who takes credit for the horse's speed and mettle. The "how"—the writer's skill—became at least as important as the "who"—the writer's subject—when biographers began to think of themselves not as chroniclers or post-mortem amanuenses but as shapers and participants, agonistic heroes and joint tenants in posthumous lives. Is the biographer a grave-robber? A harmless fantasist? "Sometimes when we think that we are rediscovering the mighty dead," the philosopher Richard Rorty says, "we are just inventing imaginary playmates." "What are you really like?" Virginia Woolf asked Vita Sackville-West, her model for *Orlando*. "Do you exist? Have I made you up?"

Consider the fable of biography one might extract from an elaborate ruse the British devised in World War II and code-named "Operation Mincemeat." They invented a complete identity and life history for a corpse they then launched from a submarine in the Mediterranean. Uniformed and documented as Major W. Martin of the Royal Marines, the corpse carried authentic-sounding but totally false documents about Allied invasion plans along with dog tags, love letters, family letters, overdraft notices, legal papers, tailor's bills, theater tickets, fiancée photo, and the like: the raw materials of biography and precisely the sort of "corroborative detail" that, as Pooh-Bah says in *The Mikado,* gives "artistic verisimilitude to an otherwise bald and unconvincing narrative." A Spanish fisherman turned "Major Martin" over to the Germans, who swallowed "Mincemeat" whole and shifted their defensive forces to the wrong landing site. "The Man Who Never Was" had gone to war, carried out his mission of duping the enemy, and lies in a Spanish cemetery under a headstone with the Horatian inscription, *Dulce et decorum est pro patria mori* (It is sweet and honorable to die for one's country). Some biographical launchings and reanimations—for example, Carl Sandburg's *Abraham Lincoln*—have had comparable histories. Edmund Wilson called Sandburg's six-volume work of mythopoesis "the cruellest thing that has happened to Lincoln since he was shot by Booth."

One consequence of the saturating presence of biography is an invasion of the body snatchers. It's getting tougher every day to find what is commonly but unfeelingly called a "subject," especially one not "taken" or "done," at least recently. Some writers get in on the ground floor with a person still kicking, but there are problems here: control, perspective, and especially closure, deathbed and interment scenes being among the ornaments of traditional biography. Better would be someone in the early stages of historical rigor mortis, with the ghost still on the premises, and furnished with private papers and compliant heirs. In any case, to write biography you need oxlike endurance, resignation to the swift passing of time without much to show for it, and the capacity to feed on your own blood when other sources run dry. You're committing a serious act of literature, that is, if you take biography as seriously as it deserves to be taken. Lives as lived don't have the shape of art, but lives as *written* ought at least to acknowledge strivings in that direction. The work doesn't get any easier as you go along from book to book. You may have acquired narrative and stylistic skills, a little bit of confidence, and some understanding of what makes people and biographies tick, but at the same time your standards go up and you demand more and more of yourself. Above all, between you and the person you write about there has to be an intimate link, not necessarily one of affection or sympathy—Adolf Hitler is an endlessly fascinating subject, as is Richard Nixon—but one of passionate, sustainable interest. In my experience, finding this link is almost as rare as seeing the legendary green flash at sundown.

I was lucky the first time. A close friend, then editor-in-chief at Pocket Books, said over a long lunch one day, "Why don't you write a biography of Mark Twain?" and I answered, "I'll do it." It was an electrifying idea, the real right thing at the right time. I resigned a perfectly good editorial job in New York and spent the next seven years with Mark Twain. A good part of that time was wasted in pure fright: I had never written a full-length book before, much less a biography of someone as masterful, iconic, and original as Mark Twain. To sustain me I had the encouragement of my wife, the novelist Anne Bernays, and several exemplars, among them Lytton Strachey, for his stylistic brilliance; Samuel Johnson, for the existential textures of his life of Richard Savage; Margaret Leach (*Reveille in Washington*) and Cecil Woodham-Smith (*The Reason Why*), for their interweaving of documentary and biography; Geoffrey Scott, for the concision and elegance of his *Portrait of Zélide;* and Erik Erikson (*Childhood and Society, Young Man Luther*), for liberating us from Sigmund Freud's cramping theology (as it seemed) of foreordination. And one fine day I realized that I was indeed able to write the sort of biography that I would have wanted to publish if I had still been an editor. After the reviews came out, and then the National Book Award and the Pulitzer Prize, someone I barely knew stopped me on the street and said, "That's all very well, but what are you going to do for an encore?" It's a question that never goes away.

I went on to write a biography of Lincoln Steffens, the grandfather of muckraking and investigative journalism; a second book about Mark Twain; and then a biography of Walt Whitman, an old interest of mine. But it took me several years to figure out how I wanted to tell Whitman's story, and this was: not to begin with an infant born in the first administration of President James Monroe but with an aged man, an invalid, living in a raddled house in Camden, New Jersey, and looking back over the well-traveled roads that had led to the writing and defense of *Leaves of Grass.*

I am also the author of many unwritten books. One of them was a biography of Ulysses Grant, general-in-chief of the Union armies, global hero, and two-term president of the United States, in his earlier life a reluctant soldier, a business failure, and a drunk. Here was the sort of archetypal figure I had been looking for: a shabby firewood peddler divinely endowed with strength and a charisma so powerful that General William Tecumseh Sherman, a nonbeliever, said he fought under Grant with "the faith a Christian has in his Savior." But after about a year of living with Grant I began to develop such a long list of reluctances (having to do with refighting the Civil War and detailing his disastrous presidencies, his bankruptcy, and his slow death of throat cancer) that I was left with an idea for what could only be a tiny book about Ulysses Grant and his rapport with horses. Finally, after reviewing for the *New Republic* a spirited and thoroughgoing new biography of Grant by William S. McFeely, I decided we wouldn't be needing another biography of Grant in this generation anyhow.

Eventually the name of Charlie Chaplin replaced Grant's on my Simon & Schuster contract. That's another story altogether, although it doesn't end any better. The year and more I spent on Chaplin had its redeeming adventures. Oona, his widow, forthcoming one moment, inaccessible the next, was as changeable as the drunk millionaire in *City Lights*. I saw her in New York and in Vevey, Switzerland, where I spent a couple of weeks rummaging through Charlie's papers and scripts, his contracts and income tax returns, which were stored in one of the dungeons of his stone manor house. The adjacent dungeon, a temperature-and-humidity-controlled vault, housed Chaplin's films and Oona's fur coats. As I worked down there, knowing that on the upper floors were the elusive chatelaine and her silent servitors, I thought of the remote castle in Ann Radcliffe's *Mysteries of Udolpho* and began to develop a serious case of the creeps. In the end I gave up on Charlie, too, for several compelling reasons.

One is that so much movie history, autobiography, memoir, and the like is pure moonshine, making it virtually impossible to tell lies from the truth. "The tragedy of film history," the actress Louise Brooks wrote, "is that it is fabricated, falsified by the very people who make film history," and those people included Chaplin, the author of several autobiographies.

Chaplin was a genius in his line, but everything brilliant and charming and original about him appears to have gone into his movies, which are gestural, speak for themselves, and so don't need the nudging of a biographer. What was left over wasn't sufficiently compelling. Even his steamy private life—his affairs and divorces, his involvements with underage women, and a paternity suit—had a certain repetitious quality. In an important sense, this man never grew beyond the age of fourteen, no matter how old and famous he got to be. In two or three early chapters I could have demonstrated—at least to my own satisfaction—that his traumatic boyhood (his drunk father and lunatic mother, his time in the orphan asylum and begging in the streets) was not only formative but supplied the text and subtext for practically every one of his movies. Having made that point, I realized that this was going to be a biography that told the same story of need and restitution over and over again. That wasn't the kind of book I wanted to write or read. So it was "Good-bye, Charlie."

Passing over in charitable silence my investigations of Gertrude Stein, Willa Cather, Stephen Crane, Edgar Allan Poe, and a few others, I come to what I still consider to have been an ideal prospect for biography. This was Irving Berlin, whose daughters offered me access to his papers, their cooperation, and the pledge of a hands-off policy as far as control or approval of the final product was concerned. Berlin had transformed American entertainment culture and made his name synonymous with American music. This immigrant Jew took over Christmas and Easter in his songs and made "God Bless America" a national anthem. He couldn't write or read scores but picked out hundreds of great tunes on his keyboard and had the musical equivalent of a stenographer take them down. English was not his first language, but he was a brilliant lyricist in English. And there was great personal and public drama in this story as well: Berlin's secret courtship of a Roman Catholic society beauty, the furor over their elopement and marriage, the unremitting enmity of his rich father-in-law. I had the impression that Irving Berlin had something of a rebarbative and recessive nature, but I felt for him, and with him, and believed that empathy if not love would conquer all things.

As it turned out, the daughters drew back when I asked for an important cycle of letters and messages their parents had exchanged during their courtship—these things were too private, too sacred, I was told, even for the most indirect background use in a biography, and if I were even to see these papers I was not to acknowledge it. I realized that if I accepted these (and some other) restrictions I would probably have to spend years of wheedling and negotiating to get whatever else I needed to see. I also realized that even the most kindly disposed biographer enters an adversarial situation when family feelings about adored parents are involved, but all the same I took this withdrawal of trust as an affront to my integrity. The venture had been irreparably compromised, and I bowed out. As Henry James's narrator would say, my "chagrin" over the loss of this unwritten book was "almost intolerable." My last working note on the Irving Berlin project reads: "Bring up violin music. Fade to blackout and curtain."

LYN LIFSHIN

THE WRITING OF "MINT LEAVES AT YADDO"

WRITER'S DIGEST

PART I

Behind the Poem, Before the Time That Stretches

I began to write early, *had* to write my own first poem a weekend
after I'd copied, at age 6, a poem of William Blake's and told
my mother it was mine. Since we lived in a small town, it's not
surprising that she ran into my teacher on Main Street, told her
she must have been an incredible inspiration.

But I knew that *I* wanted to write, knew it almost that early.
Still, even after my father gave an early poem of mine to Robert
Frost, who wrote that he liked the imagery in it, told my father
to have me bring him more, I was afraid to take a creative writing
class, afraid I couldn't write enough, couldn't write if I *had* to.
Once I began, though, after putting things like finishing a PhD
in the way like a roadblock, I found that I couldn't imagine not
writing poetry. In interviews, when asked about being so prolific
(not always as a compliment), I've found an answer: In the
Eskimo language, the words for "to breathe" and "to make a
poem" are the same.

When something terrible began happening to my mother,
writing about it was a way to breathe through it, to shape what
was happening or change it, in the only way I could. After re-
ceiving the news that what was thought first to be the flu was a
terminal disease, I sat with my mother most of the day. We
talked as much as she could. The TV was often on, a black

scratchy colorless slash of a world that seemed far away. Later, as my mother dozed, cut off from everything, I wrote poems, tried to catch her words, objects in the room, the feeling of the days burning down. I jotted down phrases, images: bringing my mother chips of ice, her hunger for steak, roast beef, lamb chops, the IV tubes with their paraphernalia, strange words that became part of our vocabulary. Angio-cath, Heplock, striated ringer. When my mother sighed that she wanted to leave my sister's house, something that would become more difficult as she got weaker and the tubes and drips became like ropes, or a leash, I often thought of the film *Midnight Cowboy*, of John Voight rescuing a scrawny Ratso Rizzo and escaping for a last feverish trip to somewhere, anywhere.

My sister and I, knowing how ill she was, still shopped giddily, hysterically, for Mother's Day gifts and, should she make it, presents for her birthday two weeks later. We knew people often hang on until their birthdays, but what do you get someone dying? We bought a black credit card holder she wanted but wouldn't need, but rejected an expensive music box. It seemed as if my sister and I were buying it for ourselves. The Christmas before, my mother, always intrigued by gadgets, had bought someone an electric iced tea maker. She was fascinated by it. Though my sister and I thought the iced tea maker was absurd, another bit of clutter, that June it seemed to be the only thing we could come up with that might amuse and please her.

Much of what I wrote during that period was especially tight, restrained, pared down. It was as if, to get through what was happening, I'd kept superfluous things at a distance, contained, controlled, but with an undercurrent. I pared away much in my daily life: Poetry readings and teaching were put on hold. I lived in chinos and a black jersey. I rarely put on contact lenses (maybe only wanting to see what was near). Fresh ground coffee in the morning and Gentle Orange tea at night were my luxuries. Ballet class, my drug of choice, was out of the question. Even with so little exercise and so little that was comforting except food, I lost weight, as if to keep up with my mother. After her death, the poems began to take on a loose, sprawling, rambling shape, and within a weekend I gained four or five pounds.

My isolation in Stowe wasn't unlike the quiet remoteness of Yaddo, the art colony I'd gone to 20 years earlier. In both Stowe and in Yaddo, the green branches clustered around the house, made rooms into jade caves. Twenty years earlier I was on the verge of divorce, on the verge of change and loss, just as I was in 1990. Outside everything was blooming. But inside, so much was shriveling. At Yaddo, magnolias and forsythia exploded, a rose bush matched the blush color of a sweater I wore. In Stowe, a huge pot of rouge petunias spilled across the redwood deck. The same stillness, the birds, the same slant of light. Hours spent standing at a window wrapped in that green, seemed to connect the two Junes.

On her birthday, my mother woke up feeling wonderful. She was animated and looked young in her jersey shift (later, I'd wash that shift, find chips of almond slivers, remnants of her last trip out to a mall). She seemed full of life, said she'd dreamt of eating all sorts of fruits on a picnic. Thrilled, we bought watermelon, peaches, cherries and took a ride up to the top of one of the tallest Stowe mountains. But the road was twisting and, with the tumor spreading inside, she became nauseated. The day was ruined. The iced tea maker she opened later, after a few hours of rest, was not the success it might have been before the ride. She was too tired to open all the cards. "There's so many," she said. "You could have saved some for next year." I wrote phrases like that in my notebook. I still have those fragments, most consisting of a line on the top of a page, the rest blank.

MINT LEAVES
AT YADDO

In frosty glasses of
tea. Here, iced
tea is what we
make waiting for

death with this
machine my mother
wanted. Not knowing
if she'd still be

here for her birth-
day we still shopped
madly, bought her
this present for.

For 20 days my
mother shows only
luke warm interest
in tea, vomits even

water, but I unpack
the plastic, intent
on trying this
sleek device while

my mother, queen
of gadgets,
—even a gun to
demolish flies—

maybe the strangest
thing she got me
can still see the
tall glasses that

seem summery on what
is the longest day.
Soon the light
will go she says,

the days get shorter.
I can't bear, she
murmurs, another
winter in Stowe and

I think how different
this isolation is,
this iced tea, this
time that stretches

where little grows
as it did, green
as that mint, except

my mother, smaller,
more distant, gaunt.

PART 2

In the Poem, In the Longest Days

It was the smell of fresh mint that triggered this poem. In workshops, I try to get students to trust their senses. As much as
music and sound and touch flash memories and feelings back,
smell does so even more vividly. When I smelled mint in the
iced tea, I felt the magical quiet of Yaddo, calm amber light from
the stained glass windows (images included in early versions of
the poem). Those honeyed shades, so full of the color that was
missing the June of the poem, were vivid but slowed the poem
down. It was the memory of those tall glasses of iced tea with
mint dripping from them that started first with the physical—
the tawny, shiny, glistening amber glass—then moved on to the
emotional, to feelings connected with the time that the image
of iced tea connects with, and then leaped on to something like
an epiphany.

In 1978 Beacon accepted my first anthology, *Tangled Vines.*
At the time I had written almost nothing about mothers and
daughters. It was my father, first emotionally and then physically absent, who was the subject of some poems. But once I'd
immersed myself in this new subject, my poems on that relationship, now a main theme, a main obsession, started. As my
mother aged, poems of rebellion changed to poems antici-
pating loss, a theme central to my poetry from the start. Images
of ''dissolving'' stud the poems from my first book of poems,

Why Is the House Dissolving?, published by Open Skull Press. My first published poem, in *Syracuse 10* (the one that Robert Frost liked), ends with an image of loss and dissolving. The poem, "Disillusions," uses the image of a child's shadow dissolving when a cloud breaks the spell of the shadow "and his dream-mate disappears."

I often think of poems as a way to hold, to keep a moment, like photographs—the first things I packed and took from my mother's. "Mint Leaves at Yaddo" is a freeze frame. An image of an afternoon. Here the mother is literally and symbolically dissolving, as is the light. Like the last two stanzas, more of her, more in her life, becomes pared down, less full, physically, emotionally and psychologically. The things she can control, where she can move, are contracting like the ice in the cubes, dying like the flies, the light. As people's ability to be effective and to interact with the world goes, their world becomes their night table, the pillows, the sheets, the bed. My mother wanted the clock just so on the pine nightstand, Life Savers candies close enough to reach for, her slippers pointed a certain way. As her life became reduced to rituals involving the basic things, getting to the bathroom, washing her hands, and all her energy was used up trying to do them, telling me how I should help her do them, our lives contracted together, were limited more and more to just her room.

The first draft of "Mint Leaves at Yaddo" was more descriptive. But I thought the poem would work better if it started, as it does now, with the image of calm evenings at Yaddo, then contrasted that with the dead, waiting, quiet in Stowe. I've tried typing the poem in longer lines, too. But in this version the enjambment and run-on lines put an emphasis on certain key words. By breaking the lines as I have, I can emphasize double meanings and twists more powerfully. For example, by breaking *birth-/day*, I can call up a birth that is really the birth of her last days, is death. By separating the eighth line, "if she'd still be," I hope for a double suggestion of "being," and "being here."

I wanted to capture both the rush of time and the sense of everything being static, frozen, of the speaker rushing toward what she is pulling back from. The repetition of *for* in lines 12 and 13 operates to show the daughter's mad search for a "present *for*" the mother slamming into the mother's apathy, "*For* 20 days my mother shows little interest," which shifts the mood. I used breathless run-on lines filled with images of things contracting and icing—the running out to shop, then the waiting to unpack—to suggest the frenzy caught in those frozen hours. I wanted to capture the rhythm of the days, the ordinary and blunt, slashed by something that startled, some beauty— the vomit bins contrasting with light on the tea reminding me of other days, just as I imagined my mother, seeing the tall glistening glass, must have drifted back to days on the front porch on North Pleasant where she grew up, or to afternoons with someone who mattered in Boston or New York City, before her children became her life. Even the poem, someone has suggested, is in the shape of a tall glass of iced tea, long and narrow as the days.

The speaker in the poem tells us it is the longest day, the longest day of summer. But *longest* is a charged word, and suggests the verb "to long," as well as something hard to get through. Because there was light to see longer, the speaker sees what she is losing. What had seemed long—life—is becoming shorter. The mother notices, as well as says, "Soon the light will go, the days get shorter." Color will be drained away like flesh, health, time, and the mother and daughter's connection. That glass only *seems* summery. There is little to make this a period of fulfillment, fruitfulness, happiness or beauty. What is ahead is the opposite of summer. Nothing will be fed, kept or maintained. The word *summery* hints at "summary," an adding up.

In the mother's murmur that she couldn't "bear another winter in Stowe," that *bear* is full of irony. In contrast with the trees leafing out, ready to bear new fruit, the mother can no longer bear new life, can barely bear life at all. The dying begin to lose modesty, to find things they'd once found embarrassing unimportant. As the mother begins to separate from her body, she is in many ways more "bare."

My mother was an actress, able to sound perky and upbeat when she was in Intensive Care. Even before she was sick, if I failed to call her when she expected me to, she might hide her disappointment expertly or become enraged. In the poem she is losing her mask, her costumes, becoming bare, unmade up. In writing so many poems about her during this period, maybe I was making her up since she no longer could.

The word *still*, in the line "can still see the tall glasses," also shimmers with suggestions. There is the stillness and the quiet, as well as the suggestion that, although she is still able to see, still alive, she won't "still be" for long. And, once again, this scene is a still, a stopped frame of what is unraveling. Like the mint trapped in the tea, the mother and daughter are held in this moment.

The word *present*, mentioned earlier, also evokes many things. It *is* a "moment in time, perceptible as intermediate between past and future, a definite now." And it is also "being at hand, being alert to circumstances, attentive, readily available." Then the mother's and daughter's presents, gifts to each other, are central to the poem; both the literal gifts of the tea maker and the gun for killing flies, as well as the emotional giving and taking. Even the legal definition of *present*, to let it be known, could be said to be implied.

There is a lot the mother in the poem can't bear, besides pain she never speaks of. I tried to capture an eerie undercurrent, the tension. How it was getting icier. Nothing was green in the middle of that summer's greenness. All the green surrounding the mother and daughter, all the ivy and the trees that were growing closer, pressing against glass, seemed to underline how the mother was only growing smaller, growing away. Traditionally, green suggests youthful, vigorous, brand new, though it can also remind the reader of the green plot of a cemetery, or even the description of someone ill who is "green," pale or wan. As in Federico García Lorca's "Somnambulistic Ballad" (a poem I focused on for half a year in college, with the haunting, recurring line "Green, green, I want you green"), green also suggests a longing for what could grow, while it foreshadows death. Repetition of words and cadences such as "this isolation is, this iced tea, this time . . ." uses *s* and *t* sounds like hisses to contribute to the dream-nightmare mood. The linking of life and death is conveyed through rhythms, assonance and

alliteration (*make waiting* and *machine my mother* and *shows only*),
which connect on a less conscious level to those in earlier
writing . . . from the Haggadah to the passages on death in Sir
Thomas Browne's "Urn Burial."

There is a contrast between the tea maker, plastic, "a sleek
device" hardly vulnerable, which is being unpacked, and the
mother, flesh disappearing, incredibly vulnerable, emotionally
and physically "packing it up." The glass of iced tea is like a
mirror, reflecting a glass that seems between the mother and
daughter: hard, fragile, brittle and breakable, a mirror the
speaker and her mother watch to see what is past and what is
coming in. The glass with tea in it also distorts, fragments, twists,
enlarges, splits, makes ripples and waves in what is perceived,
as the roles of the mother and daughter distort as they start to
reverse.

"Not knowing" underlies the poem. The speaker doesn't
know if her mother will live; the mother's words are a coded
fear that she doesn't know what is ahead and seems unable to
talk directly about it. "Shopping madly" suggests not only the
frenzy of the daughters trying to find something to show love
to the mother, but also their anger that the mother is ill, is
going to abandon them, leave them.

My mother fell for almost any new gadget, and would, when
she came to visit, always include something we'd groan and
shake our heads at, like the fly-killing gun in the poem. But the
poem shows those gadgets suddenly without power. Although
there are machines in the poem (the machine for making tea,
and the "machine" to kill flies), there is no *deus ex machina* that
will rescue her. Or us. Somehow, in luring the daughters to get
this tea maker, the mother in the poem retains some control.
Early in the poem the phrase "Here, iced tea is what we make
waiting for death," while contrasting this to what iced tea suggested at Yaddo, implies an atmosphere where the speaker
seems controlled by what is going on around her, is "in service," and there is an edge in the phrase. A mother's control
and criticisms of a daughter are often a luxury of health. Until
the end, my mother told me my skirt was too short, my hair
against her skin hurt her. In the poem, the mother is still queen.

My brother-in-law described my sister and me during those days as ladies in waiting; there, ready, waiting and waiting.

In writing about mothers and daughters in *Tangled Vines*, I made connections to mythic mothers and daughters. So often the mother is less fairy godmother than bad witch, either binding and suffocating her daughter or sending her out into wilderness. There is often a pattern of the martyr mother and the dutiful daughter. In "Mint Leaves at Yaddo," the daughter empties vomit bowls and shops for gifts while the mother suffers rather silently. I've often used the Daphne myth in my work, a woman running into trees to escape a lover. Here the myth is changed, perverted. The trees surround the speaker but offer no refuge. Instead, they flaunt their green. Nothing soothes or offers escape. Worse than not being a refuge, the green leaves are more like a cage. There is a suggestion of the Persephone and Demeter myth here, only it is not the mother sending the daughter off into the underworld and bringing darkness, but the daughter whose mother is slipping into that darkness. "I can't bear another winter," the mother sighs, but the truth is that there is only winter, and that there will be no more springs.

As noted above, I've been fascinated by the intensity and ambivalence of mother and daughter poems. There is so much emotional rawness in this relationship, even when the mother and daughter are separated or estranged, in life or by death; there seems to be energy that is never casual, unimportant or totally finished. Even in the most loving of these poems, there is an image of something darker. A child cuddled in pink is held, yes, but often feels suffocated. Vines that nourish can also strangle.

"Mint Leaves at Yaddo" stops before poems based on dreams I had in which my mother was suspended between being the woman who could open jars nobody else could and something shriveled, held almost in a cocoon. This poem is frozen in time; it shapes what was fluid the way the glass holds the tea, caught, suspended, a vial of June months before a time when I can no longer expect to hear my mother's voice on my answering machine.

It stops before the bedroom transformed by padding, walkers, a wheelchair, before rooms in which emptying each drawer is like excavating a city under ash. It stops before that house is gulped by an earthquake even as those in it are still reaching for each other.

DAVID CARKEET

DEAR REVIEWER . . .

SAN FRANCISCO REVIEW OF BOOKS

To: Reviewers of novels
From: David Carkeet, novelist
Re: The things you do

- If you don't know what's going on in the book, quickly send it back to the review editor so that someone else can get the assignment. Don't, of all things, go ahead and write the review.

- Don't begin your review with a long discussion of a general truth and then get around to the book by and by.

- Don't get all worked up just because you're reviewing a major writer. Don't pump up. Don't slobber. Don't write the history of the world. Forbidden words: "century," "decade," "era," "generation." Oh, and this one: "arguably."

- Don't get stuck on what happens in the first thirty pages and give short shrift to the rest of the book.

- Don't praise the author's style and quote an example. The example is part of a whole that your reader doesn't share with you, so it never looks as good as you say it does. You might as well whistle two notes of a melody. Don't quote any bad examples either. And don't quote any jokes. What I'm saying is don't quote anything.

- Don't steal from the language of the book to make fun of the book. If the author describes a character as "initially fetching, but a let-down after a while," don't you quote it and say the same goes for the book.

- Don't use this word to describe the author's style: "riffs."

- Yes, the author is a person, but that's no excuse: Don't try to explain things by making guesses. Don't say this part of the novel is better than that part because it's closer to the author's experience. Don't you do that. Don't look at the author's previous publication dates and say she wrote this book too fast. Forbidden words: "I suspect."

- Don't say all the writer's work thus far is just a prelude to this book. The opposite is also outlawed—damning the book because of where you think the author should be right now. Maybe, considered all by itself, it's a grand book. Forbidden words: "development," "growth," "disappointment."

- If the book is a translation, don't call it "a good translation" unless you've read the original and compared the two. If you mean the translation is pretty, or grammatical, or handsomely punctuated, you may say that. Don't say it's good.

- You are permitted, in the course of your reviewing career, to say about one author, and one author only, that he or she is "the most accomplished writer of our time."

- Don't use this word to describe a character: "loopy."

- Don't give away a single surprise of any kind, big or small. Don't say there is a major surprise at the end that you're being careful not to give away. You may say, "The book is surprising."

- Don't laundry list the characters and their salient features. This may be fun for you, but it is tedious as all hell to everyone else.

- Come to think of it, don't even say, "The book is surprising."

- Don't write your review in the prose style of the novel you're reviewing. Use some other device to tell us that the book is so mesmerizing, so utterly hypnotic, that its enchantment lingers and befogs you, even now as you write. Use a declarative sentence. Don't you go jumping in the writer's river just because it's so pretty. If the writer's style intoxicates you, go dry out before you write the review. Then use your own style.

- Don't use these words to describe the book's structure: "cobbled together."

- Don't compare the book to anything. Don't compare it to another book. Don't compare it to a movie. Don't compare it to a meal.

- Don't write a penultimate paragraph qualifying everything you've said, followed by a last paragraph that begins with, "Still" and reaffirms everything you've just qualified.

- Don't stand out in any way. Stay back there where you belong. No, further back. Further still. Further. There.

- When you finish your review, send a copy to the author right away. Ask for comments, so that you might improve your craft.

CHARLES BAXTER

DYSFUNCTIONAL NARRATIVES
OR "MISTAKES WERE MADE"

PLOUGHSHARES

Here are some sentences of distinctive American prose from our era.

> From a combination of hypersensitivity and a desire not to know the truth in case it turned out to be unpleasant, I had spent the last ten months putting off a confrontation with John Mitchell. . . . I listened to more tapes. . . . I heard Haldeman tell me that Dean and Mitchell had come up with a plan to handle the problem of the investigation's going into areas we didn't want it to go. The plan was to call in Helms and Walters of the CIA and have them restrain the FBI. . . . Haldeman and I discussed [on the "smoking gun" tape] having the CIA limit the FBI investigation for political rather than the national security reasons I had given in my public statements. . . . On June 13, while I was in Egypt, Fred Buzhardt had suffered a heart attack. Once I was assured that he was going to pull through, I tried to assess the impact his illness would have on our legal situation.

These sentences are *almost* enough to make one nostalgic for an adversary with a claim upon our attention. There he is, the late lawyer-President setting forth the brief for the defense, practicing the dogged art of the disclaimer in *RN: The Memoirs of Richard Nixon.* (I've done some cut-and-pasting, but the sentences I've quoted are the sentences he wrote.) And what sentences! Leaden and dulling, juridical-minded to the last, impersonal but not without savor—the hapless Buzhardt and his heart attack factored into the "legal situation," and that wonderful "hypersensitivity" combined with a desire "not to know the truth" that makes one think of Henry James's Lambert Strether or an epicene character in Huysmans—they present the reader with camouflage masked as objective thought.

In his memoir, Richard Nixon does not admit that he lied, exactly, or that he betrayed his oath of office. In his "public statements," he did a bit of false accounting, that was all. One should expect this, he suggests, from heads of state.

Indeed, the only surprise this reader had, trudging gamely through *RN*, looking for clues to a badly defined mystery, was the author's report of a sentence uttered by Jacqueline Kennedy. Touring the White House after RN's election, she said, "I always live in a dream world." Funny that she would say so; funny that he would notice.

Lately I've been possessed of a singularly unhappy idea: the greatest influence on American fiction for the last twenty years may have been the author of *RN*, not in his writing but in his public character. He is the inventor, for our purposes and for our time, of the concept of *deniability*. Deniability is the almost complete disavowal of intention in relation to bad consequences. This is a made-up word, and it reeks of the landfill-scented landscape of lawyers and litigation and high school. Following Richard Nixon in influence on recent fiction would be two runners-up, Ronald Reagan and George Bush. Their administrations put the passive voice, politically, on the rhetorical map. In their efforts to acquire deniability on the arms-for-hostages deal with Iran, their administrations managed to achieve considerable notoriety for self-righteousness, public befuddlement about facts, forgetfulness under oath, and constant disavowals of political error and criminality, culminating in the quasi-confessional, passive voice-mode sentence, "Mistakes were made."

Contrast this with Robert E. Lee's statement after the battle of Gettysburg, the third day and the calamity of Pickett's

Charge: "All this has been my fault," Lee said. "I asked more of men than should have been asked of them."

These sentences have a slightly antique ring. People just don't say such things anymore.

What difference does it make to writers of stories if public figures are denying their responsibility for their own actions? So what if they are, in effect, refusing to tell their own stories accurately? So what if the President of the United States is making himself out to be, of all things, a *victim*? Well, to make an obvious point, they create a climate in which social narratives are designed to be deliberately incoherent and misleading. Such narratives humiliate the act of storytelling. You can argue that only a coherent narrative can manage to explain public events, and you can reconstruct a story if someone says, "I made a mistake," or "We did that," but you can't reconstruct a story—you can't even know what the story *is*—if everyone is saying, "Mistakes were made." Who made them? Well, everybody made them and no one did, and it's history anyway, so we should forget about it. Every story is a history, however, and when there is no comprehensible story, there is, in some sense, no history; the past, under those circumstances, becomes an unreadable mess. When we hear words like "deniability," we are in the presence of narrative dysfunction, a phrase employed by the poet C. K. Williams to describe the process by which we lose track of the story of ourselves, the story that tells us who we are supposed to be and how we are supposed to act.

One spiritual godfather of the contemporary disavowal movement, the author of *RN*, set the tenor for the times and reflected the times as well in his lifelong denial of responsibility for the Watergate break-in and coverup. He claimed that misjudgments were made, though not necessarily by him; mistakes were made, though they were by no means his own, and the crimes that were committed were only crimes if you define "crime" in a certain way, in the way, for example, that his enemies liked to define the word, in a manner that would be unfavorable to him, that would give him, to use a word derived from the Latin, some culpability. It wasn't the law, he claimed; it was all just politics.

A curious parallel: the Kennedy assassination may be *the*

narratively dysfunctional event of our era: no one really knows who's responsible for it. One of the signs of a dysfunctional narrative is that we cannot leave it behind, and we cannot put it to rest, because it does not, finally, give us the explanation we need to enclose it. We don't know who the agent of the action is. We don't even know why it was done. Instead of achieving closure, the story spreads over the landscape like a stain as we struggle to find a source of responsibility. In our time, responsibility within narratives has been consistently displaced by its enigmatic counterpart, conspiracy. Conspiracy works in tandem with narrative repression, the repression of who-has-done-what. We go back over the Kennedy assassination second by second, frame by frame, but there is a truth to it that we cannot get at because we can't be sure who really did it or what the motivations were. Everyone who claims to have closed the case simply establishes that the case will stay open. The result of dysfunctional narrative, as the poet Lawrence Joseph has suggested to me, is sorrow; I would argue that it is sorrow mixed with depression, the condition of the abject, but in any case we are talking about the psychic landscape of trauma and paralysis, the landscape of, for example, two outwardly different writers, Don DeLillo (in most of *Libra*,) and Jane Smiley (in the last one hundred pages of *A Thousand Acres*).

A parenthesis: Jane Smiley's novel has been compared to *King Lear*, and its plot invites the comparison, but its real ancestors in fiction are the novels of Emile Zola. *A Thousand Acres* is Zola on the plains. Like Zola, Jane Smiley assembles precisely and carefully a collection of facts, a Naturalistic pile-up of details about—in this case—farming and land use. As for characters, the reader encounters articulate women (including the narrator, Rose) and mostly frustrated inarticulate men driven by blank desires, like Larry, the Lear figure. Lear, however, is articulate. Larry is not. He is like one of Zola's male characters, driven by urges he does not understand or even acknowledge.

Somewhat in the manner of other Naturalistic narratives, *A Thousand Acres* causes its characters to behave like mechanisms, under obscure orders. Wry but humorless, shorn of poetry or any lyric outburst, and brilliantly observant and relentless, the novel at first seems to be about 1980's greed and the destruction of resources that we now associate with Reaganism, a literally exploitative husbandry. Such a story would reveal clear if deplorable motives in its various characters. Instead, with the revelation of Larry's sexual abuse of his daughters, including the narrator, it shifts direction toward an account of conspiracy and repressed memory, sorrow and depression, in which several of the major characters are acting out rather than acting.

The characters' emotions are thus preordained, and the narrator herself gathers around herself a cloak of unreliability as the novel goes on. It is a moody novel, but the mood itself often seems impenetrable because the characters, even the men, are not acting upon events in present narrative time but are reacting obscurely to harms done to them in the psychic past, from unthinkable impulses that will go forever unexplained. Enacting greed at least involves making some decisions, but in this novel, the urge to enact incest upon one's daughter is beyond thought, and, in turn, creates consequences that are beyond thought. Rose herself lives in the shadow of thought (throughout much of the book she is unaccountable, even to herself) by virtue of her having been molested by her father. This is dysfunctional narrative as literary art, a novel that is also very much an artifact of *this* American era.

Watergate itself would have remained narratively dysfunctional if the tapes hadn't turned up, and, with them, the "smoking gun"—notice, by the way, the metaphors that we employ to designate narrative responsibility, the naming and placing of the phallically inopportune protagonist at the center. The arms-for-hostages deal is still a muddled narrative because various political functionaries are taking the fall for what the commander-in-chief is supposed to have decided himself. However, the commander-in-cheif was not told; or he forgot; or he was out of the loop. The buck stops here? In recent history, the buck doesn't stop anywhere. The buck keeps moving, endlessly; perhaps we are in the era of the endlessly traveling buck, the buck seeking a place to stop, like a story that cannot find its own ending.

We have been living, it seems, in a political culture of disavowals. Disavowals follow from crimes for which no one is capable of claiming responsibility. Mistakes and crimes tend to create narratives, however, and they have done so from the time of the Greek tragedies. How can the contemporary disavowal movement not affect those of us who tell stories? We begin to move away from fiction of protagonists and antagonists into another mode, another model. It is hard to describe this model but I think it might be called the fiction of finger-pointing, the fiction of the quest for blame.

In such fiction, people and events are often accused of turning the protagonist into the kind of person the protagonist is, usually an unhappy person. That's the whole story. When blame has been assigned, the story is over. (In writing workshops, this kind of story is often the rule rather than the exception.) Probably this model of storytelling has arisen because, for many reasons, large population groups in our time feel confused and powerless, as they often do in mass societies when the mechanisms of power are carefully masked. For people with bad jobs and mounting debts and faithless partners and abusive parents, the most interesting feature of life is its unhappiness, its dull constant weight. But in a commodity culture, people are *supposed* to be happy; this is the one tireless myth of advertising. In such a consumerist climate, the perplexed and unhappy don't know what their lives are telling them, and they don't feel as if they are in charge of their own existence. No action they have ever taken is half as interesting to them as the consistency of their unhappiness.

Natural disasters, by contrast—earthquakes and floods— have a quality of narrative relief: we know what caused the misery, and we usually know what we can do to repair the damage, no matter how long it takes.

But corporate and social power, any power carefully masked, puts its victims into a state of frenzy, the frenzy of the *Oprah* show, of *Geraldo*, and Montel Williams. Somebody must be responsible for my pain. Someone *will* be found; someone, usually close to home, *will* be blamed. TV loves dysfunctional families. Dysfunctional S&L's and banks and corporate structures are not loved quite so much. In this sense we have moved away from the Naturalism of Zola or Frank Norris or Dreiser. Like them, we believe that people are often helpless, but we don't blame the corporations so much anymore; we blame the family.

Afternoon talk shows have only apparent antagonists. Their sparring partners are not real antagonists because the bad guys usually confess and then immediately disavow. The trouble with narratives like this without antagonists or a counterpoint to the central character—stories in which no one ever seems to be deciding anything or acting upon any motive except the search for a source of discontent—is that they tend formally to mirror the protagonists' unhappiness and confusion. Stories about being put-upon almost literally do not know what to look at; the visual details are muddled or indifferently described or excessively specific in nonpertinent situations. In any particular scene, everything is significant, and nothing is. The story is trying to find a source of meaning, but in the story, everyone is disclaiming responsibility. Things have just happened.

When I hear the adjective "dysfunctional" now, I cringe. But I have to use it here to describe a structural unit (like the banking system, or the family, or narrative) whose outward appearance is intact but whose structural integrity may have collapsed, so that no one is answerable within it—every cent, every calamity, is unanswered, from the S&L collapse to the Exxon Valdez oil spill.

So we have created for ourselves a paradise of lawyers: we have an orgy of blame-finding on the one hand and disavowals of responsibility on the other.

All the recent debates and quarrels about taking responsibility as opposed to being a victim reflect some bewilderment about whether in real life protagonists still exist or whether we are all, in some sense, minor characters, the objects of terrible forces. Of course, we are often both. But look at *Oprah*. (I have, I do, I can't help it.) For all the variety of the situations, the unwritten scripts are often similar: someone is testifying because s/he's been hurt by someone else. The pain-inflicter is invariably present and accounted for onstage, and sometimes this person admits, abashedly, to inflicting the ruin: cheating, leaving, abusing, or murdering. Usually, however, there's no remorse, because some other factor caused it: bad genes, alcoholism, drugs, or—the cause of last resort—Satan. For intellectuals it may be the patriarchy: some devil or other—but an *abstract* devil. In any case, the malefactor may be secretly pleased: s/he's on television and will be famous for fifteen minutes.

The audience's role in all this is to comment on what the story means and to make a judgment about the players. Usually the audience members disagree and get into fights. The audience's judgment is required because the dramatis personae are incapable of judging themselves. They generally will not say that they did what they did because they wanted to, or because they had *decided* to do it. The story is shocking. You hear gasps. But the participants are as baffled and bewildered as everyone else. So we have the spectacle of utterly perplexed villains deprived of their villainy. Villainy, properly understood, gives someone a largeness, a sense of scale. It seems to me that that sense of scale has probably abandoned us.

What we have instead is not exactly drama and not exactly therapy. It exists in that twilight world between the two, very much of our time, where deniability reigns. Call it therapeutic narration. No verdict ever comes in. No one is in a position to judge. It makes the mind itch as if from an ideological rash. It is the spectacle, hour after hour, week after week, of dysfunctional narratives, interrupted by commercials (in Detroit, for lawyers).

Here is a koan for the 1990's: what is the relation between the dysfunctional narratives and the commercials that interrupt them?

But wait: isn't there something deeply interesting and moving and sometimes even beautiful when a character *acknowledges* an error? And isn't this narrative mode becoming something of a rarity?

Most young writers have this experience: they create characters who are an imaginative projection of themselves, minus the flaws. They put this character into a fictional world, wanting that character to be successful and—to use that word for high school—"popular." They don't want these imaginative projections of themselves to make any mistakes, wittingly or, even better, unwittingly, or to demonstrate what Aristotle thought was the core of stories, flaws of character that produce intelligent misjudgments for which someone must take the responsibility.

What's an unwitting action? It's what we do when we have to act so quickly, or under so much pressure, that we can't stop to take thought. It's not the same as an urge, which may well have a brooding and inscrutable quality. For some reason, such moments of unwitting action in life and in fiction feel enormously charged with energy and meaning.

It's difficult for fictional characters to acknowledge their mistakes, because then they become definitive: they *are* that person who did *that* thing. The only people who like to see characters performing such actions are readers. They love to see characters getting themselves into interesting trouble and defining themselves.

Lately, thinking about the nature of drama and our resistance to certain forms of it, I have been reading Aristotle's *Poetics* again and mulling over his definition of what makes a poet. A poet, Aristotle says, is first and foremost a maker, not of verses, but of plots. The poet creates an imitation, and what he imitates is an action.

It might be useful to make a distinction here between what I might call "me" protagonists and "I" protagonists. "Me" protagonists are largely objects—objects of impersonal forces or the actions of other people. They are central characters to whom things happen. They do not initiate action so much as receive it. For this reason, they are largely reactionary, in the old sense of that term, and passive. They are figures of fate and destiny, and they tend to appear during periods of accelerated social change, such as the American 1880's and 1890's, and again in the 1980's.

The "I" protagonist, by contrast, makes certain decisions and takes some responsibility for them and for the actions that follow from them. This does not make the "I" protagonist admirable by any means. It's this kind of protagonist that Aristotle is talking about. Such a person, Aristotle says, is not outstanding for virtue or justice, and she or he arrives at ill fortune not because of any wickedness or vice, but because of some mistake that s/he makes. There's that word again, "mistake."

Sometimes—if we are writers—we have to talk to our characters. We have to try to persuade them to do what they've only imagined doing. We have to nudge but not force them toward situations where they will get into interesting trouble, where they will make interesting mistakes that they may take responsibility for. When we allow our characters to make mistakes, we release them from the grip of our own authorial narcissism. That's wonderful for them, it's wonderful for us, but it's best of all for the story.

A few instances: I once had a friend in graduate school who gave long, loud, and unpleasantly exciting parties in the middle of winter; he and his girlfriend usually considered these parties unsuccessful unless someone did something shocking or embarrassing or both—*something you could talk about later.* He lived on the third floor of an old house in Buffalo, New York, and his acquaintances regularly fell down the front and back stairs.

I thought of him recently when I was reading about Mary Butts, an English writer of short fiction who lived from 1890 to 1937. Her stories have now been reissued in a collection called *From Altar to Chimneypiece.* Virgil Thomson, who was gay, once proposed marriage to her. That tells us something about the power of her personality. This is what Thomson says about her in his autobiography:

> I used to call her "storm goddess," because she was at her best surrounded by cataclysm. She could stir up others with drink and drugs and magic incantations, and then when the cyclone was at its most intense, sit down at calm center and glow. All of her stories are of moments when the persons observed are caught up by something, inner or outer, so irresistible that their highest powers and all their lowest conditionings are exposed. The resulting

action therefore is definitive, an ultimate clarification arrived at through ecstasy.

As it happens, I do not think that this is an accurate representation of Mary Butts's stories, which tend to be about crossing thresholds and stumbling into very strange spiritual dimensions. But I am interested in Thomson's thought concerning definitive action, because I think the whole concept of definitive action is meeting up with a considerable cultural resistance these days.

Thomson, describing his storm goddess, shows us a temptress, a joyful, worldly woman, quite possibly brilliant and bad to the bone. In real life people like this can be insufferable. Marriage to such a person would be a relentless adventure. They're constantly pushing their friends and acquaintances to lower their defenses and drop their masks and do something for which they will probably be sorry later. They like it when anyone blurts out a sudden admission, or acts on an impulse and messes up conventional arrangements. They like to see people squirm. They're *gleeful.* They prefer Bizet to Wagner; they're more Carmen than Sieglinde. They like it when people lunge at a desired object, and cacophony and wreckage are the result.

The morning after, you can say, "Mistakes were made," but at least with the people I've spent time with, a phrase like "Mistakes were made" won't even buy you a cup of coffee. There is such a thing as the poetry of a mistake, and when you say, "Mistakes were made," you deprive an action of its poetry, and you sound like a weasel. When you say, "I fucked up," the action retains its meaning, its sordid origin, its obscenity, and its poetry.

Chekhov says about this, in two of his letters, ". . . shun all descriptions of the characters' spiritual state. You must try to have that state emerge from their actions. . . . The artist must be only an impartial witness of his characters and what they said, not their judge." In Chekhov's view, a writer must try to release the story's characters from the aura of judgment that they've acquired simply because they're fictional. It's as if fiction has a great deal of trouble shedding its moral/pedagogical origins in fable and allegory.

In an atmosphere of constant moral judgment, characters are not often permitted to make interesting and intelligent mistakes and then to acknowledge them. It's as if the whole idea of the "intelligent mistake," the importance of the mistake made on an impulse, had gone out the window. Or, if fictional characters do make such mistakes, they're judged immediately and without appeal. One thinks of the attitudes of the aging Tolstoy here, and of his hatred of Shakespeare's and Chekhov's plays, and of his obsessive moralizing. He especially hated *King Lear*. He called it stupid, verbose, and incredible, and thought the craze for Shakespeare was like the tulip craze, a matter of mass hypnosis and "epidemic suggestion."

In the absence of any clear moral vision, we get moralizing. There's quite a lot of it around, and I think it has been inhibiting writers and making them nervous and irritable. Here is Mary Gaitskill, commenting on one of her own short stories, "The Girl on the Plane," in a recent *Best American Short Stories*. It's a story about a gang rape, and it apparently upset quite a few readers.

> In my opinion, most of us have not been taught how to be responsible for our thoughts and feelings. I see this strongly in the widespread tendency to read books and stories as if they exist to confirm how we are supposed to be, think, and feel. I'm not talking wacky political correctness, I'm talking mainstream. . . . Ladies and gentlemen, please. Stop asking "What am I supposed to feel?" Why would an adult look to me or to any other writer to tell him or her what to feel? You're not *supposed* to feel anything. You feel what you feel.

Behind the writer's loss of patience one can just manage to make out a literary culture begging for an authority figure, the same sort of figure that Chekhov refused for himself. Mary Gaitskill's interest in bad behavior is that of the observer, not the judge. Unhappy readers want her to be both, as if stories should come prepackaged with discursive authorial opinions about her own characters. Her exasperation is a reflection of C. K. Williams's observation that in a period of dysfunctional narratives, the illogic of feeling erodes the logic of stories. When people can't make any narrative sense out of their own feelings, readers start to ask writers what they are supposed to feel. Reading begins to be understood as a form of therapy. In such an atmosphere, already-moralized stories are more comforting than stories in which characters are making intelligent or unwitting mistakes.

Marilynne Robinson, in her essay "Hearing Silence: Western Myth Reconsidered," calls the already-moralized story, the therapeutic narrative, part of a "mean little myth" of our time. She notes, however, that "we have ceased to encode our myths in narrative as that word is traditionally understood. Now they shield themselves from our skepticism by taking on the appearance of scientific or political or economic discourse. . . . " And what is this "mean little myth"?

> One is born and in passage through childhood suffers some grave harm. Subsequent good fortune is meaningless because of this injury, while subsequent misfortune is highly significant as the consequence of this injury. The work of one's life is to discover and name the harm one has suffered.

As long as this myth is operational, one cannot act, in stories or anywhere else, in a meaningful way. The injury takes for itself all the meaning. The injury *is* the meaning, though it is, itself, opaque. All achievements, and all mistakes, are finessed. There is no free will. There is only acting out, the acting out of one's destiny. But acting out is not the same as acting. Acting out is behavior that proceeds according to a predetermined, invisible pattern created by the injury. The injury becomes the unmoved mover, the replacement for the mind's capacity to judge and to decide. One thinks of Nixon here: the obscure wounds, the vindictiveness, the obsession with enemies, the acting out.

It has a feeling of Calvinism to it, of predetermination, this myth of injury and predestination. In its kingdom, sorrow and depression rule. Marilynne Robinson calls this mode of thought "bungled Freudianism." It's both that and something else: an effort to make pain acquire some comprehensibility so that those who feel helpless can at least be illuminated. But unlike Freudianism it asserts that the source of the pain can *never be expunged.* There is no working-through of this injury. It has no tragic joy because within it, all personal decisions have been made meaningless, deniable. It is a life-fate, like a character disorder. Its politics cannot get much further than gender-injury; it cannot take on the corporate state.

Confronted with this mode, I feel like an Old Leftist. I want to say: the Bosses are happy when you feel helpless. They're pleased when you think the source of your trouble is your family. They're delighted when you give up the idea that you should band together for political action. They love helpless-ness (in you). They even like addicts, as long as they're mostly out of sight: after all, *addiction is just the last stage of consumerism.*

And I suppose I am nostalgic—as a writer, of course—for stories with mindful villainy, villainy with clear motives that any adult would understand, bad behavior with a sense of *scale,* that would give back to us our imaginative grip on the despicable and the admirable and our capacity to have some opinions about the two. Most of us are interested in characters who will-ingly give up their innocence and decide to act badly. I myself am fascinated when they not only do that but admit that they did it, that they had good reasons for doing so. At such moments wrongdoing becomes intelligible. It also becomes legibly polit-ical. If this is the liberal fallacy, this sense of choice, then so be it. (I know that people *do* get caught inside systems of harm and cannot maneuver themselves out—I have written about such situations myself—but that story is hardly the only one worth telling.)

It does seem curious that in contemporary America—a place of considerable good fortune and privilege—one of the most favored narrative modes, from high to low, has to do with dis-avowals, passivity, and the disarmed protagonist. Possibly we have never gotten over our American romance with innocence. We would rather be innocent than worldly and unshockable.

Innocence is continually shocked and disarmed. But there is something wrong with this. No one can go through life perpetually shocked. It's disingenuous. Writing in his journals, Thornton Wilder notes, "I think that it can be assumed that no adults are ever really 'shocked'—that being shocked is always a pose." If so, there is some failure of adulthood in contemporary American life. Our interest in victims and victimization has finally to do with our constant ambivalence about power, about being powerful, about wanting to be powerful but not having to acknowledge the buck stopping on our desk.

What I am arguing against is *not* political or social action against abusers of power, corporate or familial. I am registering my uneasiness with the Romance of Victimization, especially in this culture, and the constant disavowal of responsibility by the abuser. Romantic victims and disavowing perpetrators land us in a peculiar territory, a sort of neo-Puritanism without the backbone of theology and philosophy. After all, *The Scarlet Letter* is about disavowals, specifically Dimmesdale's, and the supposed "shock" of a minister of God being guilty of adultery. Dimmesdale's inability to admit publicly what he's done has something to do with the community—i.e., a culture of "shock"—and something to do with his own pusillanimous character.

The dialectics of innocence and worldliness have a different emotional coloration in British literature, or perhaps I simply am unable to get Elizabeth Bowen's *The Death of the Heart* (1938) out of my mind in this context. Portia, the perpetual innocent and stepchild, sixteen years old, in love with Eddie, twenty-three, has been writing a diary, and her guardian, Anna, has been reading it. Anna tells St. Quentin, her novelist friend, that she has been reading it. St. Quentin tells Portia what Anna has done. As it happens, Portia has been writing poisonously accurate observations about Anna and her husband, Thomas, in the diary. Anna is a bit pained to find herself so neatly skewered.

Bowen's portrait of Portia is beautifully managed, but it's her portrayal of Anna that fascinates me. Anna cannot be shocked. Everything she has done, she admits. In the sixth chapter of the novel's final section, she really blossoms: worldly, witty, rather mean, and absolutely clear about her own faults, she recognizes the situation and her own complicity in it. She may be sorry, but she doesn't promise to do better. Portia is the one who is innocent, who commands the superior virtues, not she herself. Speaking of reading private diaries, she says, "It's the sort of thing I do do. Her diary's very good—you see, she has got us taped. . . . I don't say it has changed the course of my life, but it's given me a rather more disagreeable feeling about being alive—or, at least, about being me."

That "disagreeable feeling" seems to arise not only from the diary but also from Anna's wish to read it, to violate it. Anna may feel disagreeable about being the person she is, but she does not say that she could be otherwise. She is the person who does what she admits to. As a result, there is a clarity, a functionality to Bowen's narrative, that becomes apparent because everybody admits everything in it and then gives their reasons for doing what they've done. It's as if their actions have found a frame, a size, a scale. As bad as Anna may be, she is honest.

Anna defines herself, not in the American way of reciting inward virtues, but in a rather prideful litany of mistakes. In her view, we define ourselves at least as much by our mistakes as by our achievements. The grace and honor of fiction is that in stories, mistakes are every bit as interesting as achievements are; they have an equal claim upon truth. Perhaps they have a greater one, because they are harder to show, harder to hear, harder to say. For that reason, they are rarer and more precious.

Speaking of a library book that is eighteen years overdue, but which she has just returned, the narrator of Grace Paley's story "Wants" says, "I didn't deny anything." She pays the thirty-two-dollar fine, and that's it. One of the pleasures of Paley's stories is that the stories, as narrated, are remarkably free of denial and subterfuge. Their characters explain themselves but don't bother to excuse themselves. City dwellers, they don't particularly like innocence, and they don't expect to be shocked. When there's blame, they take it. When they fall, there's a good reason. They don't rise; they just get back on their feet, and when they think about reform, it's typically political rather than personal. For one of her characters, this is the "powerful last-half-of-the-century way." Well, its' nice to think so. Free of the therapeutic impulse, and of the recovery movement, and of Protestantism generally, her characters nevertheless *like* to imagine various social improvements in the lives of the members of their community.

Dysfunctional narratives tend to begin in solitude and they tend to resist their own forms of communication. They don't have communities so much as audiences of fellow victims. There is no polite way for their narratives to end. Richard Nixon, disgraced, resigned, still flashing the V-for-victory from the helicopter on the White House lawn, cognitively dissonant to the end, went off to his enforced retirement, where, tirelessly, year after year, in solitude, he wrote his accounts, every one of them meant to justify and to excuse. His last book, as of this writing not yet published, is entitled *Beyond Peace*.

DAN GREENBURG

WRITERS HAVE HAD IT UP TO HERE: THE LATEST ON THE AUTHORS' STRIKE

THE NEW YORK TIMES BOOK REVIEW

It has finally happened. The poets and authors, having had it up to here, are out on strike. There will be no further putting of pen or typewriter or word processor to paper to create any sort of verse—rhymed, blank, doggerel, anything that scans. There will be no more books of fiction or nonfiction by professional authors or critics of any caliber whatsoever until this thing, whatever it is, is over.

The screenwriters are not affected, nor are the television writers, the playwrights, the composers or the lyricists, being under other unions' jurisdictions. However, all are in sympathy with the strike and have vowed not to cross the picket lines.

There has been a run on the bookstores. A panicked citizenry is salting away cases of literary first novels and shopping-cartfuls of esoteric poetry in wine cellars and fallout shelters. Complaints about hoarding have been heard. Unruly customers in the Barnes & Noble bookstore at Broadway and 82nd Street on Manhattan's Upper West Side have scuffled over the last volumes of blank verse on the shelves, and several of them have been injured in the process.

Black marketeers have been quick to exploit the current emergency. At last word, a volume of experimental fiction was being traded on the street for six cartons of Marlboros, a dozen granola bars and a pair of microfiber panty hose.

Spokesmen from the publishing houses have released a joint statement. They deplore the irresponsibility of the poets and authors and ask them to consider the effect that the strike will have upon the public. They make dire predictions about the consequences of literature deprivation. They warn that the strike could go on a long time.

The publishers have denied widely circulated reports that they are employing scabs, yet motley bands of individuals—motlier even than poets—have been seen crossing the picket lines of most New York publishing houses, oblivious to the heckling of the picketing writers.

Police officers employing riot-control devices have repeatedly trained hoses filled with Evian water upon the unruly mob. One individual who attempted to cross the picket lines was felled by several well-hurled epithets; another was treated in the emergency room of Bellevue Hospital for first-degree burns induced by scathing sarcasm.

Federal mediators have been sent to New York by the President to organize collective bargaining sessions, and they stand ready to mediate round the clock, if necessary. But both sides appear reluctant either to sit down at the table together or to order takeout.

The publishers have attempted to impose salary caps, but both poets and authors have refused to wear them. The publishers maintain that the demands of both poets and authors are preposterous.

The poets demand to not be understood too quickly. The authors demand parity with either the chimney sweeps or the shepherds, whichever is greater.

The publishers are contemptuous of these demands and maintain that if they are acceded to, poets and authors will run rampant through our streets, looting computer supply stores, taking liberties with language, committing sloppy journalism, debauching pedestrians, dangling participles, holding ad hoc poetry readings, forming personal holding companies, speaking in tongues and other unappetizing cuts of meat, threatening to unseat the Government and force lawmakers to stand, irrevocably altering the very fabric of life as we know it, causing it to attract lint and pet hair.

No one knows what the effects of a lengthy strike by poets

and authors will be. The general public is uncertain and cranky, having recently weathered strikes by the sanitation workers, the microbiologists, the upholsterers, the mimes, the Jesuits, the flutists, the three-card-monte players, the gastroenterologists, the designated drivers, the exhibitionists, the cognitive therapists and the neo-existentialist philosophers.

DOROTHY ALLISON

BELIEVING IN LITERATURE

SKIN: TALKING ABOUT SEX, CLASS AND LITERATURE

I have always passionately loved good books—good stories and beautiful writing, and most of all, books that seemed to me to be intrinsically important, books that told the truth, painful truths sometimes, in a voice that made eloquent the need for human justice. That is what I have meant when I have used the word *literature*. It has seemed to me that literature, as I meant it, was embattled, that it was increasingly difficult to find writing doing what I thought literature should do—which was simply to push people into changing their ideas about the world, and to go further, to encourage us in the work of changing the world, to making it more just and more truly human.

All my life I have hated clichés, the clichés applied to people like me and those I love. Every time I pick up a book that purports to be about either poor people or queers or Southern women, I do so with a conscious anxiety, an awareness that the books about us have often been cruel, small, and false. I have wanted our lives taken seriously and represented fully—with power and honesty and sympathy—to be hated or loved, or to terrify and obsess, but to be real, to have the power of the whole and the complex. I have never wanted politically correct parables made out of my grief, simpleminded rote speeches made from my rage, simplifications that reduce me to cardboard dimensions. But mostly that is what I have found. We are the ones they make fiction of—we queer and disenfranchised and female—and we have the right to demand our full, nasty, complicated lives, if only to justify all the times our reality has been stolen, mismade, and dishonored.

That our true stories may be violent, distasteful, painful, stunning, and haunting, I do not doubt. But our true stories will be literature. No one will be able to forget them, and though it will not always make us happy to read of the dark and dangerous places in our lives, the impact of our reality is the best we can ask of our literature.

Literature, and my own dream of writing, has shaped my system of belief—a kind of atheist's religion. I gave up God and the church early on, choosing instead to place all my hopes in direct-action politics. But the backbone of my convictions has been a belief in the progress of human society as demonstrated in its fiction. Even as a girl I believed that our writing was better than we were. There were, after all, those many novels of good and evil, of working-class children shown to be valuable and sympathetic human beings, of social criticism and subtle education—books that insisted we could be better than we were. I used my belief in the power of good writing as a way of giving meaning to some of the injustices I saw around me.

When I was very young, still in high school, I thought about writing the way Fay Weldon outlined in her essay, "The City of Imagination," in *Letters to My Niece on First Reading Jane Austen*. I imagined that Literature was, as she named it, a city with many districts, or was like a great library of the human mind that included all the books ever written. But what was most important was the enormous diversity contained in that library of the mind, that imaginary city. I cruised that city and dreamed of being part of it, but I was fearful that anything I wrote would be relegated to unimportance—no matter how finely crafted my writing might be, no matter how hard I worked and how much I risked. I knew I was a lesbian, and I believed that meant I would always be a stranger in the city—unless I performed the self-defeating trick of disguising my imagination, hiding my class origin and sexual orientation, writing, perhaps, a comic novel about the poor or the sexually dysfunctional. If that was the only way in, it made sense to me how many of the writers I loved drank or did drugs or went slowly crazy, trying to appear to be something they were not. It was enough to convince me that there was no use in writing at all.

When feminism exploded in my life, it gave me a vision of the world totally different from everything I had ever assumed or hoped. The concept of a feminist literature offered the possibility of pride in my sexuality. It saved me from either giving up writing entirely, or the worse prospect of writing lies in order to achieve some measure of grudging acceptance. But at the same time, Feminism destroyed all my illusions about Literature. Feminism revealed the city as an armed compound to which I would never be admitted. It forced me to understand, suddenly and completely, that literature was written by men, judged by men. The city itself was a city of Man, a male mind even when housed in a female body. If that was so, all my assumptions about the worth of writing, particularly working-class writing, were false. Literature was a lie, a system of lies, the creation of liars, some of them sincere and unaware of the lies they retold, but all acting in the service of a Great Lie—what the system itself labeled Universal Truth. If that truth erased me and all those like me, then my hopes to change the world through writing were illusions. I lost my faith. I became a feminist activist propelled in part by outrage and despair, and a stubborn determination to shape a life, and create a literature, that was not a lie.

I think many lesbian and feminist writers my age had a similar experience. The realizations of feminist criticism made me feel as if the very ground on which I stood had become unsteady. Some of that shake-up was welcome and hopeful, but it also meant I had to make a kind of life raft for myself out of political conviction, which is why I desperately needed a feminist community and so feared being driven out of the one I found. I know many other women who felt the same way, who grew up in poverty and got their ideas of what might be possible from novels of social criticism, believing those books were about us even when they were obviously not. What the feminist critique of patriarchal literature meant was not only that all we had believed about the power of writing to change the world was not possible, but that to be true to our own vision, we had to create a new canon, a new literature. Believing in literature—a feminist literature—became a reason to spend my life in that pursuit.

There are times I have wondered if that loss of faith was really generational, or only my own. I have seen evidence of a similar attitude in the writing of many working-class lesbians who are my age peers, the sense of having been driven out of the garden of life, and a painful pride in that exile though still mourning the dream of worth and meaning. The feminist small press movement was created out of that failed belief and the hope of reestablishing a literature that we could believe in. Daughters, Inc., Know, Inc., Diana Press, *Amazon Quarterly, Quest, Conditions* . . . right down to *OUT/LOOK*. All those magazines and presses—the ones I have worked with and supported even when I found some of the writing tedious or embarrassing—were begun in that spirit of rejecting the false ideal for a true one. This was a very mixed enterprise at its core, because creating honest work in which we did not have to mask our actual experiences, or our sexuality and gender, was absolutely the right thing to do, but rejecting the established literacy canon was not simple, and throwing out the patriarchy put so much else in question. Many of us lost all sense of what could be said to be good or bad writing, or how to think about being writers while bypassing the presses, grants, and teaching programs that might have helped us devote the majority of our time to writing, to creating a body of work.

The difficulty faced by lesbian and feminist writers of my generation becomes somewhat more understandable if we think about the fact that almost no lesbian-feminist writer my age was able to make a living as a writer. Most of us wrote late at night after exhausting and demanding day jobs, after evenings and weekends of political activism, meetings, and demonstrations. Most of us also devoted enormous amounts of time and energy to creating presses and journals that embodied our political ideals, giving up the time and energy we might have used to actually do our own writing. During my involvement with *Quest*, I wrote one article. The rest of my writing time was given over to grant applications and fund-raising letters. I did a little better with *Conditions,* beginning to actually publish short stories, but the vast majority of work I did there was editing other people's writing and again, writing grants and raising money. Imagine how few paintings or sculptures would be created if the artists all had to collectively organize the creation of canvas and paint, build and staff the galleries, and turn back all the money earned from sales into the maintenance of the system. Add to that the difficulty of creating completely new philosophies about what would be suitable subjects for art, what approaches would be valid for artists to take to their work, who, in fact, would be allowed to say what was valuable and what was not, or more tellingly, what could be sold and to whom. Imagine that system and you have the outlines of some of the difficulties faced by lesbian writers of my generation.

As a writer, I think I lost at least a decade in which I might have done more significant work because I had no independent sense of my work's worth. If Literature was a dishonest system by which the work of mediocre men and women could be praised for how it fit into a belief system that devalued women, queers, people of color, and the poor, then how could I try to become part of it? Worse, how could I judge any piece of writing, how could I know what was good or bad, worthwhile or a waste of time? To write for that system was to cooperate in your own destruction, certainly in your misrepresentation. I never imagined that what we were creating was also limited, that it, too, reflected an unrealistic or dishonest vision. But that's what we did, at least in part, making an ethical system that insists a lightweight romance has the same worth as a serious piece of fiction, that there is no good or bad, no "objective" craft or standards of excellence.

I began to teach because I had something I wanted to say, opinions that seemed to me rare and important and arguable. I wanted to be part of the conversation I saw going on all around, the one about the meaning and use of writing. The first literature classes I taught were not-for-credit workshops in a continuing education program in Tallahassee, Florida. When I moved to Washington, D.C. to work on *Quest* in 1975, I volunteered to help teach similar workshops through the women's center, and in Brooklyn in 1980 I joined with some of the women of *Conditions* to participate in a series of classes organized to specifically examine class and race issues in writing. Working as an editor, talking with other lesbian and gay writers, arguing about how fiction relates to real life—all of that helped me to systematically work out what I truly believed about literature, about writing, about its use and meaning, and the problematic relationship of writing to literature.

Starting in 1988 in San Francisco, I began to teach writing workshops because it was one of the ways I could earn rent and grocery money without taking a full-time job and still be able to write as much as possible. But teaching full time taught me how much I loved teaching itself, at least teaching writing, and how good I could be at it. Sometimes my writing classes gave me a great deal more than rent or groceries; sometimes they gave me a reason to believe in writing itself.

If you want to write good fiction, I am convinced you have to first decide what that means. This is what I always tell my students. They think I'm being obvious at the outset, and that the exercise is a waste of time, as it could be if I did not require that they apply their newly determined standards to their own work. Figure it out for yourself, I tell them. Your lovers will try to make you feel good, your friends will just lie, and your critics can only be trusted so far as they have in mind the same standards and goals that you do.

I have used one exercise in every writing class that is designed to provoke the students into thinking about what they really believe about the use of literature. In the beginning, I did not realize how much it would also challenge my own convictions. I require my students to spend the first weeks collecting examples of stories they can categorically label *good* and *bad*. I make them spend those weeks researching and arguing, exchanging favorite stories, and talking about what they have actually read, not pretend to have read. I want them to be excited and inspired by sharing stories they love, and to learn to read critically at the same time, to begin to see the qualities that make a story good and determine for themselves what makes a story bad. Near the end of the class they are asked to bring in what they think is the best and worst story they have ever read, along with a list of what constitutes a good story, and what a bad one, and to support their ideas from their examples. I tell my students to keep in mind that all such judgments, including those about craft and technique, are both passionately subjective and slyly political.

The difficult thing about this exercise is that young writers love to talk about bad writing, to make catty jokes about this writer or that, but only so long as none of that nastiness is turned on them. It is always a struggle to get students to confront what is flawed in their stories without losing heart for the struggles of writing, to help them develop a critical standard without destroying their confidence in their own work, or what their work can become. I encourage young writers to find truly remarkable work by people like them, writers who share something of their background or core identity, because I have discovered that every young writer fears that they and their community are the ones who are not as good as the more successful mainstream writing community. I prod young lesbians and gay men to find work by other queers from the small and experimental presses. Then I try to make them think about what they could be writing that they haven't even thought about before. They become depressed and scared when it is difficult for them to locate queer stories they believe are really good, but I am ruthless about making them see what hides behind some of their easy assumptions about the nature of good literature. Sometimes I feel like a literary evangelist, preaching the gospel of truth and craft. I tell them they are the generation that might be able to do something truly different, write the stories that future readers will call unqualifiedly good, but only if they understand what can make that possible, and always, that part of the struggle is a necessity to learn their own history.

In one of my most extraordinary classes the exercise worked better than I had hoped when one of the women brought in a "best" selection that was another woman's choice for "worst." The situation was made more difficult for me because her bad story was one I loved, a painful but beautifully written account of a female survival after rape in a wilderness setting. It was bad, said my student, because of how well-written and carefully done it was. It stayed in her mind, disturbed her, made her nervous and unhappy every time she went into the woods. She didn't want those ideas in her head, had enough violence and struggle in her life, enough bad thoughts to confront all the time. I understood exactly what she was saying. She was, after all, a lesbian-feminist activist of my generation, and both of us were familiar with the kind of feminist literary criticism that supported her response to the story. But many of the students were younger and frankly confused.

Subjective, I reminded myself then. We had agreed that essentially judgments about fiction are subjective—mine as well as my students'. But the storyteller seized up inside me. I thought of my stories, my characters, the albino child I murdered in "Gospel Song," the gay man who kills his lover in "Interesting Death," the little girl who tries to seduce her uncle in "Private Rituals." Bad characters, bad acts, bad thoughts— as well-written as I can make them because I want my people to be believable, my stories to haunt and obsess my readers. I want, in fact, to startle my readers, shock and terrify sometimes, to fascinate and surprise. To show them something they have not imagined, people and tales they will feel strongly about in spite of themselves, or what they would prefer to feel, or not feel. I want my stories to be so good they are unforgettable, to make my ideas live, my memories sing, and my own terrors real for people I will never meet. It is a completely amoral writer's lust, and I know that the author of that "bad" story felt it too. We all do, and if we begin to agree that some ideas are too dangerous, too bad to invite inside our heads, then we stop the storyteller completely. We silence everyone who would tell us something that might be painful in our vulnerable moments.

Everything I know, everything I put in my fiction, will hurt someone somewhere as surely as it will comfort and enlighten someone else. What then is my responsibility? What am I to restrain? What am I to fear and alter—my own nakedness or the grief of the reader?

My students are invariably determined that their stories will be powerful, effective, crafted, and unforgettable, not the crap that so embarrasses them. "Uh-huh," I nod at them, not wanting to be patronizing but remembering when I was twenty-four and determined to start my own magazine, to change how people thought about women, poor people, lesbians, and literature itself. Maybe it will be different in their lifetimes, I think, though part of me does believe it is different already. But more is possible than has yet been accomplished, and what I have done with my students is plant a seed that I expect to blossom in a new generation.

Once in a while one of my students will ask me, "Why have there been no great lesbian novels?" I do not pretend that they are wrong, do not tell them how many of the great writers of history were lesbians. They and I know that a lesbian author does not necessarily write a lesbian novel. Most often I simply disagree and offer a list of what I believe to be good lesbian writing. It is remarkable to me that as soon as I describe some wonderful story as being by a lesbian, there is always someone who wants to argue whether the individual involved really deserves that label. I no longer participate in this pointless argument. I feel that as a lesbian I have a perfect right to identify some writing as lesbian regardless of whether the academy or contemporary political theorists would agree with me.

What I find much more interesting is that so many of my gay and lesbian and feminist students are unaware of their own community's history. They may have read *Common Lives/Lesbian Lives, On Our Backs*, or various 'zines, and joke about any magazine that could publish such trivial fiction, believing the magazines contemptible because they do not edit badly written polemics and true confessions. But few of them know anything about the ideology that made many of us in the 1970s abandon the existing literary criterion to create our own.

We believed that editing itself was a political act, and we questioned what was silenced when raw and rough work by women outside the accepted literary canon was rewritten or edited in such a way that the authentic voices were erased. My students have no sense of how important it was to let real women tell their stories in their own words. I try to explain, drawing their attention to ethnographies and oral histories, techniques that reveal what is so rarely shown in traditionally edited fiction—powerful, unusual voices not recognized by the mainstream. I tell them how much could not be published or even written before the creation of the queer and lesbian presses which honored that politic. I bring in old copies of Daughters books, not *Rubyfruit Jungle*, which they know, but *The True Story of a Drunken Mother* by Nancy Hall, which mostly they haven't seen. I make it personal and tell them bluntly that I would never have begun to write anything of worth without the example of those presses and magazines reassuring me that my life, and my family's life, was a fit subject for literature.

As I drag my poor students through my own version of the history of lesbian and gay publishing, I am painfully aware that the arguments I make—that I pretend are so clear and obvious—are still completely unresolved. I pretend to my students that there is no question about the value of writing, even though I know I have gone back and forth from believing totally in it to being convinced that books never really change anything and are only published if they don't offend people's dearly held prejudices too much. So affecting confidence, I still worry about what I truly believe about literature and my writing.

Throughout my work with the lesbian and gay, feminist, and small press movements, I went on reading the enemy—mainstream literature—with a sense of guilt and uncertainty that I might be in some way poisoning my mind, and wondering, worrying, trying to develop some sense of worth outside purely political judgments. I felt like an apostate who still mumbles prayers in moments of crisis. I wanted to hear again the equivalent of the still, small voice of God telling me: Yes, Dorothy, books are important. Fiction is a piece of truth that turns lies to meaning. Even outcasts can write great books. I wanted to be told that it is only the form that has failed, that the content was still there—like a Catholic who returns to God but never the church.

The result has been that after years of apostasy, I have come to make distinctions between what I call the academy and literature, the moral equivalents of the church and God. The academy may lie, but literature tries to tell the truth. The academy is the market—university courses in contemporary literature that never get past Faulkner, reviewers who pepper their opinions with the ideas of the great men, and editors who think something is good because it says the same thing everyone has always said. Literature is the lie that tells the truth, that shows us human beings in pain and makes us love them, and does so in a spirit of honest revelation. That's radical enough, and more effective than only publishing unedited oral history. It is the stance I assumed when I decided I could not live without writing fiction and trying to publish it for the widest possible audience. It is the stance I maintain as I try to make a living by writing, supplemented with teaching, and to publish with both a mainstream publishing house and a small lesbian press. What has been extraordinarily educational and difficult to accept these past few years of doing both has been the recognition that the distinction between the two processes is nowhere near as simple or as easily categorized as I had once thought.

In 1989, when I made the decision to take my novel *Bastard Out of Carolina* to a mainstream press, I did so in part because I did not believe I could finish it without financial help. I was broke, sick, and exhausted. My vision had become so bad I could no longer assume I could go back at any time to doing computer work or part-time clerical jobs. I had to either find a completely new way to make a living and devote myself to that enterprise, or accept the fact that I was going to have to try to get an advance that would buy me at least two years to finish the book. Finally, I also knew that this book had become so important to me that I *had* to finish it, even if it meant doing something I had never assumed I would do. Reluctantly, I told Nancy Bereano what I was doing with *Bastard*, and then approached a friend to ask him to act as my agent. I had never worked with an agent before, but all my political convictions convinced me I could not trust mainstream presses and did not know enough to be able to deal with them. In fact, I learned while doing journalism in New York in the 1980s that I was terrible at the business end of writing, rotten at understanding the arcane language of contracts. In some ways my worst fears were realized. Selling a manuscript to strangers is scary.

What most surprised me, however, was learning that mainstream publishing was not a monolith, and finding there not only people who believed in literature the way I did, but lesbians and gay men who worked within mainstream publishing because of their belief in the importance of good writing and how it can change the world. Mostly younger, and without my experience of the lesbian and gay small presses, they talked in much the same way as I did about their own convictions, the jobs they took that demanded long hours and paid very poorly but let them work, at least in part, with writing and writers they felt vindicated their sacrifices. Talking to those men and women shook up a lot of my assumptions, particularly when I began to work with heterosexuals who did not seem uniformly homophobic or deluded or crassly obsessed with getting rich as quickly as possible. I found within mainstream publishing a great many sincere and hopeful people of conviction and high standards who forced me to reexamine some of my most ingrained prejudices. If I was going to continue to reject the ideology and standards of mainstream literature, I had to become a lot more clear and specific about the distinction between the patriarchal literature I had been trying to challenge all my life and the good-hearted individuals I encountered within those institutions.

As I was finishing the copyediting of *Bastard*, I found myself thinking about all I had read when Kate Millett published *Flying*: her stated conviction that telling the truth was what feminist writers were supposed to do. That telling the truth—your side of it anyway, knowing that there were truths other than your own—was a moral act, a courageous act, an act of rebellion that would encourage other such acts. Like Kate Millett, I knew that what I wanted to do as a lesbian and a feminist writer was to remake the world into a place where the truth would be hallowed, not held in contempt, where silence would be impossible.

Sometimes it seems that all I want to add to her philosophy is the significance of craft, a restatement of the importance of deeply felt, powerful writing versus a concentration on ethnography, or even a political concentration on adding certain information to the canon—information about our real lives that would make it possible for lesbians, working-class runaways, incest survivors, and stigmatized and vilified social outlaws to recognize themselves and their experiences. If I throw everything out and start over without rhetoric or a body of theory behind my words, I am left with the simple fact that what I want as a writer is to be able to tell the truth so well and so powerfully that it will have to be heard, understood, and acted on. It's why I have worked for years on lesbian, feminist, and gay publishing, for no money and without much hope, and why my greatest sorrow has been watching young writers do less than their best because they have no concept of what good writing can be and what it can accomplish.

I started this whole process—forcing my students' discussion of the good and the bad—in order to work on my own judgment, to hold it up to outside view. I can take nothing for granted with these twenty-year-olds, and there is always at least one old-line feminist there to keep me honest, to ask why and make me say out loud all the things I have questioned and tried to understand. Sometimes it helps a lot. Sometimes it drives me back down inside myself, convincing me all over again that Literature belongs to the Other—either the recognized institutions or my innocent students who have never known my self-conscious sense of sin, my old loss of faith. They question so little, don't even know they have a faith to lose. There are times I look at my writing and despair. I cannot always make it the story I think should be told, cannot make it an affirmation or anything predictable or easy or sometimes even explainable. The story tells itself, banal or not. What, then, is the point of literary criticism that tells writers what they should be writing rather than addressing what is on the page?

The novel I am working on now seems to be driving me more crazy in the actual writing of it than it ever did when I was trying to get around to the writing of it. I don't understand if it is just me or the process itself, since many other writers I have talked to are noncommunicative about the work of writing itself. Everyone discusses day jobs, teaching, what they read, music, being interviewed, groups they work with, things they want to do when this project is finished.

But over here, I am halfway done with the thing and feel like I have nothing, know nothing, am nothing. Can't sleep, and part of the time I can't even work, staying up till 4:00 or 5:00 in the morning. Thinking. About what, people ask, the book? I stare blankly, sometimes unable to explain and other times too embarrassed. I think about the book, yes, but also about my childhood, my family, and about sex, violence, what people will ask me when they read this book, about my ex-girlfriends and what they will say, about my hips and how wide they have become, my eyesight that is steadily growing worse, the friends who have somehow become strangers, even enemies, the friends who have died without ever managing to do the things they wanted to do, how old I have gotten not recognizing that time was actually passing, about why I am a lesbian and not heterosexual, about children and whether the kind of writing I do will endanger my relationship to my son—allow someone to take him away from me or accuse me of being a bad mother—and about all the things I was not told as a child that I had to make up for myself. When I am writing I sink down into myself, my memory, dreams, shames, and terrors. I answer questions no one has asked but me, avoid issues no one else has raised, and puzzle out just where my responsibility to the real begins and ends. Morality and ethics are the heart of what I fear, that I might fail in one or the other, that people like me cannot help but fail to show true ethical insight or moral concern. Then I turn my head and fall into the story, and all that thinking becomes background to the novel writing itself, the voices that are only partly my own. What I can tell my students is that the theory and philosophy they take so seriously and pick apart with such angst and determination is still only accompaniment to the work of writing, and that process, thankfully, no matter what they may imagine, is still not subject to rational determined construction.

A few years ago I gave a copy of a piece of "fiction" I had written about incest and adult sexual desire to a friend of mine, a respected feminist editor and activist. "What," she asked me, "do you want from me about this? An editorial response, a personal one, literary or political?" I did not know what to say to her, never having thought about sorting out reading in that way. Certainly, I wanted my story to move her, to show her something about incest survivors, something previously unimaginable and astounding—and not actually just one thing either, as I did not want one thing from her. The piece had not been easy for me, not simple to write or think about afterward. It had walked so close to my own personal history, my nightsweats, shame, and stubborn endurance. What did I want? I wanted the thing all writers want—for the world to break open in response to my story. I wanted to be understood finally for who I believe myself to be, for the difficulty and grief of using my own pain to be justified. I wanted my story to be unique and yet part of something greater than myself. I wanted to be seen for who I am and still appreciated—not denied, not simplified, not lied about or refused or minimized. The same thing I have always wanted.

I have wanted everything as a writer and a woman, but most of all a world changed utterly by my revelations. Absurd, arrogant, and presumptuous to imagine that fiction could manage that—even the fiction I write which is never wholly fictive. I change things. I lie, I embroider, make over, and reuse the truth of my life, my family, lovers, and friends. Acknowledging this, I make no apologies, knowing that what I create is as crafted and deliberate as the work of any other poet, novelist, or short story writer. I choose what to tell and what to conceal. I design and calculate the impact I want to have. When I sit down to make my stories I know very well that I want to take the reader by the throat, break her heart, and heal it again. With that intention I cannot sort out myself, say this part is for the theorist, this for the poet, this for the editor, and this for the wayward ethnographer who only wants to document my experience.

"Tell me what you really think," I told my friend. "Be personal. Be honest." Part of me wanted to whisper, Take it seriously, but be kind. I did not say that out loud, however. I could not admit to my friend how truly terrified I was that my story did none of what I had wanted—not and be true to the standard I have set for myself. Writing terrible stories has meaning only if we hold ourselves to the same standard we set for our readers. Every time I sit down to write, I have a great fear that anything I write will reveal me as the monster I was always told I would be, but that fear is personal, something I must face in everything I do, every act I contemplate. It is the whisper of death and denial. Writing is an act that claims courage and meaning, and turns back denial, breaks open fear, and heals me as it makes possible some measure of healing for all those like me.

Some things never change. There is a place where we are always alone with our own mortality, where we must simply have something greater than ourselves to hold onto—God or history or politics or literature or a belief in the healing power of love, or even righteous anger. Sometimes I think they are all the same. A reason to believe, a way to take the world by the throat and insist that there is more to this life than we have ever imagined.

"JCO" AND I

It is a fact that, to that other, nothing ever happens. I, a mortal woman, move through my life with the excited interest of a swimmer in uncharted waters—my predilections are few, but intense—while she, the other, is a mere shadow, a blur, a figure glimpsed in the corner of the eye. Rumors of "JCO" come to me thirdhand and usually unrecognizable, arguing, absurdly, for her historical existence. But while *writing* exists, *writers* do not—as all writers know. It's true, I see her photograph—*my* "likeness"—yet it is rarely the same "likeness" from photograph to photograph, and the expression is usually one of faint bewilderment. *I acknowledge that I share a name and a face with "JCO,"* this expression suggests, *but this is a mere convenience. Please don't be deceived!"*

"JCO" is not a person, nor even a personality, but a process that has resulted in a sequence of texts. Some of the texts are retained in my (our) memory, but some have bleached out, like pages of print left too long in the sun. Many of the texts have been translated into foreign languages, which is to say into texts at another remove from the primary—sometimes even the author's name, on the dust jacket of one of these texts, is unrecognizable by the author. I, on the contrary, am fated to be "real"—"physical"—"corporeal"—to "exist in Time." I continue to age year by year, if not hour by hour, while "JCO," the other, remains no fixed age—in spiritual essence, perhaps, forever poised between the fever of idealism and the chill of cynicism, a precocious eighteen years old. Yet, can a process be said to have an age? an impulse, a strategy, an obsessive tracery, like planetary orbits to which planets, "real" planets, must conform?

No one wants to believe this obvious truth: the "artist" can inhabit any individual, for the individual is irrelevant to "art." (And what is "art"? A firestorm rushing through Time, arising from no visible source and conforming to no principles of logic or causality.) "JCO" occasionally mines, and distorts, my personal history; but only because the history is close at hand, and then only when some idiosyncrasy about it suits her design, or some curious element of the symbolic. If you, a friend of mine, should appear in her work, have no fear—you won't recognize yourself, any more than I would recognize you.

It would be misleading to describe our relationship as hostile in any emotional sense, for she, being bodiless, having no existence, has no emotions: we are more helpfully defined as diamagnetic, the one repulsing the other as magnetic poles repulse each other, so that "JCO" eclipses me, or, and this is less frequent, I eclipse "JCO," depending upon the strength of my will.

If one or the other of us must be sacrificed, it has always been me.

And so my life continues through the decades . . . not connected in the slightest with that conspicuous other with whom, by accident, I share a name and a likeness. The fact seems self-evident that I was but the door through which she entered—"it" entered—but any door would have done as well. Does it matter which entrance you use to enter a walled garden? Once you're inside and have closed the door?

For once, not she but I am writing these pages. Or so I believe.

THOMAS E. KENNEDY

REALISM &
OTHER ILLUSIONS

AWP CHRONICLE

When we read a piece of fiction, what is it about the work that inspires the "willing suspension of disbelief" which Coleridge identified as necessary to the experience of literature? What makes us willing, even eager to believe that the artificial world into which the writer invites us is a real one? The problem may not be so acute with realistic works—if we pick up a book and begin to read, for example:

> The Jackman's marriage had been adulterous and violent, but in its last days, they became a couple again, as they might have if one of them were slowly dying,

we accept immediately the premise. With this opening to his story, "The Winter Father," Andre Dubus fills us in on the essence of a compelling situation which we automatically place in a setting in the real world, and he goes on to tell skillfully a moving story about the dissolution of family life which is or was so central to the short story of the eighties.

Likewise, we react with belief when we read the opening of Raymond Carver's "Collectors."

> I was out of work. But any day I expected to hear from up north. I lay on the sofa and listened to the rain. Now and then I'd lift up and look through the curtain for the mailman.

The scene is not unfamiliar. It is set with objects familiar to us, simple actions that we know from our own experience, charged subtly with emotions that we ourselves have experienced or could easily imagine experiencing.

Gladys Swan opens her novel *Carnival for the Gods* like this:

> It was the first time Dusty had ever backhanded her, and it was not just the blow, the pain, the blood from her lip flowing saltily into her mouth that gave Alta the shock: it was the sense that something fatal had struck at the roots of her life.

Again, a situation sufficiently grounded in recognizably real detail to be accepted without trouble as reality, as is this opening of Francois Camoin's story, "Lieberman's Father":

> Lieberman had his eyes on his chicken salad and so at first didn't see the woman. She stopped short at his table and stood swaying a little this way and that, looking like a person who has just bumped into something and is wondering if she's hurt herself.

Such openings seem immediately real enough, "normal" enough not to raise questions in our minds about where they are happening. They seem to be happening in the same world we occupy, and we accept it as such. But sometimes they seem to nudge toward the border of another dimension. Here's how Gordon Weaver's "The Interpreter" starts:

> It is as if . . . It is as if I cannot remember the things I must say to myself. It is as if all the words I know in both English and my native Mandarin have fled from me, evaporated into the cold, misty air of this wretched place, into the wet fogs that greet us each morning . . . It is as if each bitter day is the first and I wake chilled . . . knowing nothing until I can remember some words, something to say to myself that will allow me to rise.

Not *un*realistic, yet there is an edge of the other there that makes us a little unsure just where we are. And what is one to make of a short story from *Leaf Storm* by Gabriel Garcia Márquez, a story that opens with a character named Palayo walking home from the beach, entering his courtyard to find "a very old man, lying face down in the mud" and unable to rise because "his enormous wings" are in the way? How are we to suspend our disbelief and enter Márquez's world—even if we desperately want to?

Or the opening of Robert Coover's story "Beginnings":

> In order to get started, he went to live alone on an island and shot himself. His blood, unable to resist a final joke, splattered the cabin wall in a pattern that read: It is important to begin when everything is already over.

How are we to be encouraged or enabled to incorporate the conditions of that bizarre world into our own experience?

All of the examples given above can be grouped into two different categories which differ from each other in one basic manner of narrative strategy. The first five examples (Dubus, Carver, Swan, Camoin, Weaver) begin in more or less clear "realistic" modes, invite us into a world which from the start presents itself as part of the world we automatically would assume to be the setting of any occurrence related to us, be it fiction or nonfiction. The setting, we assume, is *our* world, *here*, where we live, or at least in some other land that really exists and can be "seen" in the Atlas. With Weaver, we are a little uncertain where we are, and with an opening like Márquez's or Coover's we know that the setting is not a "real" one, that the "place" in which the story occurs would seem rather to be located somewhere in the imagination than in the external world.

How, then, is the writer to persuade us of the "reality" of what he is reporting in a manner as though it is really occurring or has occurred? How does the author succeed in making us read on, in suspending our disbelief?

It is important to recognize that all of the above examples are examples of illusion, whether the illusion is a realistic one, a surrealistic one, a superrealistic one, or a so-called fabulist, metafictional, or postmodern one. It was the French novelist Émile Zola who said, "The realists of art should really be called the illusionists."

While the overall technique or strategy may vary, the basic trick, the basic illusion is generally pretty much the same, and this is what we call verisimilitude—from the Latin *verisimilitudo*—or *verus similis*—*verus* (true) and *similis* (similar), or the French *vrai semblance*—that is, something which has the appearance of being true or real, something which *seems* to be true or plausible or likely. Some theorists, like John Gardner, hold the use of verisimilitude to mean that the writer evokes, in a large sense, a "true likeness" of the world in which we live—which harkens back to Aristotle's mimetic theory of art put forth in *Poetics*—but this seems to me too narrow a view of the concept and, ultimately, one which cannot hold, for *no* writer of fiction, not even the most realistic, not even the superrealists, the Edward Hoppers or Duane Hansens or Trampedach's of prose, fashions a "true likeness" of the world. Have you ever noticed that in Hopper's wonderful evocative portraits of the city there is never any rubbish in the street? All manner of distortion, selection, rearrangement of facts and details is necessary in the writing of fiction, as will be discussed further below. Therefore, I will hold to the interpretation of the concept of verisimilitude as merely the creation of an imaginary universe which *seems* to be real, and I would suggest that *all* writers of fiction seek to create an imaginary universe which seems to be real, via the use, either continual or occasional, of verisimilitude.

What is verisimilitude? My definition is this: Verisimilitude is that quality of a work of fiction by which a physical, psychological, and spiritual reality is rendered such that the reader is persuaded to suspend disbelief in order that the author's creative discovery regarding existence—and I believe that every true work of art entails a discovery—may be explored and experienced by the reader.

How can this concept apply to the last two examples given above? Garcia Márquez and Coover. How can such pieces be given the appearance of reality, most specifically of a physical reality?

As Flannery O'Connor says, "Fiction begins where human knowledge begins—with the senses." We have only five ways of perceiving reality: we can *see* it, *hear it, taste* it, *smell* it, *touch* it.

Or, in the case of fiction, we can *seem* to do these things.

Let's look at how Márquez does this with the old man with wings. How does he make us believe in this? First of all, he is lying in the mud, about as vivid and clearly grounded an image as can be found. If he appeared flying above Palayo's head, or seated on a cloud with a harp and wearing immaculate white linen, our doubt might be so much stronger, but when we see the mud on the old angel's face, our senses begin to respond, our perception of our senses, and as we read on we learn that this old man has very few teeth in his mouth and that "his huge buzzard wings" are "dirty and half-plucked." As we get even closer, we learn further that the old angel has "an unbearable smell," and that the backs of his wings are infested with lice! This Márquez, we begin to feel, he knows his angels! By now the reader has seen and smelled this creature and has shivered at the sight of the lice chewing at the spotty pink chicken flesh of his wings, and this preposterous bizarre creature has been admitted into our imagination by Garcia's brilliant use of verisimilitude—the replica of that which our senses can perceive, even if only the imaginary counterparts of our senses perceiving the imagined aspects of an image.

Thus, Márquez has shocked us out of our normal expectations of reality, only to coax us back in again by manipulating our senses, turning them against our skepticism. We are made to *smell* the universe being painted in the sky for us. How can you deny the existence of something that *stinks*?

Interestingly, though, if we look further at some of the so called "realistic" examples given above—let's pick Camoin and Swan—we will find a strategy which is very much the reverse of that used by the Márquez example given.

In the Camoin story, we follow a half page of fairly ordinary realistic description. The woman speaks to the man at the table, addresses him by his name. He does not recognize her, asks how she could know his name, and she tells him he'll have to prepare himself for a shock. "This won't be easy for you," she says. She asks permission to sit down, to drink a glass of water, and then she tells him, "I am your father."

He says, "I already have a father," and she responds, "I am

your real father." And the remainder of this realistic story deals with the main character dealing with this incomprehensible, impossible, unreal, paradoxical yet somehow intriguing, compelling situation of a man being accosted by a woman who claims to be his real father. Camoin snares us in a realistic trap into following an impossible situation.

Similarly, Gladys Swan's realistic story begins with something about as real and concrete as can be: a smack in the mouth, a cut lip, the taste of blood on the tongue. We know that pain, discomfort of running the edge of the tongue over a sore inside the lip, the salt taste of blood, and we are with her at once. But that story turns out to be the first chapter of a novel in which the world she will lead us into will become more and more strange, surreal, a world which is deep within the imagination the deeper we follow. But we *do* follow because she has made us taste the blood of her world, "proving" its existence to us, coaxing us in by realistic details in a somewhat similar way that fairy tales do. As Bruno Bettelheim points out in his book *The Uses of Enchantment: On the Interpretation of Fairy Tales*, fairy tales "usually start out in a quite realistic way: a mother telling her daughter to go all by herself to visit grandmother. . . ." as the beginning of a series of increasingly mythical, symbolic, and often terrifying occurrences.

Interesting comparisons and contrasts can be made between the ways in which Swan employs verisimilitude and the ways it is used by Gordon Weaver and by Andre Dubus in their stories. Weaver, in his story collection *A World Quite Round* employs essentially realistic narrative in a variety of ways that veer across realism's borders into regions of intentional anti-illusionism, where he discusses the illusions he is creating and, ironically, in the process, creates an even stronger illusion—that of the truth speaker who destroys illusions. Or else he constructs a kind of shadow story exploring the nature of the language in which the story is told—as with his fine novella "The Interpreter." Or he deals subtly with the creation of art in general and its relation to identity and existence as in his story "Ah Art! Oh Life!"

In virtually all of Andre Dubus's stories, he has sought his metaphors and meanings in the daily experiences of the lives of his characters, in a realism which aims as nearly as possible to imitate a reality experienced by real people in a real world.

But what all these examples have in common is that by manipulating the details of physical or sensory "reality" of the fictional world, the writer creates a dimension to house its psychological and spiritual reality as well: Coover's linguistic island where death is the beginning and blood writes sentences on the wall, Swan's carnival, Weaver's world of language, Camoin's paradox, but also the psychological or spiritual reality of a world like our own, as in the work of Dubus, Carver, and all the other "realists" of our time.

Psychological and spiritual verisimilitude will also be achieved via the recording of a fictional character's private perceptions—as when Alta, smacked in the mouth by her husband, experiences a sense of danger having entered the roots of her existence.

Such use of verisimilitude to suspend disbelief of a world existing in whole or part beyond the world of the senses, per se, created in a dimension only of sensual *image* or imitation, also calls to mind Hawthorne's definition of fiction as "a neutral territory somewhere between the real world and fairyland where the actual and imaginary may meet and each imbue itself with the nature of the other" and Melville's reference to it as exhibiting "more reality than real life itself can show."

Earlier, I mentioned John Gardner's view of the concept of verisimilitude—his conception that a fiction of verisimilitude was a wholly realistic one meant to be experienced as occurring in the imagined reflection, if you will, of the world in which we find ourselves—recalling Aristotle's mimetic theory of art.

In contrast to this we have theories such as Jerome Klinkowitz's in *The Practice of Fiction in America*, which refers to the mimetic theory of art as "voodoo," an attempt to substitute the fiction for what is real.

Alain Robbe-Grillet has said, ". . . academic criticism in the West as in the communist countries, employs the word 'realism' as if reality were already entirely constituted . . . when the writer comes on the scene. Thus it supposes that the latter's role is limited to 'explaining' and 'expressing' the reality of his period." This, in opposition to the view of fiction as *creative* of reality.

So now we are back to the question of whether not "realism" but reality itself is a fiction forged of the language in which it is expressed.

It is interesting to think of this in relation to some examples of political propaganda. Following the troubles in the People's Republic of China a few years ago, the Chinese Government began issuing a series of booklets whose aim clearly was to write the history of the events in Tiananmen Square. As they put it in one of their press releases, "At present . . . many people are not clear about the truth. Therefore, there is a need to explain the truth about the counter-revolutionary rebellion. . . ."

There is a wild beauty in the raging naivete of this which makes me think of some of the tarter fictions of Donald Barthelme where one is hypnotized by statements of blatant paradox. "She comes to him fresh from the bath, opens her robe. 'Goodbye,' she explains. 'Goodbye.' "

One of my favorite of the Chinese propaganda booklets is the one titled "How Chinese View the Riot in Beijing," in which the anonymous propaganda writer composes a number of fictional personas and has them present their "view" of what happened. For example, there is one titled, "An Old Worker on the Riot" which begins,

> I am an ordinary old worker. In the recent period when I saw our sacred and solemn Tiananmen Square become a scene of great disorder and confusion, a filthy place that gave off a strong smell, I felt as if a fire were burning in my heart. In those days, a gang of counter-revolutionary thugs made unbridled attacks on the Chinese Communist Party. . . ."

Clearly a case of political coopting of the fictional technique of realism, verisimilitude, and persona (Greek for mask) to present a fabricated version of reality, an illusion.

Of course, the West too uses fictional technique in its propaganda. I have a nice sleek booklet entitled: *Ladies and Gentlemen:*

The 41st President of the United States, distributed immediately after George Bush was elected and which also seems aimed at the creation of a fictional persona:

> George took after his ebullient and empathetic mother. He liked pleasing people. 'He was the easiest child to bring up,' his mother says, 'very obedient.' The Bushes competed at everything—golf, tennis, tiddlywinks—anything that measured one person against another. . . .
>
> The concept of family was so powerful that it sometimes seemed to friends that the Bush children functioned as a single mind rather than as five kids fighting for parental affection.

That single mind concept is kind of scarey—like science fiction, and the concept that a tiddlywinks match measures one person against another . . .

In his fascinating book *Fiction and the Figures of Life,* William H. Gass comments on the mimetic theory of fiction by pronouncing pathetic the view of fiction as creative of living persons rather than of mere characters by pointing out that fiction is made out of words and words only. "It is shocking really," he says, to realize this—rather like discovering after all those years "that your wife is made of rubber."

In *The Art of Fiction,* John Gardner says, "In any piece of fiction, the writer's first job is to convince the reader that the events he recounts really happened . . . or might have happened (given small changes in the laws of the universe). . . . The realistic writer's way of making events convincing is verisimilitude." Gardner says that the tools of verisimilitude are "actual settings (Cleveland, San Francisco, Joplin, Missouri), precision of detail . . . streets, stores, weather, politics, etc., and plausible behavior."

As an example, Gardner names the question, "Would a mother really say that?"—a question he claimed to pose every time a mother in fiction speaks. However, if we look at a piece called "The Philosophers" by Russell Edson, we read this opening:

"I think, therefore I am," said a man whose mother quickly hit him on the head saying, "I hit my son on his head, therefore I am. . . ."

According to Gardner's formula, we are obliged to ask ourselves, "Would a mother really say that?"

Well, I don't know, yes and no, she might not *say* it, she might just thump him on the head without explaining the importance of doing so for her own existential identity. Perhaps it presents a deeper level of reality of her behavior, of the relationship between the son and the mother, of human modes of existential identification. In other words, a mother might or might not actually say and do such a thing, but one recognizes immediately that that is not the point, that a reality is being presented via details that *could* occur, even if they are absurd, and thus here exists verisimilitude: we have a son, a mother, action speech. A son speaks, is hit, answered. It *could* have happened. We laugh or curl or toes. It is absurd, but it is also true, reveals a hidden reality in a very efficient manner, and really it doesn't matter at all whether it ever happened or is meant to have happened: we have followed Edson into a dimension of the imagination as surely as when we follow Alice through the looking glass.

Russell Edson is good at this kind of thing:

Father throws the baby in the air. The baby hits the ceiling. Stop, says mother, the ceiling is crying, you're hurting the ceiling.

Would a mother really say that? Well it is not inconceivable that some mother at some time whose little boy runs headlong into her Louis Quatorze writing table and falls bleeding profusely from the scalp upon her 19th century Persian carpet may have been heard to scream, "Oh God! My poor table! My beautiful carpet! You little fool!" That, too, is a kind of verisimilitude in certain cases.

Of course, it all comes down to the question, What is real? To many people, life sometimes seems little more than a series of repetitions of meaningless events: we rise, we eat, we go to work, we come home again, we eat, look at the tube, sleep, rise again, etc. If that is what our lives really have become, a story like Robert Coover's "The Elevator," written in rebellion against realism and the conventional view of an orderly reality, and depicting a series of scenes of a man entering his office building each day to ride up to his office and the adventures he experiences during those few minutes, is perhaps more realistic than surrealistic, even though the events depicted are far from conventional ones.

Perhaps such a fiction employs verisimilitude to portray an "unreal" world that reflects something more essential of contemporary existence than a story built on linear plot and movement in which a meaningful progression of events is depicted, leading from beginning through complication of logical occurrences and cause and effect to a climax and resolution.

Jimmy Carter, about eighteen years ago, looked directly into a TV camera and, imagining the American public, said, "I want you to listen carefully now. I will never tell you a lie."

Applying John Gardner's verisimilitude test to that, we may ask ourselves, "Would an American President really say that?"

Unlike Jimmy Carter, a fiction writer must select, manipulate, eliminate, foreshorten, lie—and he must do it in the interests of a truth greater than what can be found in our confusing everyday reality. He may lie by seeming to duplicate reality or by seeming to destroy it—the anti-illusionist we see at work for example in Gordon Weaver's story "The Parts of Speech" (from *A World Quite Round*) or in John Barth's *The Floating Opera* and *Lost in the Funhouse*. Barth begins *The Floating Opera* by having his first person creative narrator tell the reader that he has never written a novel before but has read a few to try to get the hang of it—immediately convincing the reader, duping him, into believing that this is not fiction, but a straight-from-the-heart account. Anti-illusion becomes in this way an even stronger illusion.

On the matter of dogmatic realism in fiction, when Ezra Pound complained to James Joyce that *Finnegans Wake* was obscure, Joyce answered, "Well now, Ezra, the action of my work takes place at night. It is natural, isn't it, that things should not be so clear at night?''

We have probably all seen spy films in which the action at night is so realistically depicted that we are left completely in the dark as to what is happening. The point is we don't have to *use* darkness to fictionalize the dark. We use words, impressions, and our aim in fiction is to elucidate the deeper reality of darkness, not to reproduce a sensation of being in the dark for the sake of that sensation.

I believe that an examination of virtually every fictional mode will show that verisimilitude is an element at work in all of them, that in a large sense all fiction writers are "realists," in that all are dealing with reality.

Realism is only one of a number of available artistic illusions, all of which depend for their plausibility on some measure of verisimilitude.

In Gladys Swan's novel *Carnival for the Gods*, a carnival illusionist, a sleight-of-hand "artist" who, in popular terms, is known as a "magician," is approached by a boy who believes the man's magic to be real and who asks to be taught the secrets of that art. The man is so unnerved by the boy's faith in magic that he lies to him and pretends that he *can* teach magic to the child in hopes that he will divert the boy from falling into evil secrets.

But the boy is undaunted. When, finally, the illusionist dies, the boy still believes that he can find what he seeks. He takes the dead magician's cape and goes off on his own, determined to search for what he seeks and, in the closing words of the book, "if he didn't find it, to create it in an imagined land."

I find this a concise and powerful summary of the process of art. Wrapped in the mantle of a fake circus magician, the artist sets out to imagine a land in which truth can be created.

For the fiction writer, verisimilitude is the tool of the imaginative act by which that truth is sought, the soil in which an imaginary garden can grow and provide a home for the toads of that which is genuine. And it is the same for the realist and for the innovator, the experimenter, the task is the same. All is permitted.

RICHARD LEDERER

CONAN THE GRAMMARIAN

ADVENTURES OF A VERBIVORE

The owner of a small zoo lost two of his prize animal attractions in a fire. To order another pair, he wrote a letter to a zoological supply company: "Dear Sirs: Please send me two mongooses."

That didn't sound quite right, so he began again with "Dear Sirs: Please send me two mongeese."

Still not sure of this plural, he pulled the letter out of the typewriter and made this third attempt: "Dear Sirs: Please send me a mongoose. And, while you're at it, please send me another mongoose."

Many people throughout our land are like the zoo owner, unsure about their "grammar" and fearful of public embarrassment. In my role as the monthly Grammar Grappler for *Writer's Digest*, as a language commentator on National Public Radio, and as a writer of books, columns, and articles about words and phrases, I am often asked to make Solomonic judgments about matters "grammatical." But, to clear up a term, the questions usually pertain to usage, not grammar.

Scholars of language define *grammar* as a set of rules that reflect how a language is actually used. All human beings do, in fact, speak and write in accord with the structure and patterns of their native tongue. In a broad sense, there is no such thing as ungrammatical English; "bad grammar" is a contradiction in terms. Everyone who speaks must use grammar, although some uses are more unconventional than others. "Him and me ain't got no money" and "Irregardless of our warning, he laid down on the railroad tracks" are perfectly grammatical because many fluent speakers of English speak and even write such sentences. But these statements do violate the rules of standard English usage, a set of conventions accepted by the well-educated and by knowledgeable grammarians.

Often there is a yawning chasm between the so-called rules of usage and the English language in action. A clear instance of this gulf is the use of a preposition to end a sentence. The rule banishing terminal prepositions from educated discourse was invented by the late-seventeenth-century British critic and poet John Dryden, who reasoned that *preposito* in Latin means something that "comes before" and that prepositions in Latin never appear at the end of a sentence. Dryden even went so far as to reedit his own works in order to remove the offending construction, and prescriptive grammarians have been preaching the dogma ever since.

Unfortunately, Dryden neglected to consider two crucial points. First, the rules of Latin don't always apply to English. There exist vast differences between the two languages in their manner of connecting verbs and prepositions. Latin is a language of cases, English a language of word order. In Latin, it is physically impossible for a preposition to appear at the end of a sentence. Second, the greatest writers in English, before and after the time of Dryden, have freely ended sentences with prepositions. Why? Because the construction is a natural and graceful part of our English idiom. Here are a few examples from the masters:

- "Fly to others that we know not of."—William Shakespeare

- "We are such stuff / As dreams are made on."
  —William Shakespeare

- "Houses are built to live in, not to look on."—Francis Bacon

- "What a fine conformity would it starch us all into."
  —John Milton

- ". . . soil good to be born on, good to live on, good to die for and to be buried in."—James Russell Lowell

- "All words are pegs to hang ideas on."—Henry Ward Beecher

The final preposition is one of the glories of the English language. If we shackle its idioms and muffle its music with false rules, we diminish the power of our language. If we rewrite the quotations above to conform to Dryden's edict, the natural beauty of our prose and verse is forced to bow before a stiff mandarin code of structure. "Fly to others of whom we know not"; "All words are pegs upon which to hang ideas"—now the statements are artificial—people simply don't talk like that—and, in most cases, wordier.

The most widely circulated tale of the terminal preposition involves Sir Winston Churchill, one of the greatest of all English prose stylists. As the story goes, a Whitehall editor had the audacity to "correct" a proof of Churchill's memoirs by revising a sentence that ended with the outlawed preposition. Sir Winston hurled back at the proofreader a memorable rebuttal: "This is the kind of impertinence up with which I will not put!"

A variation on this story concerns a newspaper columnist who responded snappily to the accusation that he was uncouthly violating the terminal-preposition "rule": "What do you take me for? A chap who doesn't know how to make full use of all the easy variety the English language is capable of? Don't you know that ending a sentence with a preposition is an idiom many famous writers are very fond of? They realize it's a colloquialism a skillful writer can do a great deal with. Certainly it's a linguistic device you ought to read about."

For the punster there's the setup joke about the prisoner who asked a female guard to marry him on the condition that she would help him to escape. He used a proposition to end a sentence with.

Then there's the one about the little boy who has just gone to bed when his father comes into the room carrying a book about Australia. Surprised, the boy asks, "What did you bring that book that I wanted to be read to out of from about Down Under up for?"

Now that's a sentence out of which you can get a lot.

My favorite of all terminal-preposition stories involves a boy attending public school and one attending private school who happen to be sitting next to each other in an airplane. To be friendly, the public schooler turns to the preppie and asks, "What school are you at?"

The private schooler looks down his aquiline nose at the public school student and comments, "I happen to attend an institution at which we are taught to know better than to conclude sentences with prepositions."

The boy at public school pauses for a moment and then says: "All right, then. What school are you at, dingbat!"

Joining the preposition rule in the rogues' gallery of usage enormities is the split infinitive. "Many years ago, when I was a junior in Thornton Academy in Saco, Maine, I was instructed never, under pain of sin, to split an infinitive," wrote one of my column readers. Note the expression *under pain of sin*. It speaks of the priestly power of the English teacher to interpret the verbal nature of the universe and to bring down from some kind of Mount Sinai commandments for the moral and ethical use of the Word.

A split infinitive ("to better understand," "to always disagree") occurs when an adverb or adverbial construction is placed between *to* and a verb. In a famous *New Yorker* cartoon we see Captain Bligh sailing away from the *Bounty* in a rowboat and shouting, "So, Mr. Christian! You propose to unceremoniously cast me adrift?" The caption beneath the drawing reads: "The crew can no longer tolerate Captain Bligh's ruthless splitting of infinitives."

When infinitives are cleft, some schoolmarms, regardless of sex or actual profession, become exercised, even though no reputable authority on usage, either in England or in the United States, bans the split infinitive. Good writers— Philip Sidney, John Donne, Samuel Pepys, Samuel Johnson, Lord Byron, George Eliot, Matthew Arnold, Thomas Hardy, Benjamin Franklin, Abraham Lincoln, Oliver Wendell Holmes, and Henry James, to name a dozen out of thousands—have been splitting infinitives ever since the early fourteenth century, long before science learned how to split the atom. The only explosions that occur when infinitives are split issue from Robert Lowth, an Anglican bishop and self-appointed grammarian who made up the "rule" in 1762, and from those whom

Henry W. Fowler, in his dictionary of *Modern English Usage*, describes as people who "betray by their practice that their aversion to the split infinitive springs not from instinctive good taste, but from the tame acceptance of the misinterpreted opinions of others."

Like Winston Churchill, George Bernard Shaw and James Thurber had been stylistically hassled by certain know-it-alls once too often. Shaw struck back in a letter to the *Times* of London: "There is a busybody on your staff who devotes a lot of time to chasing split infinitives. . . . I call for the immediate dismissal of this pedant. It is of no consequence whether he decides to go quickly or to quickly go or quickly to go. The important thing is that he should go at once." With typical precision and concision, Thurber wrote to a meddlesome editor, "When I split an infinitive, it is going to damn well stay split!"

Many so-called rules of English grammar are founded on models in the classical languages. But there is no precedent in these languages for condemning the split infinitive because in Greek and Latin (and all the other romance languages) the infinitive is a single word that is impossible to sever. Many of our best writers—Wycliffe, Browne, Coleridge, Emily Brontë, Browning, Arnold, and Cather among them—do indeed occasionally split infinitives. Thus, when I suggest to my readers that they relax about splitting infinitives, I am not, to slightly paraphrase "Star Trek," telling them to boldly go where no one else has gone before. Several studies of modern literary and journalistic writing reveal that a majority of newspaper and magazine editors would accept a sentence using the words "to instantly trace" and that the infinitive is cleft in 19.8 percent of all instances where an adverb appears.

Rather than quoting instances from the old masters, I'll offer a new master, Dr. M. Scott Peck, a highly respected psychotherapist. Doctor Peck's books have sold millions of copies not only because of the passion and compassion of his approach to psychology and spirituality, but because of his fresh and original writing. Yet the road through Dr. Peck's best-selling book, *The Road Less Traveled* (Touchstone), is strewn with split infinitives, of which the following are but a few:

- "While it is true that one's capacity to truly listen may improve gradually with practice, it never becomes an effortless process."

- "To willingly confront a problem early, before we are forced to confront it by circumstances, means to put aside something pleasant or less painful for something more painful."

- "And in any case, it is the responsibility of a competent therapist to carefully and sometimes gradually discern those few patients who should not be led into psychoanalytic work."

Try rewriting these statements to unsplit the split constructions. In the first, "truly to listen" sounds unnatural to my ears and "capacity to listen truly may improve" produces a squinting modifier, where it is not clear what verb *truly* is modifying. In the second example, "willingly to confront" and "to confront willingly" are less natural than "to willingly confront." The third example is a close call. Dr. Peck makes the reader wait quite a while before getting from the *to* to the verb, yet that very wait reflects the patient, thoughtful essence of "to carefully and sometimes gradually discern."

Why should the alleged syntactical sin of splitting infinitives be committed with such frequency? Primarily because in modern English adjectives and adverbs are usually placed directly before the words they modify, as in "She successfully completed the course." The same people who thunder against adverbs plunked down in the middle of infinitives remain strangely silent about other split expressions: "She has successfully completed the course." (split verb phrase) "She boasted of successfully completing the course." (split prepositional phrase) "It is better to have loved and lost than never to have loved at all." (infinitive split by helping verb). We hear no objections to such sentences because in English it is perfectly natural to place adverbial modifiers before verbs, including infinitive verbs.

I do not advocate that you go about splitting infinitives promiscuously and artlessly. But there is no point in mangling a sentence just to avoid a split infinitive. Good writers occasionally employ the construction to gain emphasis, to attain the most natural and effective word order, and to avoid ambiguity. How would you gracefully rewrite these sentences from recent newspapers?: "By a 5-4 majority, the court voted to permit states to severely restrict women's rights to choose." "It took 33 seasons for Kansas to get back to number one. It took the Jayhawks one game to almost blow it." "The Red Sox shut out the Yankees 6-0 yesterday to all but clinch the American League East division title." And this last one, written by word maven William Safire: "Thus, to spell it *champing at the bit* when most people would say *chomping at the bit* is to slavishly follow outdated dictionary preferences." In my view and to my ear, you wouldn't want to revise these constructions; they are already clear and readable.

It is indeed acceptable practice to sometimes split an infinitive. If infinitive-splitting makes available just the shade of meaning you desire or if avoiding the separation creates a confusing ambiguity or patent artificiality, you are entitled to happily go ahead and split!

The usage controversy that has attracted the most attention from the press is the *like/as* debate. A generation ago the airwaves were filled with a little jingle that twanged, "Winston tastes good like a cigarette should." English teachers and other word-watchers raised such a fuss about the use of *like* in the song that the publicity was worth millions to the Winston people. So the cigarette hucksters came back with a second campaign: "What do you want—good grammar or good taste?"

My answer to that question is that the use of *like* in the Winston commercial is both good grammar (really, good usage) *and* good taste.

Among prescriptive grammarians the prevailing rule is that we may use *like* or *as* as a preposition joining a noun—"cleans like a white tornado," "blind as a bat"—but we must not use *like* as a conjunction that introduces an adverb clause: The son-of-Winston commercial song "Nobody can do it like McDonald's can" is unacceptable because the sentence doesn't sound good like a conjunction should.

Even princes have been royally reprimanded for violating this admonition. Back in the nineteenth century the poet laureate Alfred, Lord Tennyson told the linguist F. J. Furnivall, "It's a modern vulgarism that I have seen grow up within the last thirty years; and when Prince Albert used it in my drawing room, I pulled him up for it, in the presence of the Queen, and told him he never ought to use it again."

Tennyson's adamance about the "rule" is preserved by the panel for the *Harper Dictionary of Contemporary Usage* (1975, 1985). These 166 distinguished language experts condemned the use of *like* as a conjunction 72-28 percent in casual speech and 88-12 percent in writing.

Cheeky as it may appear, I take issue with the lineup of linguistic luminaries, ranging from Isaac Asimov to William Zinsser. Any open-minded, open-eared observer of the living English language cannot fail to notice that tens of everyday expressions employ *like* as a subordinating conjunction. Fill in the following blanks: "He tells it _____ it is"; "She ate _____ there was no tomorrow"; "If you knew Suzie _____ I know Suzie . . ."; "They make the food here just _____ my mother used to." And what about "Winston tastes good _____ a cigarette should" and "Nobody can do it _____ McDonald's can"? I am confident that, despite the fact that each blank kicks off an adverb clause, most native English speakers would naturally supply *like*. If I'm wrong, then I guess I don't know my *as* from a hole in the ground.

Hopefully, this discussion has stimulated your thinking about where you stand on matters pertaining to usage. And if the structure of the last sentence sets your grammatical sensibilities on edge, you are not alone.

Since the seventeenth century, *hopefully* has been employed with the meaning "in a hopeful manner," as in Robert Louis Stevenson's aphorism "To travel hopefully is better than to arrive." But during the last three decades in the United States *hopefully* has donned new clothes. Now we can scarcely get through a day without meeting statements like "Hopefully, the changes taking place in Eastern Europe will make a safer world for our children" and "Her first day on the job will hopefully not be her last."

Something has happened to *hopefully* in such sentences. First, the adverb has acquired a new meaning, roughly "it is to be hoped." Second, *hopefully* now applies to situations (as in my two examples above) rather than only to people. Third, rather than modifying a specific verb (such as *travel* in Stevenson's pronouncement), the adverb now modifies the entire sentence.

This highly fashionable (some would say *pandemic*) use of *hopefully* has provoked a ringing call to arms among self-appointed protectors of the English language. The honor of being the first to cry out against the dangers of using *hopefully* as a floating adverb seems to belong to Wilson Follett, in *Modern American Usage* (1966): "The special badness of *hopefully* is not alone that it strains *-ly* to the breaking point, but that it appeals to speakers and writers who do not think about what they are saying and pick up vogue words by reflex action."

Many linguistic traffic cops have followed Follett's lead and issued tickets and fines to all violators who use *hopefully* as a dangling adverb. Printed on these citations are the words "Abandon *hopefully* all ye who enter here." Confronted with the sentence "Hopefully, the war will soon be ended," 76 percent of the Harper usage panel responded with outbursts such as: "This is simply barbarism. What does *hopefully* modify? Does a war hope?" "I have fought this for some years, will fight it till I die. It is barbaric, illiterate, offensive, damnable, and inexcusable." "I have sworn eternal war on this adverb." "Chalk squeaking on a blackboard is to be preferred to this usage." "On my back door there is a sign with large letters which reads: THE WORD 'HOPEFULLY' MUST NOT BE MISUSED ON THESE PREMISES. VIOLATORS WILL BE HUMILIATED." "The most horrible usage of our time."

Well, well. Let's now take a deep breath and, as we have been doing, examine structure and actual use. That *hopefully* has taken on a new meaning in no way disqualifies it from respectful consideration. Almost all English nouns, verbs, and modifiers have acquired meanings that they did not possess at birth. *Silly* once meant "blessed" and *awful* "full of awe," while such words as *knight*, once "a boy," and *governor*, once a "steersman or pilot," have come up in the world. Look what has happened recently to such words as *hip, energy,* and *grass.* When words like *hopefully* stop sparking off new meanings, our language, and probably we ourselves, will have died. The fact is that, except for a few die-hard dictionaries, all contemporary lexicons accept "it is hoped" as a primary meaning of the adverb *hopefully.*

Now go back four paragraphs. Did you wince at my use of *first, second,* and *third* to kick off each sentence? That would be odd indeed; almost every speaker of English uses these adverbs as introducers. And what about these sentences: "Mercifully, the war will soon be ended"; "Apparently, the war will soon be ended"; "Fortunately, the war will soon be ended"; "Surely, the war will soon be ended." Few English speakers would criticize the architecture of such sentences, yet each begins with an adverb that modifies the entire main clause. Why among all so-called floating adverbs in our language—*apparently, evidently, first (second, third,* and so on), *fortunately, happily, however, luckily, mercifully, nevertheless, obviously, presumably, primarily, surely, thankfully, therefore, thus,* and umpteen other unexceptional expressions—should *hopefully* be singled out as being "barbaric, illiterate, offensive, damnable, and inexcusable"?

Finally (note how *finally* modifies the rest of this sentence as a perfectly acceptable floating adverb), when a new word knocks at the door of our language, we must ask, "Is it a useful addition?" I believe that the new-age *hopefully* has entered English because it does indeed fill a need of those who use the language. In these secular times, we no longer say with ease "God willing." Instead (another floating adverb), we turn to *hopefully* because it avoids the wordiness and weak passivity of "it is to be hoped that" and sidesteps, especially in writing, the egotistical intrusiveness of "I hope." As Richard Crichton puts it, "No one cares if *I* hope the war is over."

Joining *hopefully* in the list of most vilified usages that I hear about most frequently from my readers is the sentence "I feel badly." Syndicated columnist Michael Gartner, whose work on etymology I consider to be among the very best in popular linguistics, states the classic view: "Avoid the expression 'I feel badly.' Use 'I feel bad.' " *Feel*, as you'd know if you had had Miss Hall in seventh grade, is a linking or, if you'll pardon the expression, copulative verb. These verbs take the adjectival form of modifiers (*bad*), not the adverbial form (*badly*). Ask the offended why they object to "I feel badly," and the voices will slip into the tonal groove that the explanation has worn for itself: "If you feel badly, then your fingertips must have been cut off."

Again we confront the triumph of mandarin decree over reality, of mummified code over usage that actually inhales and exhales—another passionate effort by the absolutists to protect the language from the very people who speak it. In English the form of a word does not necessarily determine its part of speech. Take the word *fast*. In the sentence "Mary is a fast runner," *fast* is an adjective modifying *runner*. But in "Mary ran fast," *fast* is an adverb modifying the verb *ran*. In "Mary plans to fast tomorrow," *fast* is a verb; in "Mary went on a fast" *fast* is a noun. It is context, not morphology, that determines part of speech. That a word such as *badly* ends with *-ly* does not make it an immutable adverb modifying an action verb. While a great many adverbs do indeed wag *-ly* tails, more than a hundred adjectives do too:

beastly, beggarly, bodily, brotherly, bubbly, bully, burly, chilly, comely, costly, courtly, cowardly, crackly, creepy-crawly, crinkly, crumbly, cuddly, curly, daily, dastardly, daughterly, deadly, deathly, drizzly, early, earthly, easterly, elderly, fatherly, fleshly, friendly, frilly, gangly, gentlemanly, ghastly, ghostly, giggly, gnarly, godly, goodly, gravelly, grisly, gristly, grizzly, heavenly, hilly, holy, homely, hourly, jolly, kindly, lawyerly, leisurely, likely, lively, lonely, lovely, lowly.

That list is from just the first half of the alphabet. Clearly (yet another unattached adverb), I could go on and on. So I will:

manly, mannerly, masterly, matronly, mealy, measly, miserly, monthly, motherly, niggardly, nightly, northerly, oily, only, orderly, pearly, pimply, portly, prickly, priestly, princely, quarterly, roly-poly, scaly, scholarly, scraggly, shapely, sickly, silly, sisterly, slatternly, slovenly, smily, sniffly, southerly, spindly, sprightly, squirrely, stately, steely, straggly, surly, timely, tingly, ugly, ungainly, unmannerly, unruly, unseemly, unsightly, weekly, westerly, whirly, wiggly, wily, wobbly, womanly, wooly, worldly, writerly, yearly.

But, say the tsk-tskers, even if "I feel badly" is supported by structural precedent, doesn't the pairing of *bad* and *badly* as predicate adjectives create an unnecessary doubling up? Methinks not. Just as there are clear and important differences between the adjectives *sick* ("sick at this time") and *sickly* ("chronically sick") and *kind* ("kind at this moment") and *kindly* ("habitually kind"), a distinction between "I feel bad," meaning "I feel ill," and "I feel badly," meaning "I regret," "I'm sorry," is gradually gaining currency in our speech and writing. In English, we have long used "I feel well" and "I feel good" to signal the difference between "I feel healthy" and "I feel happy." Is it not then natural that speakers and writers should want to distinguish between physical and mental ill-being as well as physical and mental well-being? Such a change pulls up a shade and opens a window in the house of language and lets the sunshine of a new nuance in.

By now you must be thinking that I am a flaming permissivist who adopts as a household pet any new use that crawls out of the language wordwork. But this is not true; I continue to fight the good fight to maintain precise differences between the likes of *less* and *fewer* and *I, me,* and *myself.* These are useful distinctions to which the majority of educated speakers and writers continue to adhere. Words are ideas fraught with particular recognitions and energies that enlarge and quicken life. Blur shades of meaning in language and you blur shades of thinking.

For many years I have been vice president of SPELL—Society for the Preservation of English Language and Literature. Founded in 1984, SPELL is an international corps of word-watchers dedicated to the proper use and usage of the mother tongue. In the service of this lofty goal, SPELL each year confers Dunce Cap Awards on perpetrators of especially egregious errors in usage, spelling, and punctuation inflicted on the public's sensibilities. I have been the judge for that contest, a contest that nobody wants to win.

At the end of 1988 I placed the Dunce Cap on the collective heads of ad writers for Dunkin' Donuts, a company that boasts of its products' freshness. Throughout the year Dunkin' Donuts ran a radio and television commercial explaining that "the problem with supermarket doughnuts is there's no telling how long they've been laying there."

I laid the responsibility upon all advertisers to make the proper choices between *lie*, an intransitive verb that means "to repose," and *lay*, a transitive verb that means "to place." One lies in a hammock and lays a book on a table. A hen on its back is lying. A hen on its stomach may be laying. *Lie* never takes an object, *lay* almost always does. Something must be laid, and nothing can be lied. As one who is all for a SPELL of good English, I dunked Dunkin' Donuts for laying a grammatical egg, however fresh that egg may have been. And I am pleased to report that so many puzzled and outraged listeners and viewers responded to the commercial with letters and telephone calls that Dunkin' Donuts recast the sales pitch and replaced *laying* with *lying*. Who knows? If this keeps up, the company may one day change its name to Dunking Doughnuts.

In addition to confusable word pairs, I do not suffer gladly sentences riddled by structural flaws. I cringe when I hear or read dangling and misplaced modifiers, such as "Yoko Ono will talk about her husband, John Lennon, who was killed in an interview with Barbara Walters" and "Plunging a thousand feet, we saw Yosemite Falls." Was it in an interview with Barbara Walters that John Lennon was killed? Did we plummet as we gazed at the falls? Shoddily built sentences like these can only confuse, as well as amuse, listeners and readers.

What I advise my readers to do is to carefully choose their usage crusades, to avoid knee-jerk reactions and knee-bending obeisance to long-ago edicts dispensed in long-ago English classes, to present rationales that generate more light than heat, and to ask why language does what it does. Many well-meaning people concerned about the state of the English language react with horror against any noun that has turned into a verb. But part of the genius of English is words can rail-jump from one part of speech to another with no apparent change in form, that we can say "Let's wallpaper the room this morning" instead of the more cumbersome "Let's put wallpaper on the walls of the room this morning." Folks used to get huffy and puffy about the verbs *to contact* and *to process*, but who today minds? What exactly is wrong with "Tom Hanks will host 'Saturday Night Live' this week"? Is "Tom Hanks will be the host of 'Saturday Night Live' this week" demonstrably superior? I am convinced that the converted verbs *to parent, to party* and *to total* are wonderful additions to the language. On the other hand, I do wonder if *to finalize* adds anything that *to complete* or *to finish* hasn't already supplied, and I fail to see what *to author* does that *to write* doesn't. Ultimately, what I want to avoid are blanket judgments about all noun-into-verb shifts. That's because all generalizations are bad.

The hotly debated status of the word *unique* offers a unique opportunity to explore the issue of stability versus change. Until recently, *unique* did not possess a comparative or superlative form; something either was unique, "one of a kind," or it wasn't. Nowadays we hear and see *unique* compared (*more, most*), intensified (*very, quite*), or qualified (*rather, somewhat*). President Reagan praised the United Way as "a very unique opportunity to serve our local communities," and Illinois governor James Thompson called a particular case "the most unique and difficult" one that had ever come before him. Clearly, *unique* is taking on a second meaning of "unusual" to stand alongside the older meaning, "unequaled," and this upstart meaning threatens to swallow up the older one, as evidenced by the following product announcements (which are real; I did not make them up): "They are so unique, we only made a few of them" and "It's so unique, it's almost one of a kind."

When asked to respond to phrases like *a rather unique apartment* and *a most unique reaction,* the Harper usage panel condemned the relativity of *unique* 89-11 percent in writing and 76-24 percent in speaking. Among the sharpest criticisms were "No, it's dumb"; "This comes from the weakening of a great and useful word. Or perhaps I should say a 'most divine' word and 'most perfect'!"; "What corpse is ever 'a trifle dead'?"

But, say most linguists, change in language need not be equated with corruption or decay. English is alive and well and living in our voices, pens, and word processors, and that means all of us, not just the language mavens. If vox populi decrees that *unique* means "unusual" as well as "unequaled," we should listen to that vox with the utmost respect.

But what about etymology? Isn't it clear that *unique* is constructed from the Latin *unus*, meaning "one"? Yes, it is, but the etymology of a word does not necessarily fix its meaning forever. Anyone with a knowledge of Latin perceives that the etymons in *manuscript* and *manufacture* signify "hand-written" and "hand-made." Yet only the most superannuated of traditionalists would object to the phrases "a typed manuscript" and "automated manufacture." Obviously the old meaning of *manu*, "hand," has been weakened and superseded. Playing the numbers game, we find that the *tri* in *trivial*, *quar* in *quarantine*, *quint* in *quintessence*, *sept* in *September*, *oct* in *October*, *nov* in *November*, and *dec* in *December* and *decimate* no longer denote "three," "four," "five," "seven," "eight," "nine," and "ten." Why then must the *unus* in *unique* mean "one"?

But isn't *unique* an absolute adjective that will not tolerate comparison, intensification, or qualification? Here we enter a philosophical brier patch that challenges us to define what, if anything, is absolutely absolute in language. Examine these real-life sentences: "Her treatment of the civil rights movement is still the most complete on the subject." "The corpse was very dead." "Fear of spiders is nearly universal." "God is our most perfect creator." William Shakespeare used "most excellent," Thomas Gray wrote, "Full many a gem of purest ray serene, / The dark unfathomed caves of ocean bear," and our own constitution begins with the intent "to form a more perfect union." In each of these statements a so-called absolute adjective is modified by an adverb or intensified by an inflection, yet each is perfectly acceptable in modern English.

Despite such reasoning, I feel very badly when I see *unique* dying on the language vine. When I witness *unusual* gobbling up *unique*, I see, much in the manner of George Orwell's Newspeak, a precious window darkening in the house of language. *Unique* is a unique word. We have no other adjective that easily and concisely conveys the sense of "one of a kind." Because we already possess modifiers like *unusual* and *distinctive*, there is no reason why *unique* should be wordnapped into their territory. If something is indeed quite unusual and almost one of a kind, I prefer that speakers and writers say "quite unusual." Sure, I know that I may be waging a losing battle, that *unique* may have already fallen before the onslaught of *unusual.* But I shall publicly bewail the devaluing and the loss of a wonderful word. If and when *unique* is completely emptied of its uniqueness, that change will have been tested against the disapproval of people like me and the language will be the better for the give and the take.

Oh, yes. If you have been wondering about whether the zoo owner should have written *mongooses* or *mongeese,* the answer is *mongooses. Goose,* from the Old English *gos,* and *mongoose,* from the Hindi *magus,* are etymologically unrelated. While the plural of *goose* is *geese,* the preferred plural of *mongoose* is *mongooses.* Like most native or experienced users of the English language, the fellow got it right the first time.

LINDA SIMON

FOREIGN STATES OF MIND

AGNI

Those of us who write biographies—and many who read them—often question our excursions into other people's lives. What, we ask, are we doing when we assemble, from boxes and files of documents, the story of a life? Can another life ever be known? Is biography merely fiction by another name? Do lives contain an inherent narrative? Are biographers essentially voyeurs who, if they had any sense of decency, would look away? Or are they burglars foraging for marketable loot?

In her recent book, *The Silent Woman*, Janet Malcolm, investigating biographers of Sylvia Plath, sees the biographer's task as nothing less than sinister and depressing. "[N]arratives called biographies," she tells us,

> pale and shrink in the face of the disorderly actuality that is a life. . . . Each person who sits down to write faces not a blank page but his own vastly overfilled mind. The problem is to clear out most of what is in it, to fill huge plastic garbage bags with the confused jumble of things that have accreted there over the days, months, years of being alive and taking things in through the eyes and ears and heart. The goal is to make a space where a few ideas and images and feelings may be so arranged that a reader will want to linger awhile among them, rather than to flee. . . . But this task of housecleaning (of narrating) is not merely arduous; it is dangerous. There is the danger

of throwing the wrong things out and keeping the wrong things in; there is the danger of throwing too much out and being left with too bare a house; there is the danger of throwing everything out. Once one starts throwing out, it may become hard to stop. It may be better not to start.

But if we do not start, we are choosing to live in a world peopled only by those who live and breathe among us. Dead is dead, we say, if we do not dig up past lives. If the dead have written or painted or composed a thing or two, we clutch them as souvenirs, but dare not put them into the context of a life lived, because we are afraid. It is dangerous, Malcolm tells us, and she is not alone, to exert our authority over another human being, to turn a life into a *subject*.

This anxiety about examining the artifacts of another person's life seems generated, in part, by our own need for privacy—and, as writers, that need is often intense—contradicted by our equally intense desire simply to know. But this anxiety also reflects our discomfort with biography as a literary genre. We complain that critics of biographies often review the quality of the subject's life rather than the biographer's strategies or skills; we claim not to agree on criteria for evaluating biography.

But if we reflect on the ways we read biographies we may come to understand something essential about the way we write them. Reviewers of biography invariably apply two significant criteria for judging the success of a work: the resources on which the biographer bases the study; and the appropriateness of the biographer to the subject. By appropriateness, we mean not whether the biographer likes, loves, or dislikes the subject, but whether the relationship that the biographer has established will result in a portrait that serves the purpose or expectations of the reader.

Take, for example Kennedy Fraser's review of Louise DeSalvo's *Virginia Woolf: The Impact of Childhood Sexual Abuse on Her Life and Work*. Fraser, writing in *The New Yorker*, comments, "DeSalvo is a professor, and she has clearly read deeply in published and unpublished texts about her subject, which she approaches sometimes with indignation and always with a woman's heart." For Fraser, an appropriate biographer for Woolf is, crucially, a woman, and better yet, a scholar; but most vital for Fraser, she must be a protective woman, justly indignant over Woolf's treatment at the hands of her male relatives.

In reviewing V. S. Pritchett's biography of Chekhov, the poet Andrei Voznesensky tells us that he began the biography "with trepidation. . . . What, I wondered, could a man who did not know Russian and had never been in the Soviet Union tell us about Chekhov, one of my favorite authors, a master of under- statement, of concealed meaning, of twilight scenes and of prose as compressed as poetry, whose heroes don't want what they want?" Was Pritchett an appropriate biographer for Chekhov? What relationship could he establish if not that of a compatriot who could understand viscerally the texture of those twilight scenes? Fortunately, Voznesensky discovered, Pritchett was a comrade of sorts: both he and Chekhov were masterful writers of short stories. "This biographer," Voznesensky writes, "argues persuasively that the heart of Chekhov is in these sto- ries, and so is his life, and he draws the life out of the stories." So Pritchett is an appropriate biographer after all, according to Voznesensky, because he is a professional colleague of Chekhov, which allows Pritchett intimacy despite the lack of cultural connections.

As readers, we have become unanimously impatient with biographers who take the role of intimidated admirers. Laurie Lisle's biography of Louise Nevelson was not hagiographic, reviewers conceded, but still, Lisle seemed to establish no rela- tionship with the intimidating Nevelson other than observer. "Her admiration and respect for Nevelson's long struggle and enchanted cabinets and walls are always evident, but she lets the evidence speak, and sometimes she seems to be shocked herself at the abruptness, vindictiveness and cruelty of which this great personage was capable," art critic Michael Brenson decided. Dore Ashton concurred:

> [S]ince Lisle set out to write a biography and not a crit-
> ical biography, the years of Nevelson's successes are
> described in perhaps unnecessary detail. We see the

'Empress of Modern Art,' as Nevelson certainly thought of herself, traipsing around the world, quarreling with old friends and her son, bedecked in gorgeous robes and flaunting her riches . . . But we do not see into her soul, always troubled, always hungry.

Why do we not have that intimate view? What distinction is Ashton making between a biography and a critical biography? What is he getting at?

What he is getting at, I believe, is the quality of the relationship between Lisle and Nevelson, a relationship that is obscured if we insist on defining the writer as biographer and the figure written about as subject. Most of us who have written biographies use the term *subject* only as a kind of code to communicate with those who do not write biographies. The frogs that we pinned to dissecting boards in high school biology were our subjects in a way that historical figures are not. As we slit into their chest cavity, we lifted an organ and, comparing it to what we had learned about amphibians' organs, identified it as "heart." But searching a human heart is a different process: what we have learned about the heart may reflect our reading of Freud, Keats, D.H. Lawrence, or Anais Nin; but always our insights reflect our own relationships as lover and beloved. It is not the biographer's task to locate the heart and identify it by its morphology; instead the biographer is expected to declare, "Look: a heart. And it is broken." But when we make that declaration, we are entering into a relationship with our "subject" that must have another name.

It used to be that biographers wrote about heroes. Any of us who have ever identified someone as a hero know that there are only a few possibilities available for a relationship: one may admire one's hero, attempt to seduce one's hero, or hope that some of the hero's luster will rub off on one's own, lesser, life. In any case, in order to sustain the hero/worshiper relationship, the biographer needs to affirm the hero's worth, show how the hero generated heroism from early life, and set the hero in heroic settings later. Catherine Drinker Bowen, biographer of such heroic men as Justice Oliver Wendell Holmes, John

Adams, and Francis Bacon, admits that the biographer need not always *love* the hero, but then adds:

> When the biographer has chosen his subject and sits down to read, what he is actually doing for the first three or four months is to make the acquaintance of his hero. Everything comes as grist to this mill: time, place, climate; the hero's friends, his enemies, his appetites physical and spiritual. Any least word about the hero's appearance, how he looked and dressed, is cherished as a lover cherishes the most fugitive news of his beloved. There is a musical comedy song which perfectly expresses the biographer's condition at this stage. Sitting in the research library the tune goes through his head: "Getting to *know* you,/Getting to know all *about* you. . . ."

Why does a biographer choose to enter into a relationship with a hero? "When the book is done," Bowen tells us, "the author returns to the outer world, but actually he will not be the same again. The ferment of genius, Holmes said, is quickly imparted, and when a man is great he makes others believe in greatness. By that token one's life is altered. One has climbed a hill, looked out and over, and the valley of one's own condition will be forever greener."

In the twenty-five years since Bowen wrote about the hero/worshiper relationship in biography, we have come to expect something different. We understand that in our own lives we learn about human experience not by studying exemplary individuals, even if we could find one, but by entering into a variety of relationships. In our own lives, we see that people serve one another as, for example, mentor, analyst, healer, colleague, confidante, lover, parent, child, rival, sibling, guide. In each of these relationships, the participants exhibit certain patterns of behavior, reveal certain patterns of information, that sustain the particular kind of companionship. If we serve as healers, we seek patients: ill, injured, needy. The healer-biographer will produce what Joyce Carol Oates so famously called pathography, a biography that insists that the subject harbor black psychological secrets. Pathography, as I see it, results from a biographer's succumbing to the seductive role of healer in our culture; being a healer enables us to exert a kind of authority over another human being more powerful even than the parent/child relationship, which also finds its way into biography. As healer we do not protect or punish, but instead elicit confidences, unearth buried memories, hear confession. As healer-biographers, we assert, we can make sense of a life that seemed so deeply troubling to our subject. We can give a name to the ills that plagued, the demons that tormented: sexual abuse, manic-depression, unresolved Oedipal longings. We promise that the narrative will, in the end, have meaning, and thereby justify our rifling through lingerie drawers and dirty laundry.

When we read biography we intuitively respond to the relationships biographers establish, although only a few biographers are forthcoming enough to reflect openly about this experience. Mark Shorer, a biographer of Sinclair Lewis, in a revelation rare among biographers, declared that "biography itself has two subjects, and two subjects only—the figure whose life is being re-created, of course, and the mind that is re-creating it, the scrutinizing biographer no less than the object of his scrutiny." As Shorer discussed his initial attraction to Lewis, the relationship that evolved as he discovered more and more about Lewis's life, and his discoveries not only about Lewis, but about himself, we can see that *subject* is a pale, inert word for the place that Lewis filled in Shorer's life and mind. Here is Shorer, attempting to explain that place:

> I believe now that from the outset I was challenged by what I unconsciously felt to be a strange affinity. . . . There was, of course, the obvious affinity of our beginnings—the same kind of raw small Midwestern towns, probably much the same kind of inept and unsuccessful boys in that particular man's world. But I discovered many more, and many that were more subtle. Should I try to spell them out now I would be writing my autobiography, or even confession, and I have no such inclination.

Leon Edel, in his essay on transference in *Writing Lives*, argues that Shorer's experience should have been avoided.

Biographers, Edel asserts, must be on guard against identifying too fully with their subject, against losing control in interpreting material. He assumes that when Shorer confesses to his affinity with Lewis, he is admitting a "mistake" that caused the failure of his book. For some biographers, Edel tells us, "the entire biographical pursuit of certain writers [is] a drive to complete themselves in their works." Perhaps that was Shorer's drive. "As I learned about [Lewis], with all his stubborn deficiency in self-knowledge," he writes, "I believe that I gained in self-knowledge. I am not a better man, certainly, for having written his life; but I think that I am a wiser one."

Of course Shorer knew, how could he not, that the network of nerves and sinews upon which he molded the flesh of his portrait was, in effect, his own. It could be no other way. He tells us that his sense of affinity extended to

> all the careless writing, all the ill-conceived ambitions, all the bad manners, all the irrational fits of temper, all the excesses of conduct, all the immature, lifelong frivolities and regrettable follies. . . . Perhaps this is where the psychoanalyst is really needed—not in the biographer analyzing his subject, but beyond both of them, analyzing their symbiotic relationship.

I suggest that biographers do not choose subjects, but companions, just as they choose, from among the living, individuals who will somehow enrich—or as Edel says, "complete"—their lives; that their choice of companion reflects their own needs as human beings and assumptions about other human beings; that their relationship with those companions reflects their relationships with other living beings; that biography cannot be separated from autobiography: that is, the life written about is inextricably entangled with the life of the biographer. The inevitable "symbiotic relationship" between writer and subject allows us privileged views of past lives, views that we, as readers, could not have in any other way. Biography is not a violation, not an intrusion, but a triumph.

In an unusually candid preface to her biography of the flamboyant jazz dancer Josephine Baker, biographer Phyllis Rose responds to a question she was asked many times during her research for the book: What had drawn her to Baker? "The truth was," she writes,

> my choice was made as instinctively as it is when you fall in love. You do not compose a list of qualities and accomplishments you admire and look for a person to embody them. You see someone. You light up inside. If the choice is a deep one, the lists, reasons, and rationalizations come later, along with new interests and a larger frame of reference for life. For the commitment to a different person— whether imaginative, as in the case of biography, or physical, as in the case of love—is often renewing.

Rose wanted to share in Baker's "spontaneity, fearlessness, energy, joy." But there was more. When a particularly boorish questioner asked her, "What is a white intellectual like you doing writing about a black nymphomaniac?" Rose immediately retorted, "You'd be surprised how much we have in common." The answer, it seems, surprised even Rose. But in the course of discovering Baker, she affirmed something about herself. "If I did not have my say about Josephine Baker," she tells us,

> people might not credit the degree to which, in our fantasies at least, we cross, the degree to which she wanted to be remembered for her ideas or the degree to which in my dreams I am onstage in fox and feathers with an audience madly applauding. To consider us so different that we could have nothing to say about each other flattens us both and minimizes our common cultural heritage, not to say our humanity.

And now about my relationship with William James.

I first met James in the 1960s, when, by chance, as an undergraduate I found myself taking courses from John McDermott, then as now a pre-eminent James scholar, whose own identification and infatuation with James allowed us, his students, to come away with an indelibly vivid, even tangible, impression of

James. Discovering James led us to redefine our conceptions of what it means to be a philosopher: there he was, lively, witty, down-to-earth, eager to connect with his readers, even with the inexperienced minds of college freshmen. There was something right and relevant and modern about James's need to test philosophy against daily life, about his tolerance for varieties of religious experiences, about his intellectual irreverence. While other philosophers—Kant, say, or the unfortunate Nietzsche—seemed tormented and sour, James was exuberant.

We met again, James and I, about a decade later while I was researching and writing a biography of Alice B. Toklas, the companion of Gertrude Stein, who herself had been a student of James in the 1890s. Stein adored James. "Is life worth living?" she asked. "Yes, a thousand times yes when the world still holds such spirits as Prof. James. He is truly a man among men; . . . a scientist of force and originality embodying all that is strongest and worthiest in the scientific spirit; . . . a metaphysican skilled in abstract thought, clear and vigorous and yet too great to worship logic as his God, and narrow himself to a belief merely in the reason of man." Of course, a scientist who does not worship logic would have a short career in any age, but Stein did not love James because of his theories of psychology, but because of the range of his imagination. "Now James," wrote another of his students, "was an illuminating ray, a dissolvent force. He looked freshly at life and read books freshly." He simply delighted people: "he was a sportive, wayward, Gothic sort of spirit, who was apt, on meeting a friend, to burst into foolery, and whose wit was always three parts poetry."

Still a decade later, I embarked on research for a book focused on the year 1906 as a way to explore the cultural climate of the early twentieth century, the world that gave birth to modernism in literature and art. Although the choice of 1906 seemed arbitrary to some, it was not to me. It was the year, after all, when Picasso began his revolutionary *Demoiselles d'Avignon* and when James delivered his lectures on pragmatism. How could I relate these two apparently disparate events? That was the question with which I began my research, in which James featured significantly. I found him striding onto the set, so to speak, in Boston and New York, the friend of many other players in my study. In 1906 James was the foremost philosopher in America. "There was James first, and no second," his student John Dewey exclaimed.

Encountering James as philosopher and teacher spurred my interest in him as friend, colleague, son, brother, husband, father. I had already read several biographies of James; his brothers Henry, Robertson and Wilkie; and his sister Alice, but one relationship beckoned: that between James and his wife, also named Alice, only peripherally addressed by the writers I had read. One summer, then, simply to satisfy my own curiosity, I spent my mornings at Harvard's Houghton Library reading James's unpublished correspondence with Alice Gibbens James, some fifteen hundred letters—letters which no biographer, at the time, had yet mined.

Theirs was a strong and close marriage, and to few other correspondents did James so eagerly reveal his thoughts and feelings. So I read of James's recurring depressions, fits of hypochondria, and inner resilience; his impatience with colleagues and the demands of the academic life, yet his enormous concern for his students; his irreverence toward the institutionalization of philosophy and psychology, yet his respect for their modes of inquiry; his need for affirmation and even adoration, yet his charming modesty; his love of family, his craving for solitude.

Whatever he experienced, he experienced intensely, even illness, fatigue, homesickness—and the 1906 San Francisco earthquake. Like Phyllis Rose writing about Josephine Baker, I wanted to share in James's "spontaneity, fearlessness, energy, joy." And also in his contradictions and complexities. I wanted to understand how a man born in 1842 and dead by 1910 could have invented for us key terms by which we still define our world: pluralism and pragmatism, stream of consciousness and continuous present. He recognized for us the possibility of multiple perspectives long before artists depicted such vision in their cubist works. He guided his own generation from the rigidity and stability of the nineteenth century to the ambivalence, unpredictability, and indeterminacy of the twentieth.

"We ought to say a feeling of *and,* a feeling of *if,* a feeling of *but,* and a feeling of *by,* quite as readily as we say a feeling of *blue* or a feeling *cold,*" he once wrote. "Yet we do not: so inveterate has our habit become of recognizing the existence of the substantive parts alone, that language almost refuses to lend itself to any other use." How, I wondered, did James imagine freedom from such intellectual prescriptions? "The word 'or,' " he said, "names a genuine reality." How did James know that reality?

Like Rose, I am "crossing" in writing about James, because my scholarly training, like hers, is in literature, not philosophy or psychology; and, no doubt, some readers would find a different biographer more appropriate. But in exploring his relationships, I have seen that he revealed his personality most unaffectedly with companions other than his professional colleagues. Nor did he believe that his ideas could be communicated only to especially trained minds. He resented, even derided, the cloister of the academy and the contrived boundaries between disciplines. And so, I confess, do I.

The professorial role irritated him—not because of the demands of his students, but because of the conventions of the classroom. His own students celebrated his defiance of those conventions. He did not look or act like a college professor. Here is how one student remembers James:

> Brilliant, high-strung, dynamic, vivacious, resilient, unexpected, unconventional, picturesque—these are some of the terms that at once recur in recalling James. Among many incidents, I remember his fetching embarrassment when baffled while figuring on the black-board; his remark in the college Yard when congratulating me on securing my Ph.D.: "*but,* you've probably read what bosh I think it all is"; the startled turning of heads toward him in crowded Sanders Theatre as he conspicuously beat the audience to its applause of General Booth at the close of a moving address on the work of the Salvation Army among the poor; his fidgeting at a department symposium in Royce's house, and his silent exit, in carpet slippers, when

Munsterberg was in full teutonic swing; his entrance, with elaborate stealth, clad in brown Norfolk jacket, striped trousers, *and* silk hat, into Royce's morning metaphysics class already under way, his attentive listening to Royce on The Absolute—and the departure of the two from the room. We left them on the steps of Sever Hall as we slowly trailed away, still arguing, as they so often did—James animated and Royce quiet, with his whimsical tolerant smile.

James's interests—in psychical research, for example—and his lack of interest—in laboratory science and faculty meetings—sometimes embarrassed biographers who preferred thinkers with more respect for verifiable data and committees. If James were alive today, he might be among those who stop in to see John Mack to ask about those reports of abduction by extra-terrestrial aliens. I suspect he would be keenly interested in pharmo-psychology, in research into the biochemical basis of consciousness and the mapping of the brain. And also in movies, computer games, and virtual reality. As a companion, James urges us not to close our minds to possibilities. Including the possibility that someone who has never known you in life can understand you.

Some subjects—J.D. Salinger, for one, or W.H. Auden—seem hostile to the enterprise of biography. But James does not resist, even seems to welcome, inquiry. "Philosophic study," he once wrote, "means the habit of always seeking an alternative, of not taking the usual for granted, of making conventionalities fluid again, of imagining foreign states of mind." He might have been defining the biographer's task.

He loved biographies, and I suspect that he would have been disappointed by the first attempt in this direction by his former student Ralph Barton Perry, James's self-proclaimed intellectual heir, who used the biography as an opportunity to defend his own intellectual heritage. Perry located James in the context of Great Men of Philosophy: this for the colleague that George Santayana noticed was "attentive, puzzled, and suspicious" of theories. "He lived his life among them," Santayana wrote, "as a child lives among grown-up people; what a relief to turn from those stolid giants, with their prohibitions and exactions and tiresome talk, to another real child or a nice animal!'' When Perry felt forced to offer some assessment of James's personality, he nodded briefly toward the psychological schematization of the day to dissect and label James's attitudes and behavior.

Not surprisingly, one critic of the biography was Perry's rival as heir-apparent, another of James's former students, Horace Kallen. Kallen complained that Perry's ''systematic account'' obscured and distorted James. ''Abounding and unbounded,'' Perry calls him, in a moment of unconscious personal reminiscence, and then, according to Kallen, Perry forces James into ill-fitting psychological categories. Because Kallen saw his own relationship with James as that of a kindred spirit, he believed that an appropriate biographer would have a ''less rationalist and somewhat more imaginative and intuitive appreciation of the Jamesian tempo. . . .''

Yet whether or not Perry misread something essential about James, his study has served generations of readers who emerge with their own portrait of James from the many rich sources that Perry compiled. And each of James's biographers after Perry has given us a different portrait, depending on their relationship with James, depending on what they needed from him. R.W.B. Lewis, biographer of Edith Wharton, sees James as a patrician gentleman and bathed the James family in the mellow glow of gaslight. Psychiatrist and historian Howard Feinstein, biographer of James's early years, sees James as combatant in a primal struggle with his father. Just as in his life James sat for several painters whose portraits reflect their own artistic vision, he has sat for many writers—F.O. Matthiessen, Gay Wilson Allen, Jacques Barzun, Daniel Bjork, Gerald Myers—all of whom have engaged in different conversations with him, asking different questions inspired by different needs.

And my own portrait?

The William James that I know seems something like Fred Astaire. Remember, if you will, the silk hat that James wore to Royce's lecture. Lithe and trim, the two men seem not to be affected by the same force that binds the rest of us to earth. Like Astaire, James was debonair and dashing, courtly and flirtatious. He was as elegant a writer as Astaire was a dancer. More than once, I have looked up from *The Principles of Psychology* to imagine him standing before a mirror knotting a brightly colored, flowing tie, in preparation to go to the theater, or to Commonwealth Avenue for dinner with friends, or to catch the train to New York, slightly flushed in anticipation of the excursion. There was in James a certain buoyancy of spirit that has its purest expression in dance. When James suggested that his dear friend James Jackson Putnam might have done better to run away with a ballerina than marry the prosaic woman who, James thought, was more like a sister than a lover, I believe that James was recognizing that a buoyant spirit gives us permission to see and understand in a fresh, even idiosyncratic way; to liberate ourselves from schemes, from systems, and even from gravity.

Recalling James, friends portray him as a liberator ("a birthright member of . . . 'the great society of encouragers,' " as one student put it) who freed them from a constricting self-image. He had the rare ability of making people believe that they could find within themselves lush new corners in the garden of their own spirit. He encouraged them to make decisions with passion and courage, and not to fear change. The next book, the next encounter, the next mountain top, he told them, would reveal, surely, an unexpected vista. A vista that, in barely perceptible or profound ways, could change their sense of self.

The Jamesian quest to reinvent the self in response to new experiences, encounters, and relationships is the biographer's quest: to discover the possibilities of two lives—our subject's and, as we respond to our subject, our own; to imagine foreign states of mind—within our subject and ourselves. Many of us, in the middle of our lives, would like to believe that who we have become is not all that we will ever be; we would like to seek alternatives, to make conventionalities fluid, to light out into new territory. Alice James once remarked, after her husband's death, that no one could ever know just how exciting it was to *travel* with him. I think I understand.

MENIAL LABOR AND THE MUSE

WOMEN, ANIMALS, AND VEGETABLES

An all-day rain of the mizzly seductive sort, compounded by snow fog; twilight began this day and will mediate it until fully dark.

Before settling in at my desk I've distributed an extra bale of hay to the horses, making a quick trip from house to barn in my slicker and muck boots. The whole main floor of the barn is packed, this time of year, with last August's second cutting, a mix of timothy and brome grass, mostly without the seed heads. The bales are still green, so sweet it makes me salivate as I inhale their aroma which cries *summer!* on the winter air. I have never understood why some entrepreneur has yet to capture the scent and market it as a perfume. Doesn't everyone melt, smelling new hay? I must have been a horse in the last incarnation or had a profound love affair in some sixteenth-century hayloft.

A perspicacious student once pointed out to me that it rains or snows in a large percentage of my poems. She's right, of course, though I hadn't even thought of the connection.

Stormy days are my best writing days. The weather relieves me of my Jewish-Calvinist urgency to do something useful with one or another of the young stock, to longe or drive or ride the current two-, three-, or four-year-old. Or, in season, to cut around the perimeters of the pastures, work that's known as *brushing out.* Or clean out and re-bed the run-in sheds and the central area under the barn my friend Robin calls the motel lobby. No need to bring the vegetable garden into this, or the sugar bush of a hundred maple trees. We probably won't be setting any taps this March. Acid rain and the depredations of the pear thrip that followed have so weakened the trees that they need a rest period.

This year's wood is in, all split and stacked. Next year's is already on the ground, split in four-foot lengths to dry. It snowed before we could get two truckloads of manure on the garden, though. Victor says we'll have a thaw, that there is still time. He's still puttying and caulking as we button up for the hard months. *Still* is the wrong word, as there is no beginning and no apparent end. Outside water faucets are drained and closed off, heating element installed in the watering trough, and so on.

Writing and well-being. In the most direct, overt, and uncomplicated way, my writing depends on the well-being that devolves from this abbreviated list of chores undertaken and completed.

One set of self-imposed deadlines nurtures the other: something harshly physical each day, the reward being a bone-tired sense of equipoise at nightfall. A daily session at the desk even when, as Rilke warned, nothing comes. I must keep holy even disappointment, even desertion. The leaven of the next day's chores will redeem the failed writing, infuse it with new energy or at the very least allow me to shred it while I await the Rilkean birth-hour of a new clarity.

The well-being of solitude is a necessary component of this equation. A "Good! No visitors today" mentality isn't limited to snowstorms or Monday mornings. On the contrary, this feeling of contentment in isolation pervades every good working day. My writing time needs to surround itself with empty stretches, or at least unpeopled ones, for the writing takes place in an area of suspension as in a hanging nest that is almost entirely encapsulated. I think of the oriole's graceful construction.

This is why poems may frequently begin for me in the suspended cocoon of the airplane, or even in the airport lounge during those dreary hours of layovers. There's the same anonymity, the same empty but enclosed space, paradoxical in view of the thousands of other travelers pulsing past. But I have no repsonsibility here. I am un-called upon and can go inward.

My best ruminations take place in the barn while my hands (and back) are busy doing something else. Again, there's the haunting appeal of enclosure, the mindless suspension of doing simple, repetitive tasks—mucking out, refilling water buckets, raking sawdust—that allows those free-associative leaps out of which a poem may occasionally come. And if not, reasons the Calvinist, a clean barn is surely a sign of the attained state of grace. Thus I am saved. And if the Muse descends, my androgynous pagan Muse, I will have the best of both worlds.

ABOUT THE AUTHORS

DOROTHY ALLISON was a finalist for the 1992 National Book Award for her novel *Bastard Out of Carolina*, published by NAL-Dutton. She also has published a collection of essays titled *Skin: Talking About Sex, Class, and Literature*, published by Firebrand Books and from which "Believing in Literature" is taken.

MARGARET ATWOOD has published twenty-five volumes of fiction, poetry and essays, including the best-selling novels *The Handmaid's Tale, Cat's Eye* and, most recently, *The Robber Bride,* all published by Doubleday.

CHARLES BAXTER is the author of three collections, most recently *A Relative Stranger*, published by W.W. Norton & Company. He also has published two novels—*First Light,* by Viking Penguin, and *Shadow Play,* by W.W. Norton & Company. He teaches creative writing at the University of Michigan.

T. ALAN BROUGHTON is the author of four novels, a collection of short stories and five volumes of poetry. In 1994 his collection of poems titled *In the Country of Elegies* was published by Carnegie-Mellon.

DAVID CARKEET is the author of four novels, most recently *The Full Catastrophe*, published by Simon & Schuster.

WILLIAM GASS is author of several books of fiction, including *In the Heart of the Heart of the Country*, published by Godine, and, most recently, *The Tunnel*, published by Alfred A. Knopf. He teaches at Washington University in St. Louis.

WILLIAM GOLDMAN wrote the screenplays for such films as *Butch Cassidy and the Sundance Kid, All the President's Men, Marathon Man* and *Mercy*. He is also the author of numerous novels as well and books of nonfiction.

ANNETTE GRANT is currently an editor of the "Arts and Leisure" section of *The New York Times*.

DAN GREENBURG is the author of eighteen books, ranging from novels to humorous nonfiction. His articles have appeared in *The*

New Yorker, Esquire, MS Magazine, Time, Newsweek, Life, Vanity Fair, Playboy and many other publications.

JUSTIN KAPLAN is the author of the biography *Mr. Clemens and Mark Twain*, published by Simon & Schuster, for which he won the Pulitzer Prize and the National Book Award. He also is the author of several other biographies, and he edited the sixteenth edition of *Bartlett's Familiar Quotations*.

THOMAS E. KENNEDY is the author of the novel *Crossing Borders*, published by Watermark Press, and four books of literary criticism. His short stories have appeared in numerous literary magazines. He lives in Copenhagen, Denmark, and acts as European editor for *Cimarron Review*.

MAXINE KUMIN has published ten volumes of poetry, four novels, two collections of essays and a collection of stories. *Women, Animals, and Vegetables*, published by W.W. Norton & Company and from which "Menial Labor and the Muse" is taken, is a collection of essays and stories.

RICHARD LEDERER is the author of ten books about language and writing. His best known books are *Anguished English* and *More Anguished English*, both published by Wyrick & Company.

LYN LIFSHIN has written more than ninety books and chapbooks of poetry, most recently *Marilyn Monroe Poems*, published by Quiet Lion Press. Her poems have appeared in numerous periodicals, including *American Poetry Review, Ploughshares, Rolling Stone* and *The Christian Science Monitor*.

MICHAEL NORMAN is an associate professor of journalism at New York University and a former reporter for *The New York Times*. He is the author of *These Good Men*, a memoir published in 1990 by Crown and in 1991 by Pocket Books.

KATHLEEN NORRIS is the author of *Dakota: A Spiritual Geography*, published by Ticknor & Fields. Her most recent book of poems is *Little Girls in Church*, published by the University of Pittsburgh Press.

JOYCE CAROL OATES has published twenty-four novels as well as numerous story, poetry and play collections. Her work has won many awards, including a National Book Award for *them*. She is the Roger S. Berlind Distinguished Professor in the Humanities at Princeton University.

ROGER ROSENBLATT is the author of several books of nonfiction. His most recent book is *The Man in the Water*, a collection of essays and stories, published by Random House. "Nine Antirules of Journalism" is based on a lecture he gave at the University of Michigan as part of the school's Hopwood series.

LINDA SIMON is the author of *The Biography of Alice B. Toklas* and *Gertrude Stein Remembered*, both published by the University of Nebraska Press. She is the director of the Writing Center at Harvard University and is at work on a biography of William James.

STEPHEN SPENDER has published numerous works of fiction, nonfiction and poetry, most recently a collection of poems titled *Dolphins*, published by St. Martin's Press. He was awarded the Queen's Gold Medal for Poetry in 1971 and was knighted in 1982.

CALVIN TRILLIN is a staff writer for *The New Yorker*. He is the author of eighteen books, most recently *Too Soon to Tell*, a collection of essays published by Farrar, Straus & Giroux.

LEE UPTON is the author of three collections of poetry. Her newest is *Approximate Darling*, published by the University of Georgia Press. She teaches at Lafayette College in Easton, Pennsylvania.

NANCY WILLARD has published collections of stories, poetry and essays, as well as novels and books for children. Her children's books *The Sorcerer's Apprentice*, published by Scholastic, and *The Marzipan Moon*, published by Harcourt Brace & Company, are considered classics.

ABOUT THE EDITOR

JACK HEFFRON is senior editor of Story Press and former associate editor of *Story* magazine. His short stories have appeared in such literary journals as *High Plains Literary Review*, *North American Review* and *TriQuarterly*. His book reviews have appeared in *Black Warrior Review* and *Utne Reader*. He lives in Cincinnati, Ohio.

INDEX

Art of Fiction, The, 204
Ashton, Dore, 226-227
Aspern Papers, The, 136
Atlas, James, 103-104

Babel, Isaac, 124-125
Barker, Pat, 99
Barth, John, 206
Bastard Out of Carolina, 188-189
"Beginnings," 198
Blockbuster Complex, The, 48
Bogan, Louise, 106, 109-110
Borchardt, Georges, 43, 52-53, 56, 63, 65, 69
Bowen, Catherine Drinker, 227-228
Bowen, Elizabeth, 172-173
Brock, Dave, 134
Burlingame, Edward, 50-51, 70
Butts, Mary, 167-168

Camoin, Francois, 197, 200-201
Carnival for the Gods, 197, 207
Carver, Raymond, 196
Cave, Ray, 16
Chekhov, Anton, 125-126, 168-169
Citizen Kane, 19-20
"Collectors," 196-197
Coover, Robert, 198, 206
Coren, Alan, 16

Death of the Heart, The, 172-173
DeSalvo, Louise, 225-226
Dryden, John, 209
Dubus, Andre, 196, 201-202

Edel, Leon, 229-230
Eder, Richard, 57-61
Edson, Russell, 204-205
Education of Henry Adams, The, 136
"Elevator, The," 206
Elkin, Stanley, 52

"Faces of Madness," 127
Fenton, James, 98
Fiction and the Figures of Life, 204
Finnegans Wake, 78, 206-207
"First Love," 124-125
Floating Opera, The, 206
Flying, 189
"For People With Problems About

How to Believe," 37
Ford, Ford Madox, 21
Forster, E.M., 101
Fosca, 113
Fraser, Kennedy, 225-226
From Altar to Chimneypiece, 167
Futter, Deborah, 70

Gaitskill, Mary, 169-170
Gardner, John, 199, 202, 204-205
Gass, William H., 204
"Girl on the Plane, The," 169
Goldstein, Larry, 15
Good Soldier, The, 21

Haber, Leigh, 67
Hall, Radclyffe, 100
Hamilton, Ian, 135
Hamilton, Nigel, 134
Harris, Robert, 61-62
Hoeft, Jack, 52
Hopwood, Avery, 15-16
Howard, Gerald, 45, 48

Ice at the Bottom of the World, The, 43, 68-69
Ingall, Rachel, 127
Inherit the Wind, 34-35
"Interpreter, The," 197
Isherwood, Christopher, 102

James, Henry, 136
James, William, 231-237
Jenks, Tom, 51, 53, 64-65
JFK: Reckless Youth, 134
Joyce, James, 100, 104, 206-207

King, Stephen, 91-92
Klinkowitz, Jerome, 202
Knox, Bernard, 97-98

Lady Chatterley's Lover, 100
"Lady With the Pet Dog, The," 126
Language and Silence, 34
Lapine, James, 113-115
Last Brother, The, 134-135
Lawrence, D.H., 100
Leaf Storm, 197-198
Leavitt, David, 96-105
"Lieberman's Father," 197, 200-201

Lish, Gordon, 65
Living End, The, 52
"Love Song for a Moog Synthesizer,"
 123-124
"Lover, The," 124

Malcolm, Janet, 135-136, 224-225
Mann, Thomas, 129
Marathon Man, 88-91
Márquez, Gabriel Garcia, 197-198, 200
Maugham, Somerset, 23
McCarthy, Cormac, 54-55
McCullough, David, 134
McGinniss, Joe, 134-135
Middlebrook, Diane, 135
Mifflin, Margot, 62-63
Millett, Kate, 189-190
Milofsky, David, 12-13
Misery, 91-95

O'Brien, Meg, 64

Paley, Grace, 173-174
Passion, 113-119
Peck, M. Scott, 212-213
Persian Boy, The, 99
"Philosophers, The," 204-205
Plath, Sylvia, 135-136
Pound, Ezra, 77
Practice of Fiction in America, The, 202
Pritchett, V.S., 226

Real Anita Hill, The: The Untold Story,
 134
Regeneration, 99
Reiner, Rob, 91-95
Renault, Mary, 99
Richard, Mark, 42-47, 49-51, 53-60,
 62-70
RN: The Memoirs of Richard Nixon,
 158-160
Road Less Traveled, The, 212-213
Robbe-Grillet, Alain, 202-203
Robinson, Marilynne, 170-171
Rose, Phyllis, 230-231
Roth, Philip, 51
Rusoff, Marly, 49-50, 55-57, 59-60,
 66-67, 69

Salinger, J.D., 135

Scarlet Letter, The, 172
Scheinman, Andy, 92-95
Secret History, The, 44
Shorer, Mark, 229-230
Siegel, Marvin, 61-62
"Silent Woman, The," 224-225
Sinkler, Rebecca, 61-62
Sister Water, 130
Skin of Our Teeth, 23
Smiley, Jane, 161-162
Solotaroff, Ted, 48-50
Sondheim, Stephen, 113-119
Sontag, Susan, 99
Stafford, Bill, 37
Steiner, George, 34
Swan, Gladys, 197, 200-201, 207

"Tale, A," 109
Talese, Nan, 42-47, 49, 51-52, 53-56,
 60, 66-67, 69-70
Tangled Vines, 148, 153
Tartt, Donna, 44
Temple, The, 104
Tennyson, Alfred, Lord, 215
Thomson, Virgil, 167-168
Thousand Acres, A, 161-162
Tillinghast, Richard, 17
"Tonio Kroger," 129
Twain, Mark, 23, 139-140

Ulysses, 100, 104
Updike, John, 123-124

*Virginia Woolf: The Impact of Childhood
 Sexual Abuse on Her Life and Work,*
 225-226
Volcano Lover, The, 99
Von Mehren, Jane, 50
Voznesensky, Andrei, 226

Walker, Alice, 124
"Wants," 173-174
Well of Loneliness, The, 100
"What I Believe," 101
While England Sleeps, 96-105
Whiteside, Thomas, 48
Why Is the House Dissolving?, 148-149
Wilder, Thornton, 23, 172
"Winter Father, The," 196
Writing Lives, 229-230